mini atlas

Bartholomew

Edinburgh

1973

Printed and Published in Great Britain by
John Bartholomew & Son Ltd. 1973
ISBN 0 85152 595 4

Contents

Contents

THE EARTH
Showing Continents

Star Projection by Berghaus

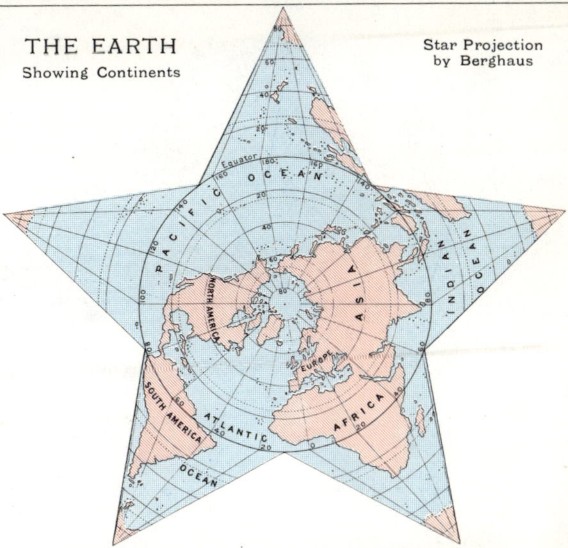

COMPARATIVE DISTANCES OF PLANETS FROM SUN

in millions of miles

COMPARATIVE SIZES OF PLANETS AND SUN

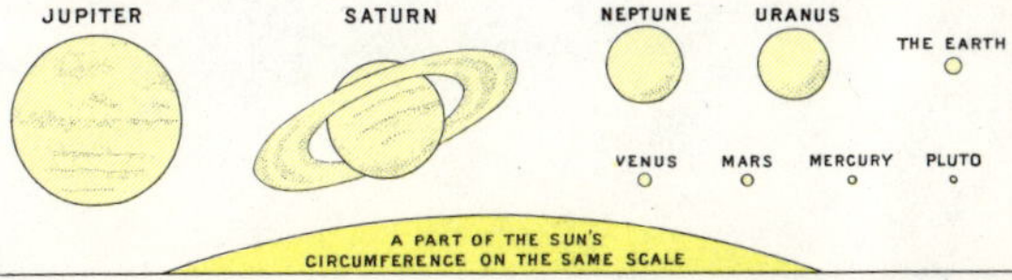

5571

Equatorial Sca

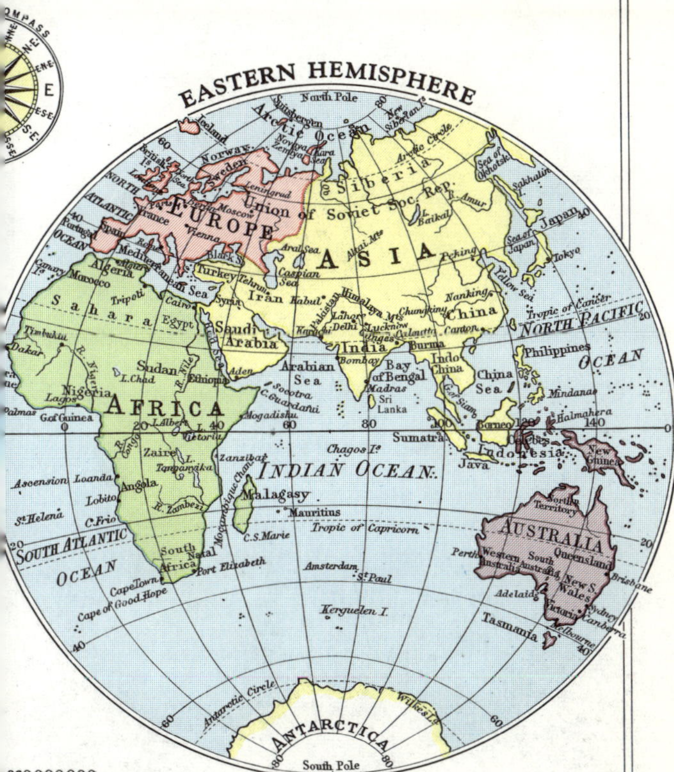
EASTERN HEMISPHERE
North Pole
Arctic Ocean
Spitsbergen
Iceland
Norway
Sweden
British Is.
NORTH ATLANTIC OCEAN
Portugal
Spain
France
EUROPE
Leningrad
Moscow
Vienna
Rome
Black Sea
Union of Soviet Soc. Rep.
Siberia
Arctic Circle
Sea of Okhotsk
Sakhalin
L. Baikal
R. Amur
Japan
Sea of Japan
Tokyo
Peking
ASIA
Aral Sea
Caspian Sea
Turkey
Mediterranean Sea
Algeria
Morocco
Tripoli
Cairo
Egypt
Syria
Iran
Kabul
Pakistan
Himalaya Mts
Lahore
Delhi
Lucknow
Karachi
Calcutta
Saudi Arabia
Red Sea
Aden
India
Bombay
Madras
Bay of Bengal
Arabian Sea
Sri Lanka
Burma
Indo China
China
Nanking
Chungking
Canton
Yellow Sea
Tropic of Cancer
NORTH PACIFIC OCEAN
Philippines
China Sea
Mindanao
Halmahera
Borneo
Celebes
Sumatra
Java
Indonesia
New Guinea
Sahara
Timbuktu
Dakar
R. Niger
Nigeria
Lagos
Sudan
R. Nile
Ethiopia
L. Chad
AFRICA
G. of Guinea
L. Albert
L. Victoria
R. Congo
Zaire
L. Tanganyika
Angola
Loanda
Lobito
R. Zambezi
Socotra
C. Guardafui
Mogadishu
Zanzibar
Mozambique Chan.
Malagasy
Mauritius
Chagos Is.
INDIAN OCEAN
Tropic of Capricorn
C.S. Marie
Ascension
St. Helena
C. Frio
SOUTH ATLANTIC OCEAN
South Africa
Natal
Port Elizabeth
Cape Town
Cape of Good Hope
Amsterdam
St. Paul
Kerguelen I.
AUSTRALIA
Northern Territory
Western Australia
South Australia
Queensland
New S. Wales
Victoria
Perth
Adelaide
Brisbane
Sydney
Canberra
Melbourne
Tasmania
Antarctic Circle
Wilkes Ld.
ANTARCTICA
South Pole

230,000,000

RELIEF

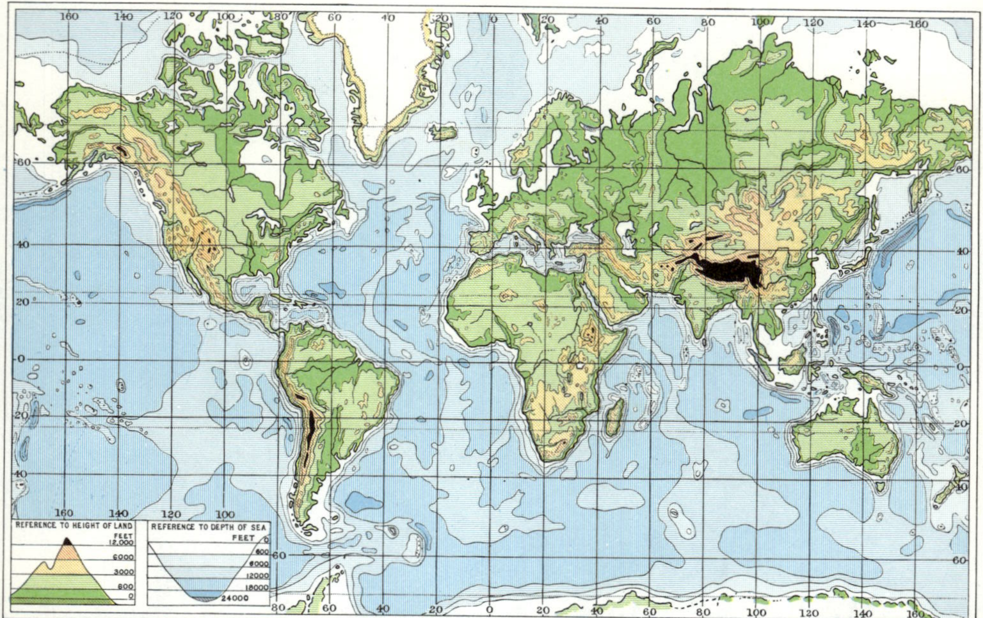
REFERENCE TO HEIGHT OF LAND
FEET
12,000
6000
3000
600
0
REFERENCE TO DEPTH OF SEA
FEET
0
600
6000
12000
18000
24000

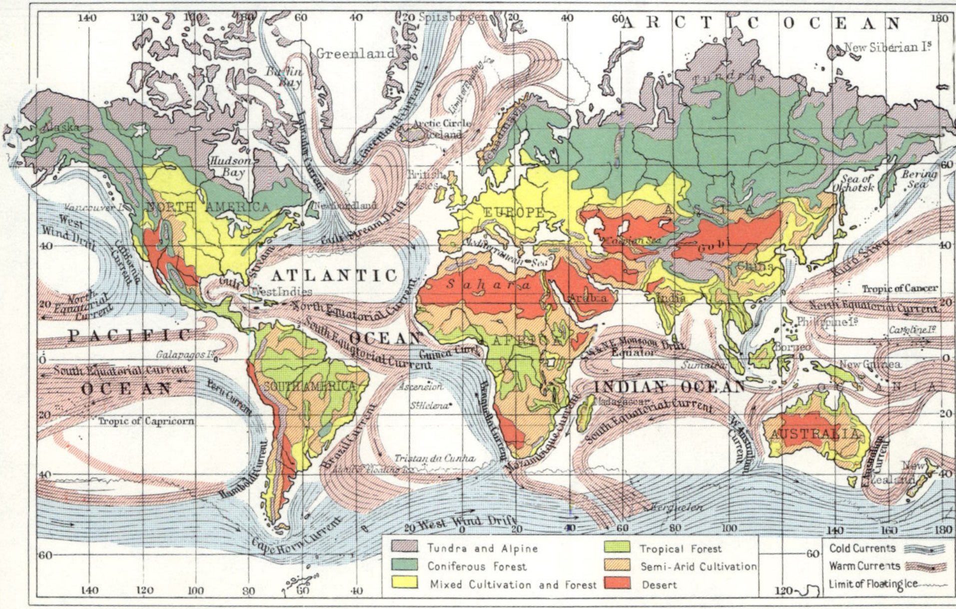
ARCTIC OCEAN
New Siberian Is
Spitsbergen
Greenland
Baffin Bay
Hudson Bay
Alaska
Arctic Circle
Iceland
British Isles
Newfoundland
NORTH AMERICA
EUROPE
ASIA
Tundras
Sea of Okhotsk
Bering Sea
Vancouver I.
West Wind Drift
California Current
Labrador Current
E. Greenland Current
Limit of Floating Ice
Gulf Stream Drift
Gulf Stream
Mediterranean Sea
Caspian Sea
Gobi
China
Kuro Siwo
Tropic of Cancer
North Equatorial Current
ATLANTIC
West Indies
Sahara
Arabia
India
North Equatorial Current
Philippine Is
Caroline Is
PACIFIC
OCEAN
AFRICA
S.W. & N.E. Monsoon Drift
Equator
Borneo
Galapagos Is
South Equatorial Current
Guinea Curr.
Sumatra
New Guinea
South Equatorial Current
OCEAN
SOUTH AMERICA
Peru Current
Ascension
INDIAN OCEAN
OCEANIA
Madagascar
St Helena
Tropic of Capricorn
Brazil Current
Benguela Current
Mozambique Current
South Equatorial Current
W. Australian Current
AUSTRALIA
E. Australian Current
Tristan da Cunha
Humboldt Current
New Zealand
Kerguelen
West Wind Drift
Cape Horn Current
Tundra and Alpine
Coniferous Forest
Mixed Cultivation and Forest
Tropical Forest
Semi-Arid Cultivation
Desert
Cold Currents
Warm Currents
Limit of Floating Ice

TEMPERATURE—JANUARY

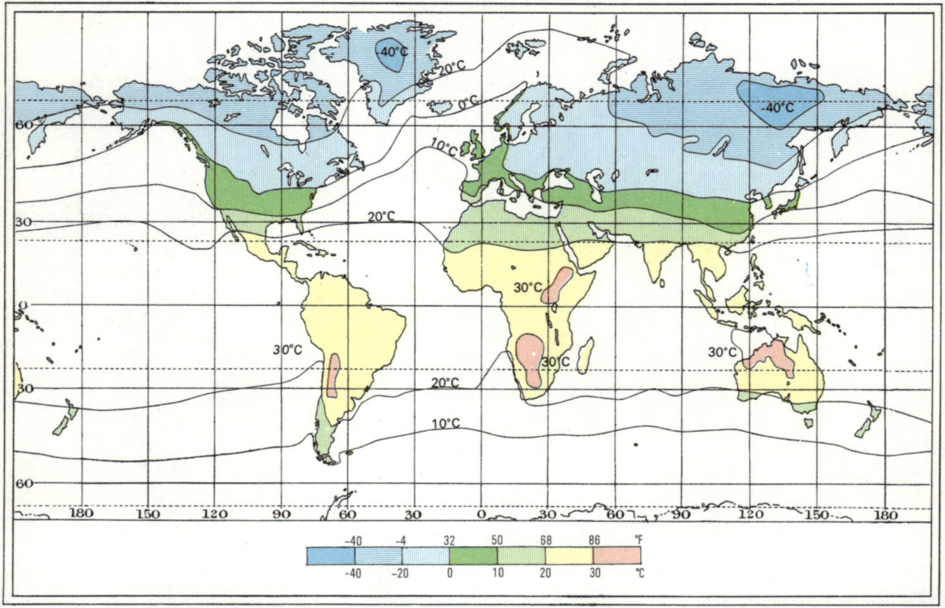

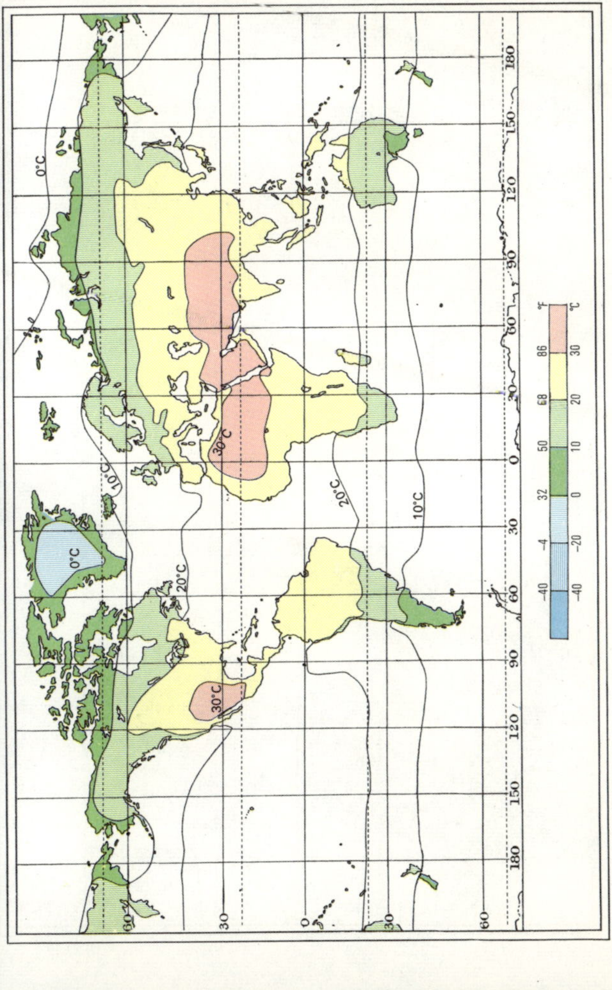

0°C
10°C
20°C
30°C
0°C
10°C
20°C
30°C
20°C
10°C
180
150
120
90
60
30
0
30
60
90
120
150
180
60
30
0
30
60
°F
-40
-4
32
50
68
86
°C
-40
-20
0
10
20
30

COMMUNICATIONS

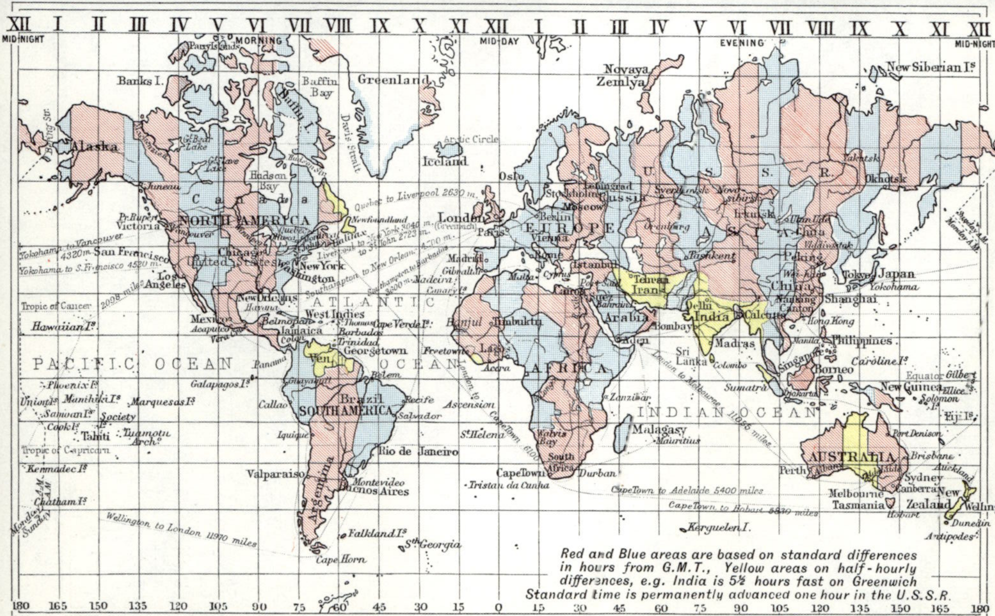

Red and Blue areas are based on standard differences in hours from G.M.T., Yellow areas on half-hourly differences, e.g. India is 5½ hours fast on Greenwich Standard time is permanently advanced one hour in the U.S.S.R.

NORTH AMERICA

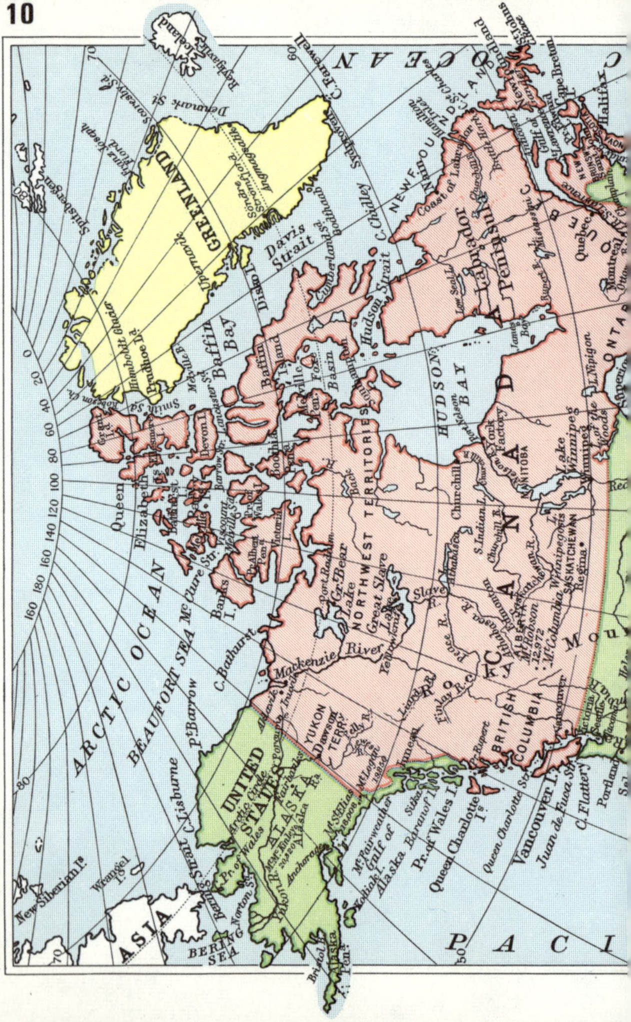

UNITED STATES
MEXICO
CENTRAL AMERICA
SOUTH AMERICA
WEST INDIES
CARIBBEAN SEA
GULF OF MEXICO
ATLANTIC
PACIFIC OCEAN
Bahama Islands
Bermudas
CUBA
JAMAICA
HAITI
DOMINICAN REP.
Puerto Rico
Florida
Yucatan
Lower California
Gulf of California
Sierra Madre
Sierra Nevada
Rio Grande
Tropic of Cancer
Gulf of Campeche
G. of Tehuantepec
BELIZE
GUATEMALA
HONDURAS
SALVADOR
NICARAGUA
COSTA RICA
PANAMA
Panama Canal
San Francisco
Los Angeles
San Diego
Phoenix
El Paso
Santa Fé
Albuquerque
Denver
Salt Lake City
Carson City
Great Salt Lake
Omaha
Kansas City
St. Louis
Chicago
Detroit
Pittsburgh
Cincinnati
Indianapolis
Louisville
Memphis
Atlanta
Little Rock
Dallas
Austin
New Orleans
Mobile
Galveston
Brownsville
Jacksonville
Charleston
Savannah
Raleigh
Richmond
Wilmington
WASHINGTON
Philadelphia
New York
Havana
Monterrey
Chihuahua
Zacatecas
Guanajuato
Guadalajara
MEXICO
Veracruz
Tampico
Acapulco
Mazatlan
C. S. Lucas
C. Corrientes
Socorro I.
Guadalupe
C. Catoche
C. Hatteras
C. Sable
C. Gracias a Dios
Statute Miles
0 100 200 300 400 500 1000
10
20
30
70
80
90
100
110
120

UNITED STATES
Alaska
Camden B.
Mackenzie B.
C. Bathurst
C. Kellett
Banks Id.
Viscount Melville Sound
Cornwallis
Pr. Albert Pena.
Victoria Id.
Wollaston Pena.
Pr. of Wales Id.
McClintock Ch.
Amundsen Gulf
Dolphin Str.
Coronation G.
Great Bear L.
Ft. McPherson
Aklavik
Inuvik
Ft. Norman
Ft. Good Hope
Port Radium
Bathurst Inlet
Coppermine R.
Northwest Terri
Mackenzie
Ft. Simpson
Yellowknife
Gt. Slave L.
Ft. Resolution
Hay River
Ft. Liard
Clinton Colden L.
Dubawnt L.
Baker L.
Back R.
Ft. Smith
Yukon Terr.
Dawson
Whitehorse
Mt. Logan
Mt. St. Elias
Fairbanks
Eagle
Porcupine R.
Peel R.
Stewart R.
Pelly R.
Teslin L.
Watson Lake
Juneau
Sitka
Chichagof I.
Baranof I.
Pr. of Wales I.
Ketchikan
Prince Rupert
Queen Charlotte Is.
Qn. Charlotte Sound
Skeena
British Columbia
Pr. George
Mt. Waddington
Vancouver Island
Nanaimo
Vancouver
New Westminster
Victoria
Kamloops
Nelson
Juan de Fuca Str.
C. Flattery
PACIFIC OCEAN
Ft. Nelson
Ft. St. John
Peace River
Lesser Slave L.
Alberta
Athabasca R.
Mc Murray
Mt. Robson 12,972
Mt. Columbia
Edmonton
Red Deer
Calgary
Bow R.
Macleod
Lethbridge
Medicine Hat
Coutts
Fond du Lac
L. Athabasca
Wollaston L.
Lynn Lake
Reindeer L.
Churchill R.
Flin Flon
Saskatchewan
Pr. Albert
N. Battleford
Saskatoon
Moose Jaw
Regina
Swift Current
Weyburn
Kamsack
The Pas
Winnipegosis
Manitoba
L. Manitoba
Winnipeg
Brandon
Portage la Prairie
Seattle
Olympia
Mt. Olympus
Bellingham
Spokane
Astoria
Portland
Salem
Columbia
Walla Walla
Mt. Rainier 14,408
Mt. Hood 11,225
Snake R.
Boise
Butte
Helena
Missouri R.
Ft. Peck Res.
Northern Pacific Railway
Bismarck
Yellowstone R.
Yellowstone L.
Big Horn Mts.
Pierre
Dakota
Yankton
Niobrara
Fremont Pk. 13,790
Mt. Shasta 14,380
Humboldt
Gt. Salt L.
Ogden
Salt Lake City
Austin
UNITED STATES

Statute Miles
0 100 200 300 400
GREENLAND
Baffin Bay
Upernavik
Bylot I.
Lancaster Sound
Pond Inlet
C. Adair
Scott Inlet
R. Clyde
Cockburn Land
Baffin Id
C. Hr. Kater
Home Bay
Disko I.
Disko B.
Holstensborg
Søndre Strømfjord
Kung Frederick VI Land
Davis Strait
Cumberland Peninsula
C. Walsingham
Cumberland Sd
Godthaab
Lichtenfels
Frederikshaab
Julianehaab
Sydprøven
C. Desolation
Fury & Hecla Str.
G. of Boothia
Melville Penin.
Foxe Basin
Prince Charles I.
L. Nettilling
Amadjuak
Rae Isthmus
Foxe Channel
Foxe Pen.
Hall Pen.
C. Murchison
Frobisher Bay
Resolution I.
Southampton I.
Rowes Welcome
Evans Str.
Charles I.
Hudson Str.
C. Chidley
Akpatok I.
Marble I.
Coats I.
Mansel I.
C. Southampton
C. Smith
C. Wolstenholme
Payne L.
Ungava Bay
Fort Chimo
Newfoundland
Coast of Labrador
Okhak
Nain
Hopedale
Indian Harb.
Rigolet
Hudson Bay
C. Dufferin
Churchill
The Sleepers
Belcher Is.
C. Henrietta Maria
Ft. Severn
York Factory
Minto L.
Leaf R.
Lr. Seal L.
Up. Seal L.
L. Bienville
Labrador Peninsula
Schefferville (Knob Lake)
Mishikamau L.
Churchill R.
Goose Bay
Gt. Whale R.
Fort George R.
Labrador City
Ashuanipi L.
Gagnon
Moisie R.
Mingan
Anticosti
James Bay
Akimiski I.
E. Main R.
Rupert Ho.
Rupert R.
L. Mistassini
Sept Iles
Port Cartier
Gulf of St. Lawrence
Quebec
Chibougamau
Saguenay
L. St. John
Chicoutimi
Gouin Res.
Campbellton
Bathurst
Newcastle
Pr. Edward I.
Charlottetown
Sydney
Cape Breton I.
New Brunswick
Fredericton
Saint John
Moncton
Nova Scotia
Halifax
B. of Fundy
C. Sable
Quebec
Trois Rivières
Sherbrooke
Montreal
Ottawa R.
Bangor
Augusta
Burlington
Mt. Washington 6293
Portland
Concord
Boston
Cape Cod
Lowell
Hartford
Providence
Nantucket
Severn R.
Attawapiskat R.
Albany R.
Moosonee
St. Joseph Lake
Sioux Lookout
L. Seul
L. Nipigon
Moose R.
Abitibi
Cochrane
L. of the Woods
Thunder Bay
Timmins
Sudbury
Ontario
Lake Superior
Sault Ste Marie
North Bay
OTTAWA
Georgian Bay
Kingston
L. Huron
Toronto
L. Ontario
Syracuse
Rochester
Albany
Hudson
Niagara Falls
Buffalo
Hamilton
Windsor
L. Erie
Cleveland
Pittsburgh
Superior
Minneapolis
St. Paul
Mississippi
Green Bay
Milwaukee
Madison
Racine
Dubuque
L. Michigan
Saginaw
Gr. Rapids
Lansing
Detroit
Chicago
S. Bend
Toledo
New Haven
Newark
Trenton
NEW YORK
Long Island
ATLANTIC OCEAN
60 50 40 70

WESTERN PROVINCES

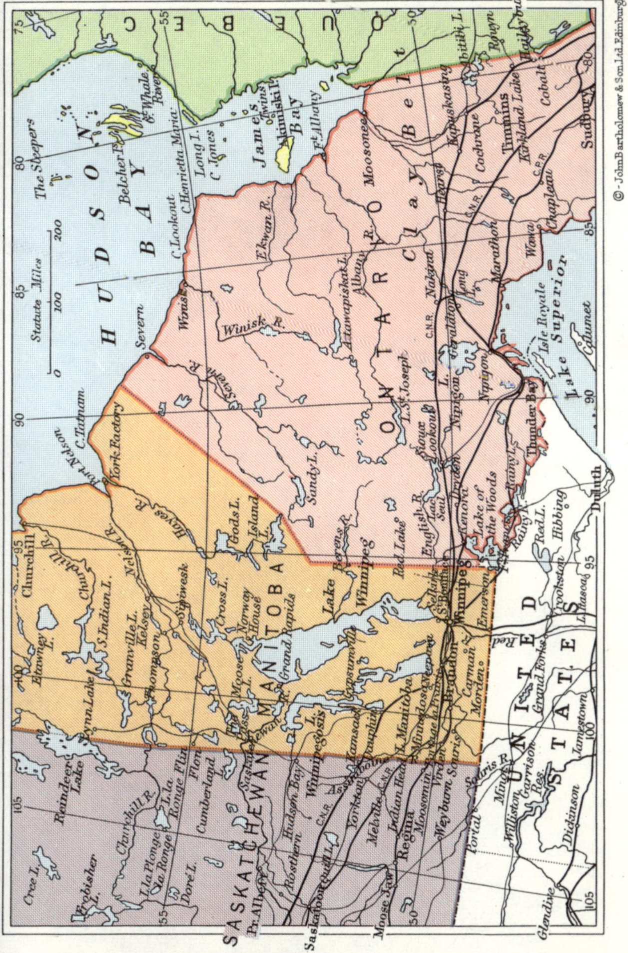
HUDSON BAY
James Bay
ONTARIO
MANITOBA
SASKATCHEWAN
UNITED STATES
QUEBEC
Clay Belt
Statute Miles
0 100 200
The Sleepers
Belcher Is.
Whale R.
C. Henrietta Maria
C. Lookout
Long I.
C. Jones
Akimiski I.
Twins
Ft. Albany
Moosonee
Ekwan R.
Winisk R.
Winisk
Severn
Severn R.
C. Tatnam
Port Nelson
York Factory
Hayes R.
Nelson R.
Churchill
Churchill R.
Gods L.
Island L.
Cross L.
Norway House
Sipiwesk
Kelsey
Thompson
Granville L.
S. Indian L.
Lynn Lake
Etawney L.
Reindeer Lake
Lake Winnipeg
Berens R.
Grand Rapids
The Pas
Moose L.
L. Winnipegosis
L. Manitoba
Dauphin
Brandon
Winnipeg
St. Boniface
Selkirk
Emerson
Carman
Morden
Portage la Prairie
Minnedosa
Virden
Souris
Flin Flon
Cumberland
L. la Ronge
La Ronge
L. la Plonge
Doré L.
Cree L.
Frobisher L.
Pr. Albert
Saskatoon
Rosthern
Hudson Bay
Yorkton
Melville
Indian Head
Regina
Moosomin
Weyburn
Moose Jaw
Assiniboine R.
C.N.R.
C.P.R.
Red Lake
English R.
Lac Seul
Sioux Lookout
L. St. Joseph
Sandy L.
Attawapiskat L.
Albany R.
Kenora
Dryden
Lake of the Woods
Rainy L.
Nipigon
L. Nipigon
Geraldton
Nakina
Long L.
Marathon
Hearst
Kapuskasing
Cochrane
Timmins
Kirkland Lake
Chapleau
Wawa
Sudbury
Cobalt
Haileybury
Rouyn
Abitibi L.
Thunder Bay
Isle Royale
Lake Superior
Calumet
Duluth
Hibbing
Red L.
Crookston
Grand Forks
Jamestown
Minot
Garrison Res.
Williston
Dickinson
Glendive
Portal
Souris R.
Red R.
Lake of the Woods
© - John Bartholomew & Son Ltd. Edinburgh

Whitefish Bay
Batchawana
Mekatina
Biscotasing
Rock Island Lake
Ruel
Sturgeon R.
Pogamasing
Mississagi R.
Sable R.
Wabos
Bellevue
Cartier
Capreol
Sault Ste Marie
White R.
Larchwood
Copper Cliff
Worthington
Sudbury
Markstay
Sault Ste Marie
St Mary R.
Bruce Mines
Thessalon
Elliot Lake
Webbwood
Spanish
Algoma
Massey
Panache
Burwash
Warren
Verner
French R.
St Joseph I.
Blind R.
North Channel
St Ignace
Mackinac Str. of Mackinac
Mackinaw
Drummond I.
Cockburn I.
Gore Bay
Little Current
Killarney
Philip Edward I.
Bois Blanc I.
Manitoulin I.
Manitowaning
Byng Inlet
Cheboygan
Duck Is
Mullet L.
Burt L.
Onaway
Rogers City
South Baymouth
Fitzwilliam I.
Georgian Bay
LAKE HURON
Cove I.
Flowerpot I.
Cabot Hd
C. Hurd
Tobermory
Depot Harbor
Parry I.
Sans Souci
Gaylord
1348
Hillman
Alpena
Atlanta
Lewiston
Thunder B.
581
Bruce Pen.
Blackriver
Colpoy B.
Christian I.
Owen Sd
Penetanguishene
Au Sable R.
Lincoln
Grayling
Mio
Bamfield
Harrisville
Wiarton
Nottawasaga Bay
Meaford
Owen Sound
Roscommon
Au Sable
Oscoda
Southampton
Port Elgin
Collingwood
Houghton L.
Tawas City
Paisley
Chesley
Meredith
West Branch
Saginaw Bay
Kincardine
Hanover
Durham
Harrison
Omer
Walkerton
Mt Forest
44
Gladwin
Standish
Grindstone
Caseville
Port Hope
Lucknow
Harbor Beach
Orangeville
Palmerston
W. Bay City
Bay City
Wingham
Bad Axe
Sebewaing
Palms
Goderich
Listowel
Fergus
MICHIGAN
Saginaw
Clinton
Guelph
Caro
Sandusky
Mitchell
Waterloo
Kitchener
Marlette
Ithaca
Stratford
Galt
Vassar
St Marys
St Charles
U. S.
Woodstock
Yale
Paris
Owosso
Lapeer
Port Huron
Forest
London
Brantford
St Johns
Flint
Strathroy
Ingersoll
Sarnia
Tillsonburg
St Clair
Simcoe
Fenton
Holly
Lansing
Petrolia
Rochester
Aylmer
810
Marine City
Oil Spr.
Thames
St Thomas
Pontiac
Mt Clemens
Mason
Howell
Dresden
Port Stanley
Birmingham
Wallaceburg
Eaton Rapids
Lake St Clair
DETROIT
Chatham
Ridgetown
Long Point
925
Jackson
Ann Arbor
Walkerville
Blenheim
Windsor
Rondeau
Ypsilanti
Wyandotte
Erieau
ERIE
Essex
572
Erie
Tecumseh
Sandwich
42
Amherstburg
Leamington
L.
Hudson
Denton
Pt Pelee
Conneaut
84
82
80

Statute Miles
0 20 40 60 80 100
Q U E B E C
O N T A R I O
NEW YORK
UNITED STATES
LAKE ONTARIO
246
Lake du Moine
Wolf L.
Kipawa L.
Kipawa R.
Timiskaming
Crest
Mattaw
Rapides des Joachims
Deux Rivieres
Brent
Corisune
Petawawa
Chalk River
Achray
Algonquin Park
Pembroke
Ottawa R.
Black R.
R. du Moine
Baskatong Res.
Mont Laurier
Maniwaki
Gracefield
Thirtyone Mile L.
Aylwin
Waltham
Ft. Coulonge
Calumet I.
Bryson
Quyon
Buckingham
Gatineau R.
Hull
OTTAWA
Rockland
Hawkesbury
Lachute
Montebello
Ripon
Simon L.
Arundel
Rouge R.
L. Remi
Labelle
Nominingue
Mont Tremblant Park
Trembling Mt.
St. Jovite
R. du Lievre
Alexandria
Cornwall
Seaway
Whitney
Wilno
Golden Lake
Eganville
Renfrew
Arnprior
Almonte
Madawaska R.
Maynooth
Carleton Place
Winchester
Aultsville
Smiths Falls
Mississippi R.
Perth
Morrisburg
Iroquois
Prescott
Brockville
Westport
Tweed
Madoc
Gananoque
Kingston
Napanee
Thousand Isles
Clayton
Watertown
Carthage
Sackets H.
Henderson
Amherst I.
Wolfe I.
Picton
Prince Edward Pena.
Belleville
Trenton
Campbellford
Lakefield
Peterborough
Rice L.
Pontypool
Cobourg
P. Hope
Bowmanville
Whitby
Ajax
Oshawa
TORONTO
Lindsay
Trent Canal
Balsam L.
Stony L.
Kawartha L.
Coe Hill
Millbridge
Bancroft
Gooderham
Irondale
Haliburton
Bracebridge
Muskoka
Gravenhurst
Bobcaygeon
Sutton
Scugog L.
L. of Bays
Madawaska
Princes L.
Scotia
St. Lawrence
Massena
Norwood
Ogdensburg
Canton
Raquette R.
Gouverneur
Edwards
Benson Mines
Lowville
Adams
Pulaski
Black R.
Boonville
Oswego
Fulton
Camden
Oneida L.
Rome
Utica
Mohawk R.
Charlotte
Port Dalhousie
Port Weller
Niagara on the Lake
Niagara Fs.
Albion
Rochester
Baldwinsville
Wampsville
Oneida
Herkimer
Little F.
Lockport
N. Tonawanda
Lyons
Seneca Falls
Geneva
Syracuse
Morrisville
Batavia
Canandaigua
LeRoy
Auburn
Lancaster
E. Aurora
Lackawanna
Cooperstown
Warsaw
Mt. Morris
Perry
Penn Yan
Seneca L.
Cayuga L.
Homer
Cortland
Springville
I.R.
Norwich
Oneonta
Gowanda
Arcade
Dansville
Oxford
Tredonia
Bath
Watkins
Ithaca
Sidney
Delhi
Cuba
Hornell
Belmont
Salamanca
Elmira
Binghamton
Deposit
Walton
Addison
Olean
Wellsville
Corning
Waverly
Owego
Johnson City
Athens
Sayre
Susquehanna
Hancock
78
76
46
44
42

QUEBEC

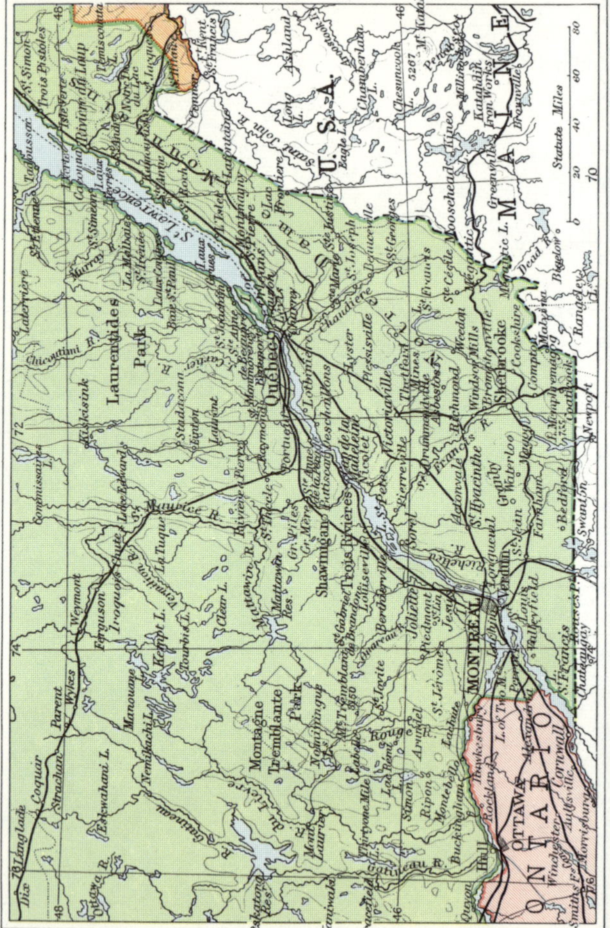

U.S.A.
MAINE
ONTARIO
Laurentides Park
Montagne Tremblante Park
Quebec
MONTREAL
OTTAWA
Trois Rivières
Sherbrooke
St. Lawrence
St. Maurice R.
Chicoutimi R.
Gatineau R.
Ottawa R.
Richelieu R.
Chaudière R.
St. Francis R.
Shawinigan
La Tuque
Rivière du Loup
Trois Pistoles
Hull
Cornwall
Granby
St. Hyacinthe
Drummondville
Victoriaville
Thetford Mines
Asbestos
Lake Edward
Kiskisink
Parent
Weymont
Lévis
Joliette
Sorel
Verdun
Longueuil
St. Jean
Valleyfield
Lachute
St. Jérôme
Mont Laurier
Buckingham
Baskatong Res.
Maniwaki
Gracefield
Moosehead L.
Greenville
Katahdin Iron Works
Brownville
Statute Miles

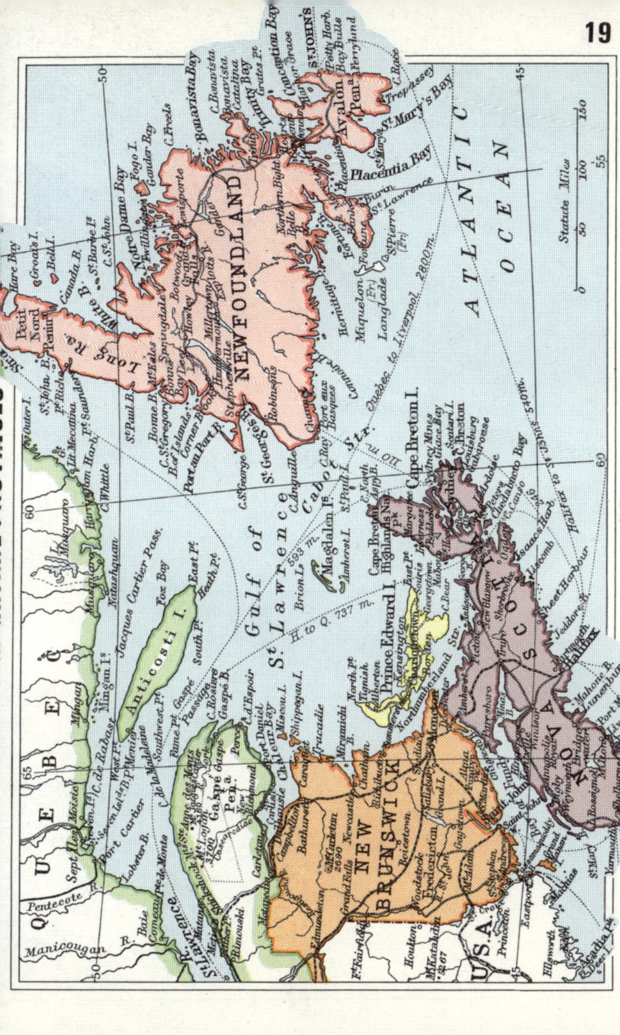
NEWFOUNDLAND
QUEBEC
NEW BRUNSWICK
NOVA SCOTIA
Prince Edward I.
Cape Breton I.
Anticosti I.
Gulf of St. Lawrence
ATLANTIC OCEAN
U.S.A.
Gaspé Pen.
Avalon Pen.
Placentia Bay
St. Mary's Bay
Trinity Bay
Conception Bay
Bonavista Bay
Notre Dame Bay
White B.
Long Ra.
Petit Nord
St. JOHN'S
Halifax
Magdalen Is.
Cabot Str.
Northumberland Str.
Jacques Cartier Pass.
Mingan Is.
St. Pierre (Fr.)
Miquelon (Fr.)
Quebec to Liverpool 2800 m.
H. to Q. 737 m.
Statute Miles
0 50 100 150

Vancouver Island
Juan de Fuca Str.
C. Flattery
Victoria
Mt. Olympus
Olympia
Astoria
Portland
Salem
Seattle
Washington
Bellingham
Spokane
Columbia
Walla Walla
Oregon
Mt. Hood 11,225
C. Blanco
Klamath R.
C. Mendocino
Mt. Shasta 14,162
California
Sierra Nevada
Coast Range
Santa Rosa
Oakland
San Francisco
Sacramento
Stockton
S. Joaquin
Monterey
San Luis Obispo
Santa Barbara
Pt. Conception
San Pedro
Long Beach
Los Angeles
San Diego
Mexicali
Mt. Whitney 14,495
Nevada
Humboldt
Carson City
Bullion V.
Mead L.
Hoover Dam
Gt. Salt L.
Salt Lake City
Ogden
Utah
Wasatch
L. Powell
R. Grand
Idaho
Boise
Idaho Falls
Pocatello
Snake R.
Montana
Gt. Falls
Helena
Butte
Missouri R.
Ft. Peck Res.
Yellowstone R.
Yellowstone L.
Wyoming
Big Horn Mts.
Gannett Pk. 13,785
Cheyenne
Rocky Mountains
Colorado
Long's Pk.
Mt. Elbert 14,420
Denver
Pueblo
Blanca Pk. 14,363
Arizona
Colorado Plateau
Lit. Colorado
Prescott
Phoenix
R. Gila
Tucson
Yuma
New Mexico
Santa Fe
Albuquerque
El Paso
Rio Grande
R. Pecos
Llano Estacado
Apache Mts.
North Dakota
Bismarck
South Dakota
Pierre
Nebraska
North Platte
Niobrara
Kansas
Cimarron
Canadian
Oklahoma
Wichita Falls
Ft. Worth
Texas
Colorado
Austin
S. Antonio
Edmonton
Pr. Albert
Saskatchewan
The Pas
Battleford
Saskatoon
Kamsack
Regina
Moose Jaw
Swift Current
Weyburn
Brandon
Medicine Hat
Lethbridge
Calgary
Red Deer
Ft. Macleod
Mt. Robson 12,972
Mt. Columbia
Kamloops
Thompson
Nelson
New Westminster
CANADA
PACIFIC OCEAN
Guadalupe
Sebastian Vizcaino B.
Cedros I.
Lower California
Gulf of California
Ballenas B.
S. Juanico
Loreto
Alijos.
Tropic of Cancer
La Paz
C. San Lucas
Caborca
Ures
Hermosillo
Guaymas
Alamos
Sinaloa
Culiacan
Altata
Mazatlan
Ojinaga
Chihuahua
Guerrero
Presidio
S. Vicente
Parral
Sierra Mojada
Bolson de Mapimi
R. Salado
R. de Nazas
Aviles
Saltillo
Salada
Durango
Fresnillo
Zacatecas
San Blas
R. Grande
Aguas Calientes
San Luis Potosi
Leon
Guanajuato
L. Chapala
Guadalajara
Queretaro
Las Tres Marias
MEXICO
Statute Miles
0 100 200 300 400 500
130
120
110
100
40
30
20

CANADA
Lake Superior
L. Michigan
L. Huron
L. Ontario
L. Erie
Georgian Bay
Ottawa
OTTAWA
Montreal
Quebec
Trois Rivières
Toronto
Hamilton
Kingston
Cochrane
Timmins
Sudbury
North Bay
Sault Ste Marie
Moosonee
Albany R.
Attawapiskat
Rupert Ho.
Rupert R.
E. Main R.
Mistassini L.
L. St. John
Gouin Res.
Chicoutimi
Saguenay
Campbellton
Bathurst
Newcastle
Fredericton
St. John
Gulf of St Lawrence
B. of Fundy
L. Nipigon
Lake Seul
Sioux Lookout
St. Joseph Lake
L. of the Woods
Moose R.
Abitibi
Minnesota
Duluth
Superior
Minneapolis
St. Paul
Wis.
Green Bay
Milwaukee
Madison
Racine
Mich.
Saginaw
Gr. Rapids
Lansing
Detroit
Windsor
Iowa
Dubuque
Des Moines
Davenport
Chicago
Gary
Illinois
Springfield
Ind.
Indianapolis
Ohio
Toledo
Sandusky
Cleveland
Columbus
Dayton
Cincinnati
Keokuk
Missouri
St. Joseph
Kansas City
Jefferson City
St. Louis
Cairo
Ky.
Louisville
Lexington
Cumberland
Pittsburgh
Pa.
Harrisburg
Philadelphia
Trenton
Newark
NEW YORK
N.J.
Atlantic C.
Delaware R. & Bay
Md.
Baltimore
WASHINGTON
W.Va.
Wheeling
Va.
Richmond
Petersburg
Norfolk
Portsmouth
Newport News
Chesapeake Bay
C. Hatteras
N.Y.
Buffalo
Niagara Falls
Rochester
Syracuse
Albany
New Haven
Long Island
Mass.
Boston
Cape Cod
Nantucket
Providence & R.I.
Conn.
Hartford
Lowell
Concord
N.H.
Vt.
Burlington
Portland
Me.
Bangor
Augusta
Sherbrooke
Tenn.
Nashville
Knoxville
Memphis
Norris R.
Winston Salem
Raleigh
N.C.
Mt. Mitchell 6710
Wilmington
C. Lookout
C. Fear
S.C.
Columbia
Charleston
Georgetown
Beaufort
Savannah
Ga.
Atlanta
Augusta
Macon
Columbus
Albany
Altamaha R.
Brunswick
Jacksonville
Arkansas
Little Rock
Camden
Miss.
Vicksburg
Jackson
Columbus
Ala.
Birmingham
Montgomery
Mobile
Tombigbee
Alabama
Tennessee
Mississippi
Red R.
Louisiana
Baton Rouge
New Orleans
Natchitoches
Sabine
Galveston
Beaumont
Tulsa
Muskogee
Ozark Mts.
Pensacola
Tallahassee
Apalachee Bay
Florida
Tampa
L. Okeechobee
Palm B.
Miami
C. Sable
Pine Is.
Key West
Florida Str.
ATLANTIC
OCEAN
Bahama Is.
Gr. Bahama
Lit. Bahama
Gr. Abaco
New Providence
Eleuthera
Nassau
Andros Is.
Cat I.
Watling I.
Long I.
Acklins I.
Mariguana
Gr. Inagua
Bahama Chan.
Nuevitas
GULF OF MEXICO
Havana
Matanzas
Bahia Honda
Pinar del Rio
C. San Antonio
Yucatan Str.
C. Catoche
Progreso
Merida
Valladolid
Cozumel I.
Triangulos
Pinos I.
Trinidad
Camaguey
CUBA
Manzanillo
Santiago de Cuba
Windward P.
Haiti
Port au Prince
Lit. Cayman
Brownsville
Matamoras
90
80
70
50
40
30
20

EASTERN STATES

ATLANTIC OCEAN
GULF OF MEXICO
TENNESSEE
NORTH CAROLINA
SOUTH CAROLINA
GEORGIA
ALABAMA
MISSISSIPPI
FLORIDA
C. Hatteras
Raleigh B.
C. Lookout
Onslow B.
Long B.
Greensboro
Durham
Raleigh
Winston Salem
Charlotte
Mt. Mitchell
Asheville
New Bern
Jacksonville
Fayetteville
Wilmington
Florence
Columbia
Greenville
Orangeburg
Charleston
Port Royal
Savannah
Savannah R.
Augusta
Athens
Gainesville
Atlanta
Macon
Dublin
Columbus
Albany
Thomasville
Waycross
Brunswick
Darien
Fernandina
Jacksonville
St. Augustine
Daytona Beach
Titusville
C. Kennedy
Orlando
Ocala
Gainesville
Lake City
Tallahassee
Apalachee B.
Cedar Keys
St. Petersburg
Tampa
Tampa B.
Fort Pierce
Palm Beach
L. Okeechobee
Miami
Key Largo
Ten Thousand Is.
C. Sable
Florida Bay
Key West
Florida Keys
Gt. Bahama I.
Gt. Abaco
Berry Is.
Nassau
New Providence
Eleuthera
Knoxville
Johnson City
Chattanooga
Nashville
Clarksville
Hopkinsville
Paducah
Columbia
Jackson
Memphis
Paris
Milan
Huntsville
Decatur
Gadsden
Birmingham
Anniston
Tuscaloosa
Selma
Montgomery
Monroeville
Brewton
Mobile
Pensacola
Westville
Apalachicola
Rome
Dalton
Holly Springs
Pontotoc
Grenada
Greenwood
Greenville
Vicksburg
Meridian
Jackson
Brookhaven
Hattiesburg
Natchez
New Orleans
Mississippi R.
L. Pontchartrain
Statute Miles
0 50 100 200 300
35
30
25
85
80
75

MIDDLE ATLANTIC COAST

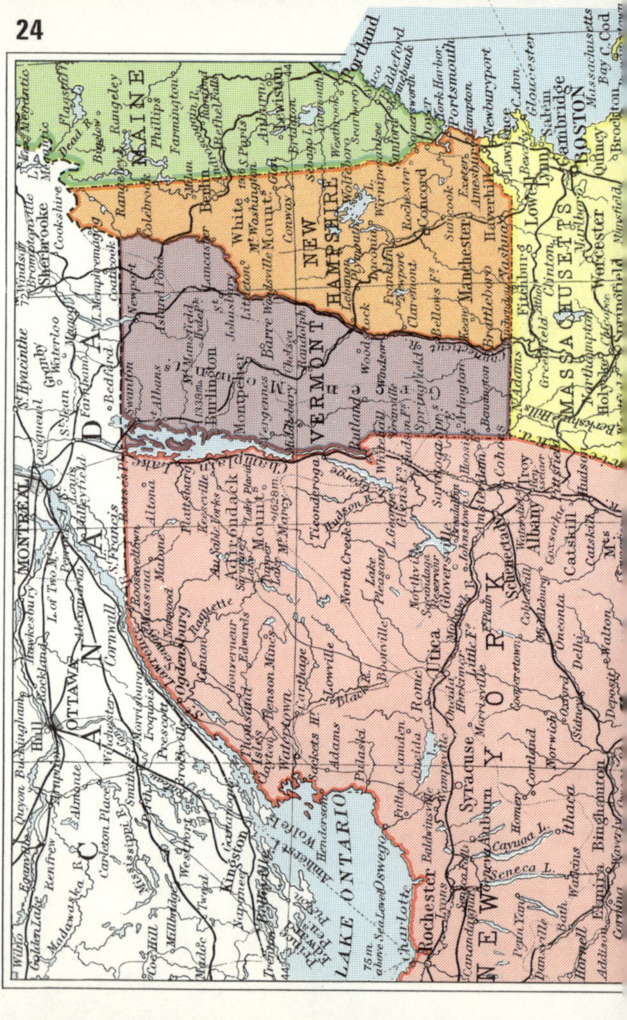

ATLANTIC
OCEAN
Statute Miles
0
20
40
60
80
100
40
74
NEW YORK
Brooklyn
Long Island
Staten I.
CONNECTICUT
Hartford
NEW HAVEN
Bridgeport
RHODE ISLAND
FALL RIVER
New Bedford
Martha's Vineyard
Nantucket
Block I.
Montauk Pt.
NEW JERSEY
Jersey City
Newark
Paterson
Trenton
Camden
Atlantic City
Cape May
PHILADELPHIA
PENN
Harrisburg
Scranton
Wilkes Barre
Allentown
Reading
Lancaster
Williamsport
DELAWARE
Wilmington
Dover
Delaware Bay
MARYLAND
BALTIMORE
Annapolis
WASHINGTON D.C.
VA

ERIE AND OHIO BASINS

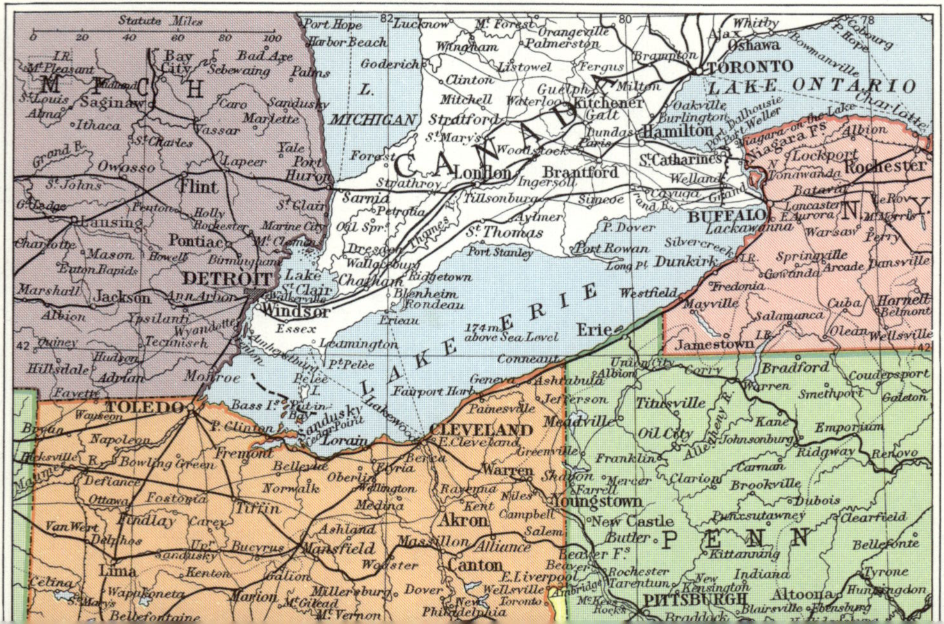

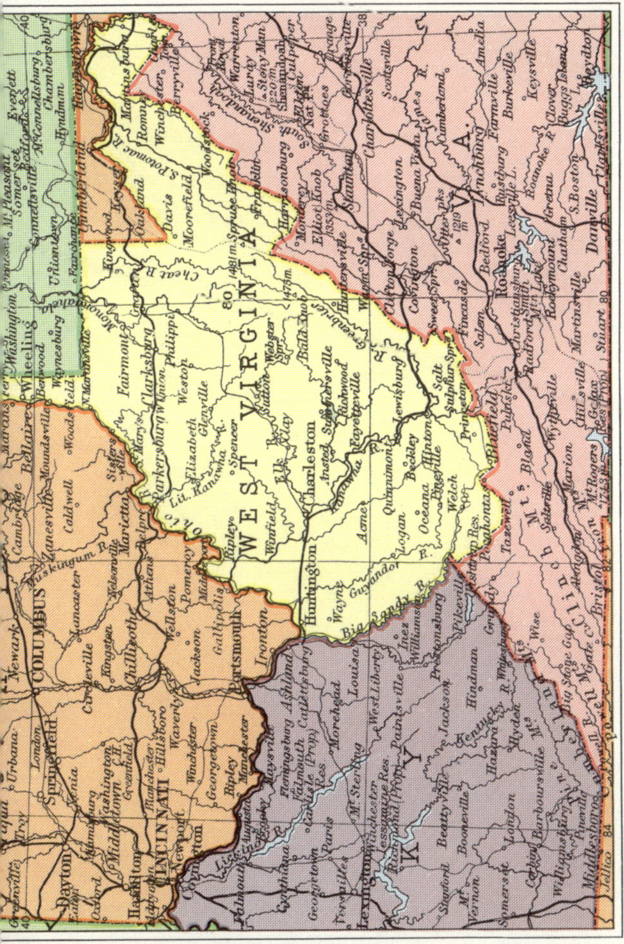
WEST VIRGINIA
V A.
K Y.
COLUMBUS
CINCINNATI
Charleston
Huntington
Roanoke
Wheeling
Lexington
Portsmouth
Springfield
Dayton
Parkersburg
Clarksburg
Danville
Lynchburg
Charlottesville

MISSOURI
ILLINOIS
INDIANA
KENTUCK
ARKANSAS
TENNESSEE
MISSISSIPPI
ALABAMA
LOUISIANA
GULF OF MEXICO
Statute Miles
0 50 100 150
St Louis
Jefferson City
Springfield
Louisville
Evansville
Paducah
Nashville
Memphis
Jackson
Chattanooga
Little Rock
Pine Bluff
Vicksburg
Natchez
Meridian
Birmingham
Montgomery
Mobile
Pensacola
New Orleans
Baton Rouge
Tallahas
Columbus
Anniston
Huntsville
Greenville
Columbia
Gadsden
Selma
Hattiesburg
Alexandria
Shreveport
Breton Sound
Chandeleur Is
Palos I.
The Delta
Barataria B.
Terrebonne B.
Timbalier B.
Isle Dernière
Atchafalaya B.
Marsh I.
Choctawhatchee B.
St Andrews B.
St Joseph's B.
C. San Blas
Apalachee
Mobile B.
Panama City

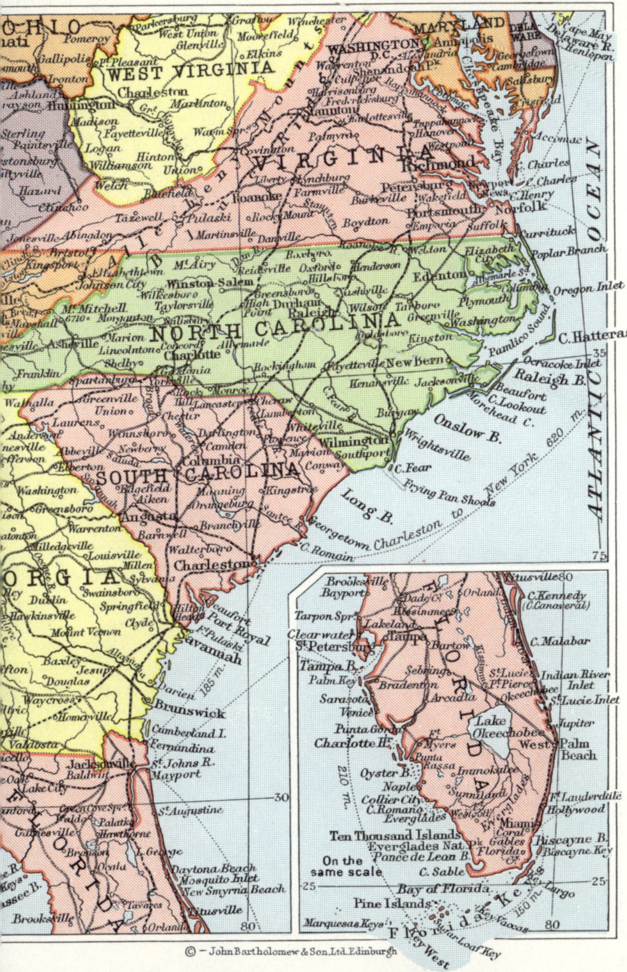
OHIO
WEST VIRGINIA
MARYLAND
DELAWARE
WASHINGTON D.C.
VIRGINIA
NORTH CAROLINA
SOUTH CAROLINA
GEORGIA
FLORIDA
ATLANTIC OCEAN
Charleston
Parkersburg
Huntington
Richmond
Petersburg
Norfolk
Portsmouth
Roanoke
Lynchburg
Danville
Winston-Salem
Greensboro
Durham
Raleigh
Charlotte
Wilmington
New Bern
C. Hatteras
Pamlico Sound
Oregon Inlet
Ocracoke Inlet
Raleigh B.
Onslow B.
C. Lookout
C. Fear
Frying Pan Shoals
Long B.
Columbia
Augusta
Charleston
Savannah
Brunswick
Jacksonville
St. Augustine
Daytona Beach
Titusville
Orlando
Tampa
St. Petersburg
Lake Okeechobee
West Palm Beach
Ft. Lauderdale
Hollywood
Miami
C. Sable
Bay of Florida
Florida Keys
Key West
Charleston to New York 620 m.
On the same scale
Chesapeake Bay
C. Kennedy (C. Canaveral)

CENTRAL STATES

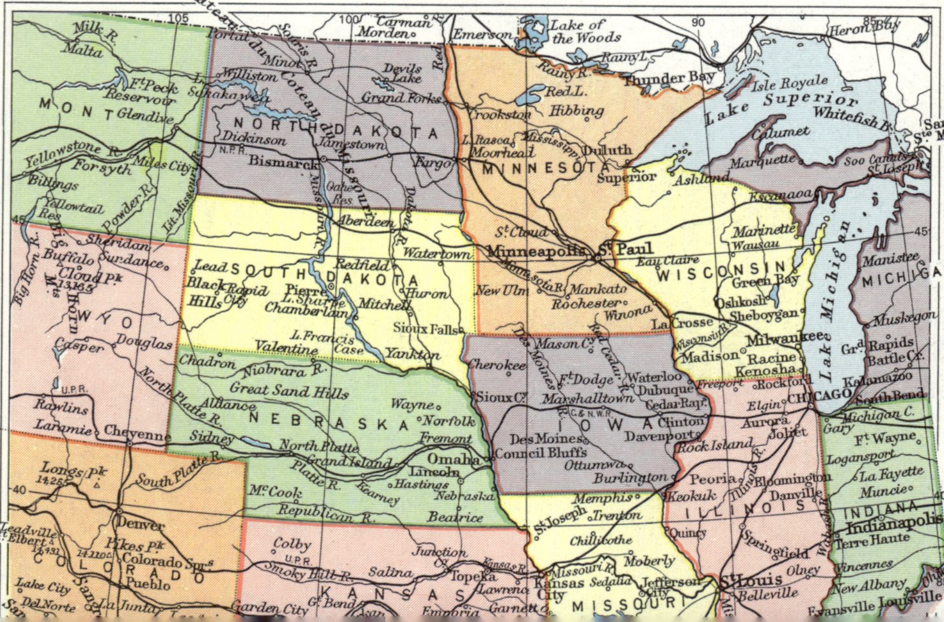

TENN
ALA
MISSISSIPPI
ARKANSAS
LOUISIANA
OKLAHOMA
TEXAS
NEW MEXICO
MEXICO
GULF OF MEXICO
Llano Estacado
Bolson de Mapimi
Nashville
Clarksville
Columbia
Memphis
Jackson
Paris
Milan
Huntsville
Gadsden
Birmingham
Decatur
Tuscaloosa
Selma
Montgomery
Monroeville
Brewton
Pensacola
Mobile
Daphne
Holly Springs
Pontotoc
Grenada
Greenwood
Greenville
Vicksburg
Meridian
Jackson
Brookhaven
Hattiesburg
Natchez
Baton Rouge
New Orleans
Mississippi R.
Morgan
Donaldsonville
Lake Charles
Pt Arthur
Alexandria
Monroe
Shreveport
Red R.
Charleston
Jonesboro
Newport
Norfolk Lake
Dardanelle
Little Rock
Pine Bluff
Arkansas City
Camden
Hot Springs
Texarkana
Fayetteville
Joplin
Carthage
Bull Shoals Res.
Tahlequah
Ft Smith
Vinita
Tulsa
Muskogee
Oklahoma C.
Shawnee
McAlester
Atoka
L. Texoma
Arkansas C.
Ponca City
Enid
Guthrie
Cimarron R.
Chickasha
Lawton
Ardmore
Red R.
Woodward
Canadian R.
Borger
Amarillo
Childress
Wichita Falls
Denison
Paris
Greenville
Dallas
Ft Worth
Tyler
Longview
Sabine R.
Lufkin
Corsicana
Waco
Temple
Hearne
Trinity R.
Orange
Beaumont
Houston
Galveston
Austin
Colorado R.
Columbus
S. Antonio
Kerrville
Brazos R.
Abilene
Cisco
S. Angelo
Sherwood
Lubbock
Colorado City
Midland
Farwell
Matagorda L.
Corpus Christi
Padre I.
L. Madre
Pt Isabel
Rockport
Laredo
Falcon Res.
Brownsville
Brackettville
Eagle Pass
Rio Grande
Nuevo Laredo
Cerralvo
Monclova
Monterrey
Villaldama
Piedras Negras
Allende
Nueva Rosita
Sierra Mojada
Pecos
Marfa
Presidio
Rio Bravo del Norte
El Paso
Ciudad Juarez
Santa Fe
Albuquerque
Las Vegas
Roswell
Lincoln
Rio Pecos
Chihuahua
Camargo
Conchos R.
Jimenez
Hidalgo del Parral
Escalon
Mapimi
Gómez Palacio
Lerdo
El Oro
Statute Miles
0 50 100 200 300 400
95
100
105
30
35

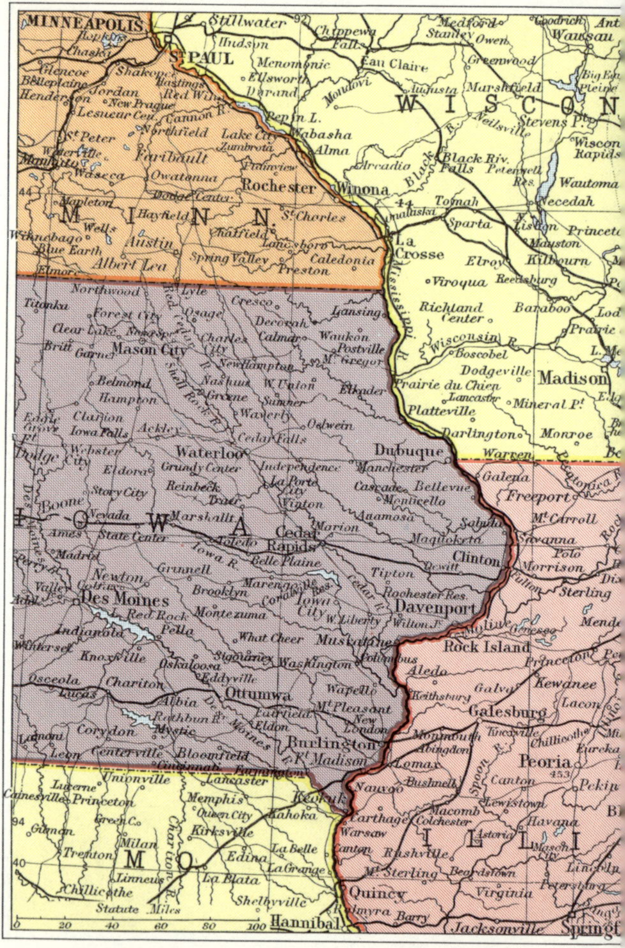
MINNEAPOLIS
St PAUL
Stillwater
Hudson
Menomonie
Ellsworth
Durand
Chippewa Falls
Eau Claire
Mondovi
Augusta
Medford
Stanley
Owen
Greenwood
Marshfield
Goodrich
Wausau
WISCONSIN
Neilsville
Stevens Pt.
Wiscon Rapids
Black Riv. Falls
Arcadia
Alma
Wabasha
Pepin L.
Glencoe
Belleplaine
Henderson
Jordan
New Prague
Hastings
Red Wing
Lesuear Cen.
Cannon R.
Northfield
Lake City
Zumbrota
St Peter
Faribault
Waseca
Owatonna
Rochester
Winona
Dodge Center
Mapleton
Hayfield
St Charles
MINN.
Wells
Chatfield
Winnebago
Blue Earth
Austin
Lanesboro
Spring Valley
Caledonia
Preston
Albert Lea
La Crosse
Tomah
Sparta
Elroy
Kilbourn
Mauston
Wautoma
Necedah
Viroqua
Reedsburg
Richland Center
Baraboo
Mississippi R.
Wisconsin R.
Boscobel
Dodgeville
Madison
Prairie du Chien
Lancaster
Mineral Pt.
Platteville
Darlington
Monroe
Warren
Northwood
Lyle
Cresco
Titonka
Forest City
Osage
Decorah
Lansing
Clear Lake
Charles City
Calmar
Waukon
Postville
Britt
Mason City
New Hampton
Mc Gregor
Belmond
Nashua
W. Union
Elkader
Hampton
Greene
Sumner
Shell Rock R.
Waverly
Clarion
Iowa Falls
Ackley
Cedar Falls
Oelwein
Webster City
Waterloo
Dubuque
Eldora
Grundy Center
Independence
Manchester
Story City
Reinbeck
La Porte City
Cascade
Bellevue
Boone
Traer
Vinton
Monticello
IOWA
Nevada
Marshallt
Anamosa
Marion
Cedar Rapids
Ames
State Center
Toledo
Maquoketa
Madrid
Iowa R.
Belle Plaine
Clinton
Newton
Grinnell
Tipton
Dewitt
Des Moines
Brooklyn
Marengo
Iowa City
Davenport
Red Rock
Montezuma
W. Liberty
Indianola
Pella
What Cheer
Muscatine
Knoxville
Oskaloosa
Sigourney
Washington
Eddyville
Osceola
Chariton
Ottumwa
Wapello
Lucas
Albia
Mt Pleasant
Rathbun R.
Fairfield
New London
Corydon
Mystic
Eldon
Burlington
Leon
Centerville
Bloomfield
Ft Madison
Galena
Freeport
Mc Carroll
Savanna
Polo
Morrison
Sterling
Fulton
Moline
Rock Island
Geneseo
Princeton
Aledo
Galva
Kewanee
Keithsburg
Galesburg
Lacon
Monmouth
Abingdon
Knoxville
Chillicothe
Eureka
Peoria
Lomax
Nauvoo
Bushnell
Canton
Pekin
Macomb
Lewistown
Carthage
Colchester
Havana
Warsaw
Astoria
Mason City
ILLI
Rushville
Mt Sterling
Beardstown
Quincy
Virginia
Petersburg
Barry
Jacksonville
Springf
Unionville
Lancaster
Lucerne
Princeton
Memphis
Keokuk
Queen City
Kahoka
Green C.
Gilman
Milan
Kirksville
Chariton R.
Trenton
MO
Edina
La Belle
La Grange
Linneus
La Plata
Chillicothe
Shelbyville
Palmyra
Hannibal
Statute Miles
0 20 40 60 80 100

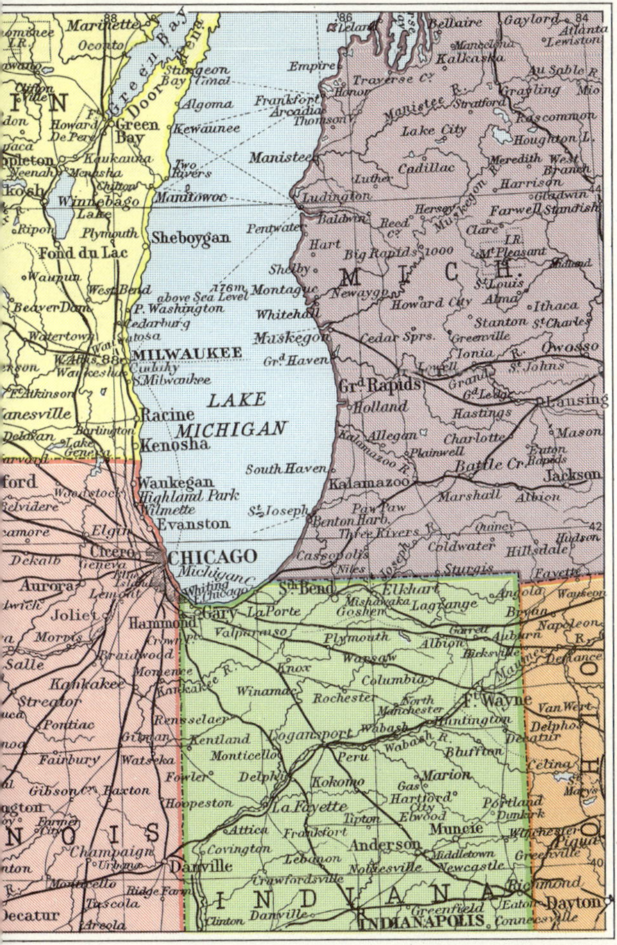

Marinette
Oconto
Green Bay
Door Pena.
Sturgeon Bay
Algoma
Kewaunee
Howard
De Pere
Green Bay
Kaukauna
Menasha
Neenah
Chilton
Two Rivers
Manitowoc
Winnebago Lake
Ripon
Plymouth
Sheboygan
Fond du Lac
Waupun
West Bend
P. Washington
Cedarburg
Beaver Dam
Watertown
MILWAUKEE
Cudahy
S. Milwaukee
Waukesha
Ft. Atkinson
Janesville
Delavan
Burlington
Lake Geneva
Racine
Kenosha
LAKE MICHIGAN
176m above Sea Level
Waukegan
Highland Park
Wilmette
Evanston
Woodstock
Belvidere
Elgin
Sycamore
Dekalb
Cicero
Geneva
CHICAGO
Aurora
Lemont
Joliet
Hammond
Whiting
E. Chicago
Gary
Crown Pt.
Morris
Braidwood
Momence
Kankakee
Streator
Pontiac
Fairbury
Watseka
Gilman
Gibson C.
Paxton
Fowler
Hoopeston
Champaign
Urbana
Danville
Monticello
Tuscola
Ridge Farm
Decatur
Arcola
Leland
Empire
Traverse C.
Honor
Frankfort
Arcadia
Thompsonv.
Manistee
Manistee R.
Ludington
Pentwater
Hart
Shelby
Montague
Whitehall
Muskegon
Gr.d Haven
Gr.d Rapids
Holland
South Haven
Kalamazoo
Kalamazoo R.
St. Joseph
Benton Harb.
Paw Paw
Three Rivers
Cassopolis
Niles
St. Bend
Elkhart
Mishawaka
Goshen
Lagrange
Bellaire
Gaylord
Atlanta
Lewiston
Mancelona
Kalkaska
Au Sable R.
Grayling
Mio
Stratford
Roscommon
Houghton L.
Lake City
Cadillac
Meredith
West Branch
Luther
Harrison
Gladwin
Hersey
Muskegon R.
Farwell
Standish
Baldwin
Reed C.
Clare
Big Rapids
I.R.
Mt. Pleasant
Midland
MICH.
Newaygo
St. Louis
Alma
Ithaca
Howard City
Stanton
St. Charles
Cedar Sprs.
Greenville
Ionia
Owosso
Lowell
St. Johns
Grand R.
Gd. Ledge
Lansing
Hastings
Allegan
Charlotte
Mason
Plainwell
Eaton Rapids
Battle Cr.
Jackson
Marshall
Albion
Quincy
Coldwater
Hillsdale
Hudson
Sturgis
Fayette
Angola
Wauseon
Bryan
Napoleon
LaPorte
Valparaiso
Plymouth
Albion
Garrett
Auburn
Warsaw
Kirksville
Defiance
Maumee
Knox
Kankakee R.
Columbia
Winamac
Rochester
North Manchester
Ft. Wayne
Van Wert
Rensselaer
Wabash
Huntington
Delphos
Kentland
Logansport
Wabash R.
Decatur
Peru
Bluffton
Monticello
Delphi
Kokomo
Marion
Celina
Gas City
Hartford
St. Marys
La Fayette
Tipton
Elwood
Portland
Dunkirk
Attica
Frankfort
Muncie
Winchester
Piqua
Covington
Anderson
Middletown
Greenville
Lebanon
Noblesville
Newcastle
Crawfordsville
Richmond
INDIANA
Greenfield
Eaton
Dayton
Clinton
Danville
INDIANAPOLIS
Connersville
OHIO
ILLINOIS
WISCONSIN
88
86
84
44
42
40

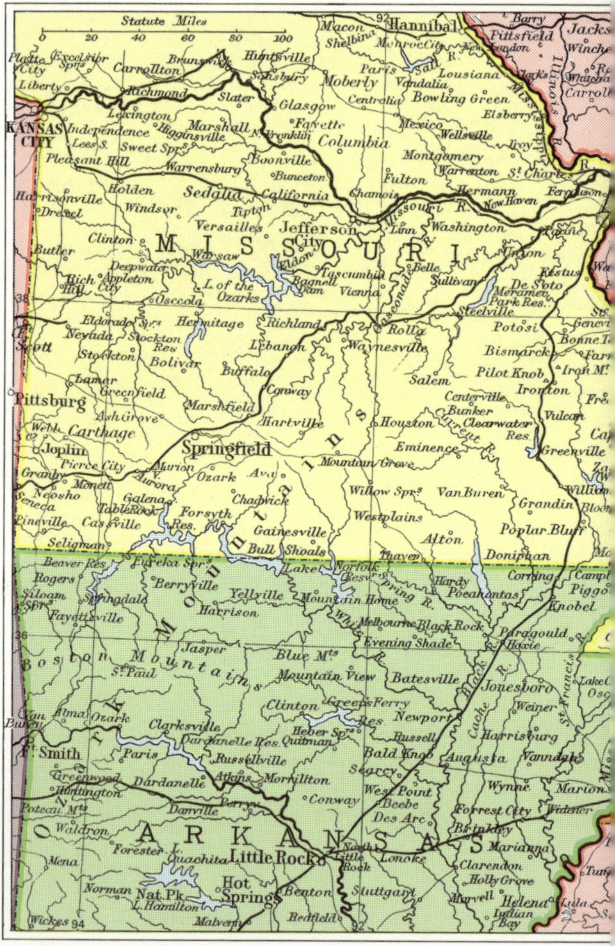
Statute Miles
0 20 40 60 80 100
MISSOURI
ARKANSAS
KANSAS CITY
Platte City
Excelsior Sprs
Liberty
Carrollton
Brunswick
Huntsville
Macon
Shelbina
Hannibal
Monroe City
New London
Pittsfield
Barry
Salt R.
Paris
Moberly
Salisbury
Vandalia
Lousiana
Richmond
Slater
Glasgow
Centralia
Bowling Green
Mississippi R.
Illinois R.
Lexington
Independence
Higginsville
Marshall
Fayette
N. Franklin
Columbia
Mexico
Wellsville
Elsberry
Troy
Lees S.
Sweet Sprs
Pleasant Hill
Warrensburg
Boonville
Bunceton
Montgomery
Warrenton
St Charles
Fulton
Harrisonville
Holden
Sedalia
California
Chamois
Hermann
New Haven
Ferguson
Drexel
Windsor
Tipton
Missouri R.
Versailles
Jefferson City
Linn
Washington
Pacific
Clinton
Butler
Warsaw
Eldon
Gasconade R.
Union
Deepwater
Appleton City
Rich Hill
Bagnell Dam
Tascumbia
Belle
Sullivan
De Soto
Festus
L. of the Ozarks
Vienna
Meramec Park Res.
Osceola
Steelville
Eldorado Sprs
Hermitage
Richland
Rolla
Potosi
Nevada
Stockton Res
Stockton
Lebanon
Waynesville
Bismarck
Ft Scott
Bolivar
Buffalo
Salem
Pilot Knob
Iron Mt
Lamar
Greenfield
Conway
Centerville
Ironton
Pittsburg
Ash Grove
Marshfield
Bunker
Clearwater Res.
Vulcan
Webb
Carthage
Hartville
Houston
Current R.
Joplin
Springfield
Eminence
Greenville
Pierce City
Marion
Mountain Grove
Granby
Monett
Aurora
Ozark
Ava
Willow Sprs
Van Buren
Neosho
Seneca
Galena
Chadwick
Grandin
Table Rock
Forsyth
Westplains
Pineville
Cassville
Res.
Gainesville
Poplar Bluff
Seligman
Bull Shoals
Alton
Thayer
Doniphan
Beaver Res
Eureka Sprs
Lake
Norfolk Resv
Spring R.
Hardy
Corning
Rogers
Berryville
Yellville
Pocahontas
Piggott
Siloam Sprs
Springdale
Mountain Home
Knobel
Fayetteville
Harrison
White R.
Melbourne
Black Rock
Paragould
Evening Shade
Hoxie
Jasper
Boston Mountains
Ozark Mountains
Blue Mts
St Paul
Black R.
St Francis R.
Mountain View
Batesville
Jonesboro
Clinton
Greers Ferry Res.
Newport
Weiner
Cache R.
Van Buren
Alma
Ozark
Clarksville
Heber Sprs
Quitman
Harrisburg
Russell
Ft Smith
Paris
Dardanelle Res.
Russellville
Bald Knob
Augusta
Vanndale
Searcy
Greenwood
Dardanelle
Atkins
Morrillton
Wynne
Huntington
Conway
West Point
Beebe
Marion
Poteau Mts
Danville
Perry
Forrest City
Des Arc
Waldron
Brinkley
Forester
L. Ouachita
North Little Rock
Lonoke
Marianna
Mena
Little Rock
Clarendon
Holly Grove
Hot Springs
Benton
Stuttgart
Norman
Nat. Pk
L. Hamilton
Marvell
Helena
Indian Bay
Wickes
Malvern
Redfield
92
94
38
36

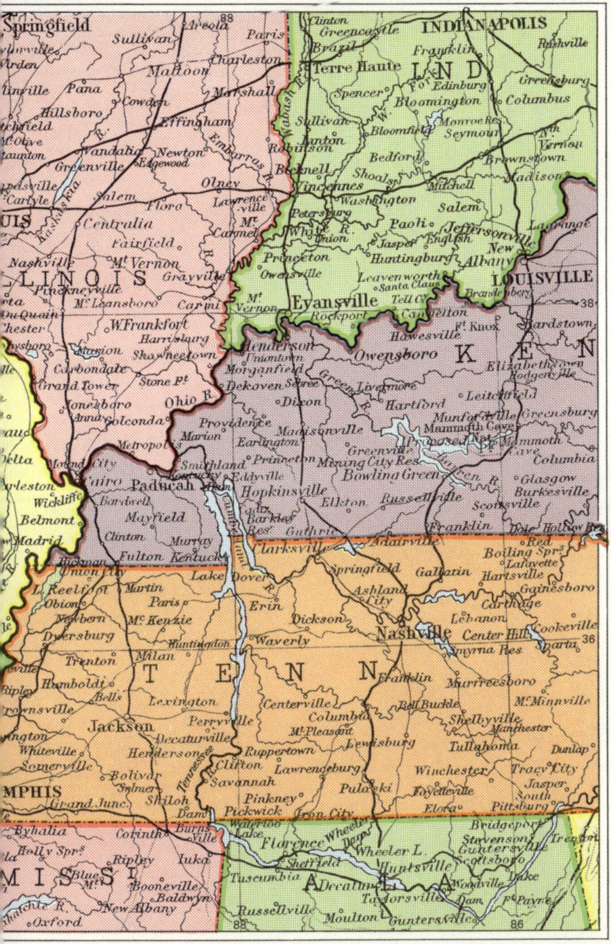

Springfield
Sullivan
Areola
Paris
Charleston
Mattoon
Pana
Cowden
Marshall
Hillsboro
Effingham
Vandalia
Newton
Edgewood
Greenville
Embarras R.
Olney
Salem
Flora
Lawrenceville
Mt Carmel
Centralia
Fairfield
Nashville
Mt Vernon
Grayville
LINOIS
Pinckneyville
McLeansboro
Carmi
W.Frankfort
Harrisburg
Shawneetown
Carbondale
Grand Tower
Stone Ft
Ohio R.
Jonesboro
Anna
Golconda
Metropolis
Mound City
Cairo
Paducah
Smithland
Wickliffe
Belmont
Bardwell
Mayfield
Clinton
Murray
Fulton
Kentucky
Hickman
Union City
Clinton
Greencastle
INDIANAPOLIS
Rushville
Brazil
Franklin
Terre Haute
IND
Edinburg
Greensburg
Spencer
Bloomington
Columbus
Wabash R.
Sullivan
Linton
Bloomfield
Monroe Res.
Seymour
Nth Vernon
Robinson
Bedford
Brownstown
Bicknell
Shoals
Madison
Vincennes
Mitchell
Washington
Salem
Petersburg
White R.
Paoli
Jeffersonville
Union
Jasper
English
New Albany
Princeton
Huntingburg
Owensville
Leavenworth
Santa Claus
LOUISVILLE
Mt Vernon
Evansville
Tell City
Rockport
Cannelton
Brandenburg
Hawesville
Ft Knox
Bardstown
Henderson
Owensboro
KEN
Morganfield
Elizabethtown
Hodgenville
Dekoven
Sebree
Green R.
Livermore
Leitchfield
Dixon
Hartford
Munfordville
Greensburg
Mammoth Cave
Providence
Madisonville
Marion
Earlington
Greenville
Mammoth Cave
Columbia
Princeton
Mining City Res.
Eddyville
Bowling Green
Glasgow
Hopkinsville
Elkton
Russellville
Burkesville
Scottsville
Cadiz
Barkley Res.
Guthrie
Franklin
Dale Hollow Res.
Clarksville
Adairville
Red Boiling Sprs
Lafayette
Springfield
Gallatin
Hartsville
Lake
Dover
Ashland City
Gainesboro
Carthage
Reelfoot
Martin
Obion
Paris
Erin
Lebanon
Newbern
McKenzie
Dickson
Nashville
Center Hill
Cookeville
Dyersburg
Huntingdon
Waverly
Smyrna Res.
Sparta
Trenton
Milan
TENN
Franklin
Murfreesboro
Humboldt
Bells
Lexington
Centerville
Bell Buckle
McMinnville
Columbia
Shelbyville
Jackson
Perryville
Mt Pleasant
Manchester
Decaturville
Lewisburg
Tullahoma
Whiteville
Henderson
Ruppertown
Dunlap
Somerville
Clifton
Lawrenceburg
Winchester
Tracy City
Bolivar
Savannah
Pulaski
Jasper
Selmer
Tennessee R.
Pinkney
Fayetteville
South Pittsburg
MPHIS
Grand Junc.
Shiloh
Dam
Pickwick
Iron City
Elora
Byhalia
Corinth
Burnsville
Waterloo
Lake
Wheeler Dam
Bridgeport
Stevenson
Holly Sprs
Ripley
Iuka
Florence
Wheeler L.
Guntersville
Scottsboro
MISSI
Blue Mt
Sheffield
Huntsville
Booneville
Tuscumbia
Decatur
Woodville
Baldwyn
ALA
New Albany
Taylorsville
Dam
Ft Payne
Oxford
Russellville
Moulton
Guntersville
88
38
36
86

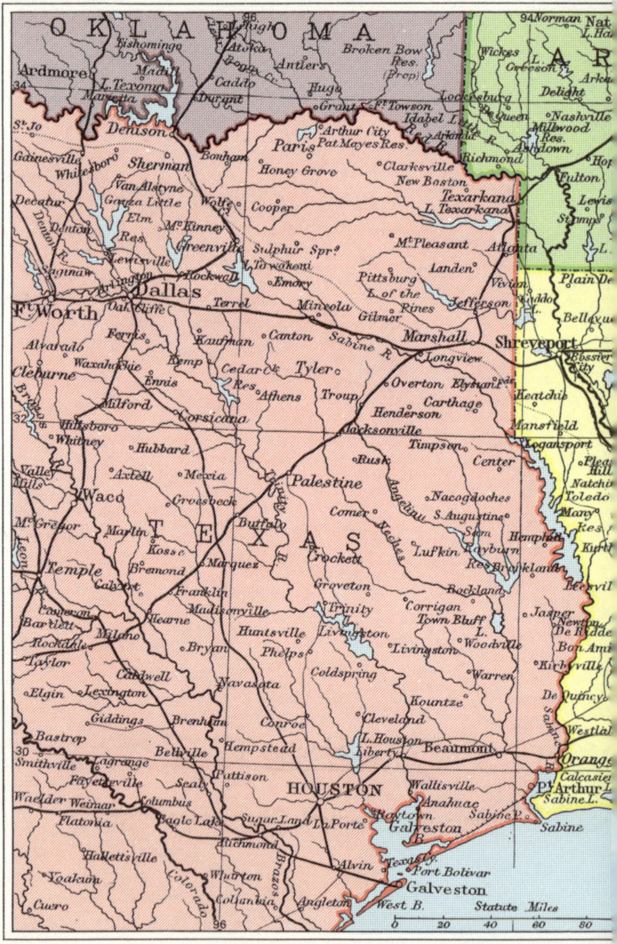
O K L A H O M A
T E X A S
Ardmore
Tishomingo
Atoka
Antlers
Broken Bow Res. (Prop)
Caddo
Durant
Hugo
Grant
Ft Towson
Idabel
Marietta
L. Texoma
Madill
Denison
Sherman
Bonham
Paris
Pat Mayes Res.
Arthur City
Honey Grove
Clarksville
New Boston
Texarkana
L. Texarkana
St Jo
Gainesville
Whitesboro
Van Alstyne
Decatur
Denton
McKinney
Greenville
Cooper
Sulphur Spr.
Mt Pleasant
Lewisville
Rockwall
L. Tawakoni
Emory
Pittsburg
Linden
Atlanta
Saginaw
Arlington
Dallas
Ft Worth
Oak Cliffe
Terrel
Mineola
L. of the Pines
Jefferson
Gilmer
Vivian
Marshall
Shreveport
Longview
Alvarado
Ferris
Kaufman
Canton
Sabine R.
Cleburne
Waxahachie
Kemp
Cedar Ck Res.
Tyler
Ennis
Athens
Troup
Overton
Carthage
Milford
Corsicana
Henderson
Hillsboro
Whitney
Jacksonville
Mansfield
Timpson
Logansport
Hubbard
Rusk
Center
Axtell
Mexia
Palestine
Waco
Groesbeck
Nacogdoches
Valley Mills
Comer
S. Augustine
Mc Gregor
Marlin
Buffalo
Trinity R.
Lufkin
Neches
Angelina
Hemphill
Kosse
Crockett
Temple
Bremond
Marquez
Cabert
Franklin
Groveton
Rockland
Madisonville
Trinity
Corrigan
Jasper
Cameron
Hearne
Town Bluff
Bartlett
Milano
Huntsville
Livingston
Woodville
Rockdale
Bryan
Phelps
Taylor
Caldwell
Coldspring
Warren
Elgin
Lexington
Navasota
Kountze
Giddings
Brenham
Conroe
Cleveland
Bastrop
Hempstead
L. Houston
Liberty
Beaumont
Smithville
Lagrange
Bellville
Orange
Fayetteville
Sealy
Pattison
HOUSTON
Wallisville
Pt Arthur
Waelder
Weimar
Columbus
Anahuac
Sabine L.
Flatonia
Eagle Lake
Sugar Land
La Porte
Raytown
Galveston B.
Sabine
Richmond
Hallettsville
Brazos
Alvin
Texas Cy.
Port Bolivar
Galveston
Yoakum
Colorado
Wharton
Columbia
Angleton
West B.
Cuero
Statute Miles
0
20
40
60
80
96
94
34
32
30

MISSISSIPPI
LOUISIANA
NEW ORLEANS
Baton Rouge
Jackson
Vicksburg
Natchez
Monroe
Alexandria
Pine Bluff
El Dorado
Greenville
Greenwood
Hattiesburg
Gulfport
Biloxi
Lafayette
Opelousas
Lake Pontchartrain
Mississippi R.
Red R.
Pearl R.
Big Black R.
Yazoo R.
Chandeleur Sound
Vermilion Bay
92
90
34
32
30

WESTERN STATES

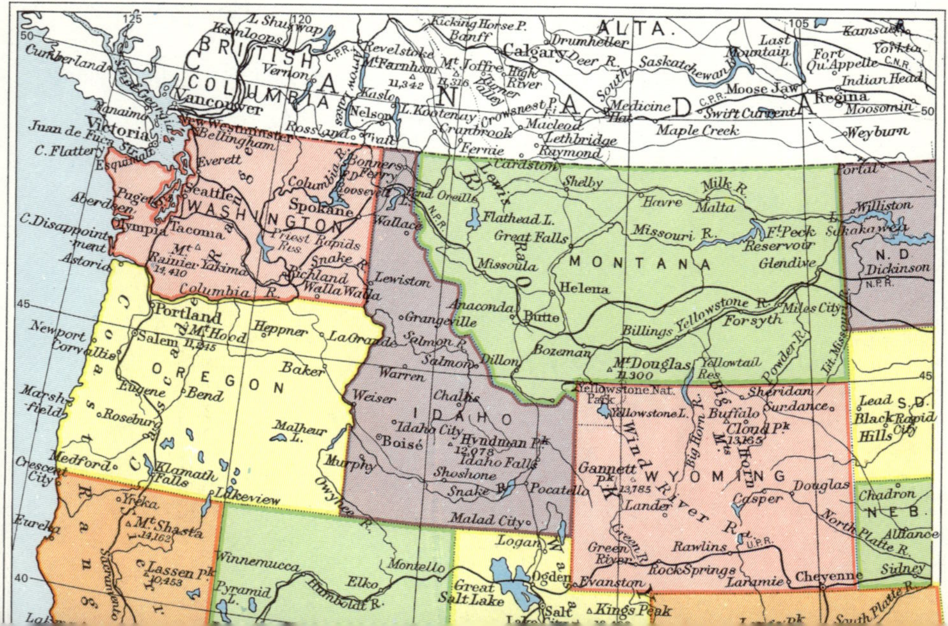

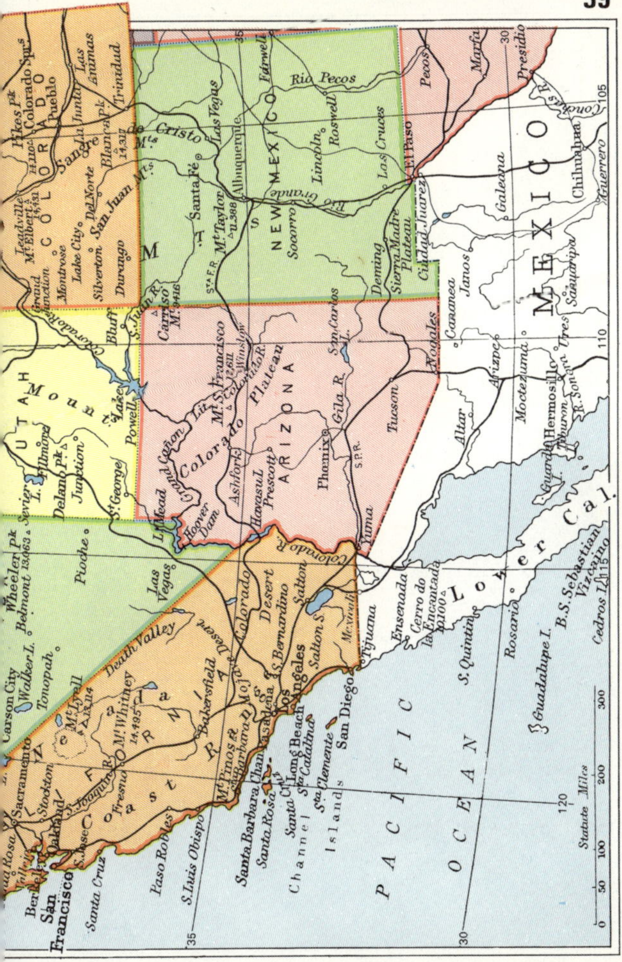
UTAH
COLORADO
NEW MEXICO
ARIZONA
MEXICO
PACIFIC OCEAN
Lower Cal.
Channel Islands
Colorado Plateau
Mount Lake Powell
Sangre de Cristo Mts
San Juan Mts
Sierra Madre Plateau
Death Valley
Mojave Desert
Colorado Desert
Coast Ra.
Grand Canon
Hoover Dam
L. Mead
Rio Grande
Rio Pecos
Colorado R.
Gila R.
S. Juan R.
Salton S.
Pikes Pk
Colorado Sps
Pueblo
Las Animas
La Junta
Trinidad
Leadville
Mt Elbert 14,431
Blanca Pk 14,317
Del Norte
Lake City
Silverton
Durango
Montrose
Grand Junction
Las Vegas
Santa Fé
Albuquerque
Mt Taylor 11,388
Socorro
Lincoln
Roswell
Farwell
Las Cruces
Deming
El Paso
Ciudad Juarez
Pecos
Marfa
Presidio
Carrizo Mt 9416
Mt S. Francisco 12,611
Winslow
Ashfork
Prescott
Havasu L.
Phœnix
San Carlos L.
Tucson
Nogales
Yuma
S.P.R.
St. George
Junction
Delano Pk
L. Fillmore
Sevier L.
Bluff
Wheeler Pk
Belmont 13,063
Pioche
Las Vegas
Tonopah
Walker L.
Carson City
Mt Lyell 13,114
Mt Whitney 14,495
Sacramento
Stockton
Oakland
Berkeley
San Francisco
S. Jose
Santa Cruz
Fresno
S. Joaquin R.
Bakersfield
Paso Robles
S. Luis Obispo
Mt Pinos
Santa Barbara
Santa Barbara Chan.
Santa Rosa
Santa Cruz
Sta Catalina
Sta Clemente
Pasadena
Los Angeles
Long Beach
S. Bernardino
San Diego
Tijuana
Mexicali
Ensenada
Cerro do la Encantada 10100
S. Quintin
Rosario
Guadalupe I.
B. S. Sebastian Vizcaino
Cedros I.
Guardia I.
Tiburon I.
Hermosillo
Moctezuma
Arizpe
Altar
Cananea
Janos
Galeana
Chihuahua
Guerrero
Sahuaripa
Ures
R. Sonora
Conchos R.
Statute Miles
0 50 100 200 300
35
30
105
110
115
120

PACIFIC COAST

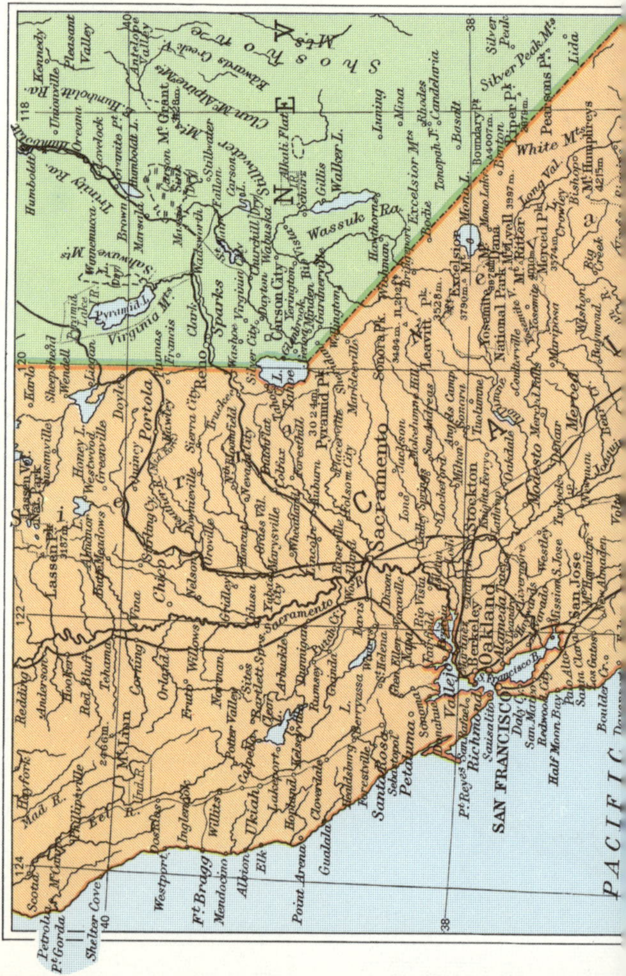

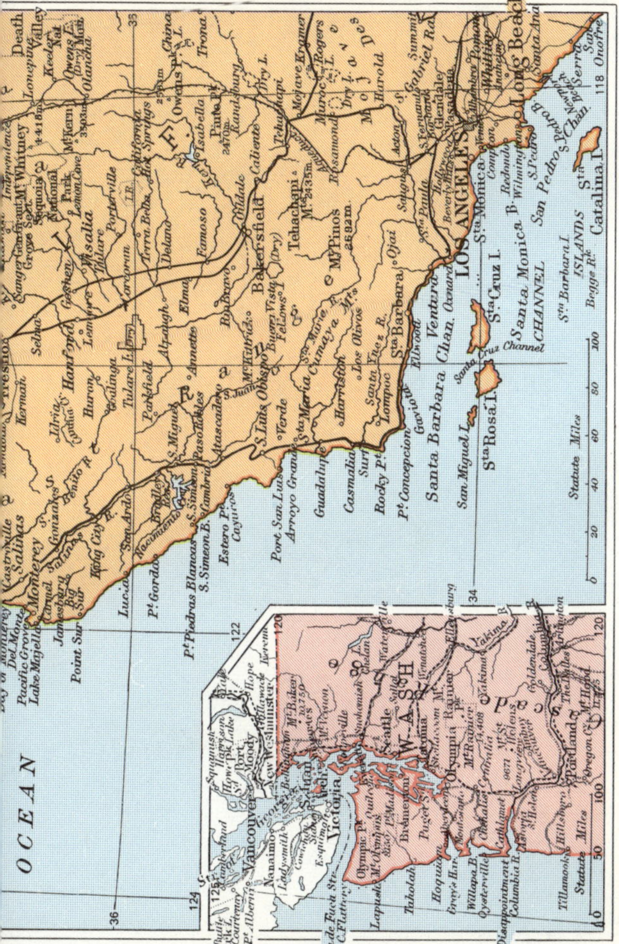
OCEAN
LOS ANGELES
Long Beach
Pasadena
Glendale
Santa Monica
San Pedro
Bakersfield
Tehachapi
Mt Pinos
Hanford
Visalia
Tulare
Fresno
Monterey
Salinas
Santa Barbara
Ventura
Santa Barbara Chan.
Santa Cruz Channel
Santa Monica CHANNEL
Sta Cruz I.
Sta Rosa I.
San Miguel I.
Sta Catalina I.
Pt Concepcion
Point Sur
Statute Miles
Vancouver
Victoria
Seattle
Tacoma
Olympia
Portland
Mt Rainier
Mt Hood
Statute Miles

ALASKA

U. S. S. R.
Arctic Circle
Chukotskiy Pen.a
Anadyr Gulf
Anadyr
Meynypilgyno
Bering Sea
St. Lawrence I.
St. Matthew I.
Hall I.
Nunivak I.
Pribilof Is
St. Paul I.
St. George I.
Aleutian Is
Unalaska
Dutch Harbor
Umnak I.
Fox Is
Unimak I.
Atka
Amlia
Adak
Kanaga
Tanaga
Amchitka
Andreanof Is
Rat Is
Kiska
Attu
Agattu
Bristol Bay
Kuskokwim B.
Kuskokwim
Kwigillingok
Bethel
Mountain Village
Hooper Bay
C. Romanzof
Norton Sd.
St. Michael
Unalakleet
Nome
Seward Pen.a
C. Pr. of Wales
Bering Str.
Kotzebue Sd.
C. Lisburne
Point Hope
Noatak R.
Noorvik
Wainwright
Pt. Barrow
Barrow
Colville
Brooks Range
Endicott Mts
Koyukuk
Kaktovik
Prudhoe B.
Halkett C.
Ft. Yukon
Circle
Yukon
Eagle
Big Delta
Tanana
Fairbanks
Nenana
Ruby
Kaltag
Holy Cross
Flat
McGrath
Mt. McKinley Nat. Pk
Alaska Range
Curry
Palmer
Anchorage
Cook Inlet
Kenai Pen.a
Homer
Seward
Valdez
Cordova
Prince William Sd.
Mt. Sanford
Mt. Wrangell
Mt. St. Elias
Mt. Logan
Mt. Fairweather
Gulf of Alaska
Kodiak I.
Kodiak
Afognak I.
Katmai
Alaska Pen.a
Shumagin Is
Ft. Randall
L. Iliamna
Platinum
Chichagof I.
Alexander Arch.
Sitka
Baranof I.
Juneau
Skagway
Telegraph Creek
Petersburg
Wrangell
Ketchikan
Prince of Wales I.
Metlakatla
Prince Rupert
Graham I.
Queen Charlotte Is
Moresby I.
Skeena
B. C.
Stikine Mts
Rocky Mts
Whitehorse
Teslin
Yukon Territory
Ft. Selkirk
Dawson
Mayo
Klondike
Mackenzie Mts
Ft. Simpson
Liard
Ft. Norman
Mackenzie
Great Bear Lake
Coppermine
Inuvik
Aklavik
Ft. McPherson
Tuktoyaktuk
Mackenzie Bay
Bathurst C.
Alaska Highway
Statute Miles
0 50 100 200 300

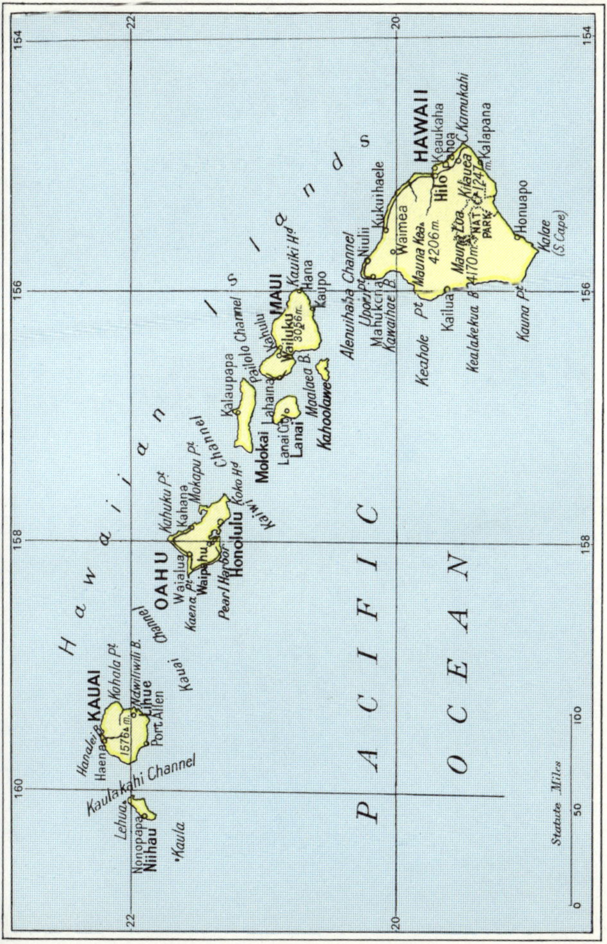

Hawaiian Islands
PACIFIC OCEAN
KAUAI
OAHU
MAUI
HAWAII
Niihau
Molokai
Lanai
Kahoolawe
Kaula
Lehua
Nonopapa
Kaulakahi Channel
Kauai Channel
Kaiwi Channel
Pailolo Channel
Alenuihaha Channel
Haena
Hanalei B.
Kahala Pt
1576 m.
Nawiliwili B.
Lihue
Port Allen
Kaena Pt
Waialua
Kahuku Pt
Kahana
Mokapu Pt
Koko Hd
Wahiawa
Pearl Harbor
Honolulu
Kalaupapa
Lahaina
Lanai City
Maalaea B.
Wailuku
Kahului
3056 m.
Hana
Kauiki Hd
Kaupo
Upolu Pt
Mahukona
Kawaihae B.
Niulii
Kukuihaele
Waimea
Mauna Kea
4206 m.
Mauna Loa
4170 m.
NAT PARK
Kilauea
1247 m.
Hilo
Keaukaha
Kapoho
C. Kumukahi
Kalapana
Honuapo
Kalae (S. Cape)
Kauna Pt
Keahole Pt
Kailua
Kealakekua B.
Statute Miles
0
50
100
154
156
158
160
20
22

MEXICO AND C. AMERICA

ATLANTIC OCEAN
WEST INDIES
CARIBBEAN SEA
GREATER ANTILLES
LESSER ANTILLES
CUBA
BAHAMA ISLANDS
HISPANIOLA
DOMINICAN REP.
JAMAICA
Puerto Rico (United States)
SOUTH AMERICA
Tropic of Cancer
Windward Passage
Mona Passage
Leeward Is.
Windward Is.
Virgin Is.
G. of Venezuela
Isla de Pinos
Havana
Cienfuegos
Camaguey
Santiago de Cuba
Port au Prince
Sto Domingo
Kingston
San Juan
Guadeloupe
Martinique
Dominica
St. Lucia
St. Vincent
Grenada
Barbados
TRINIDAD & TOBAGO
Port of Spain
Curaçao
Aruba
Bonaire
Margarita
Maracaibo
Barranquilla
Cartagena
Paraguana Pena
Guajira Pena
Statute Miles
0 100 200 300

SOUTH AMERICA

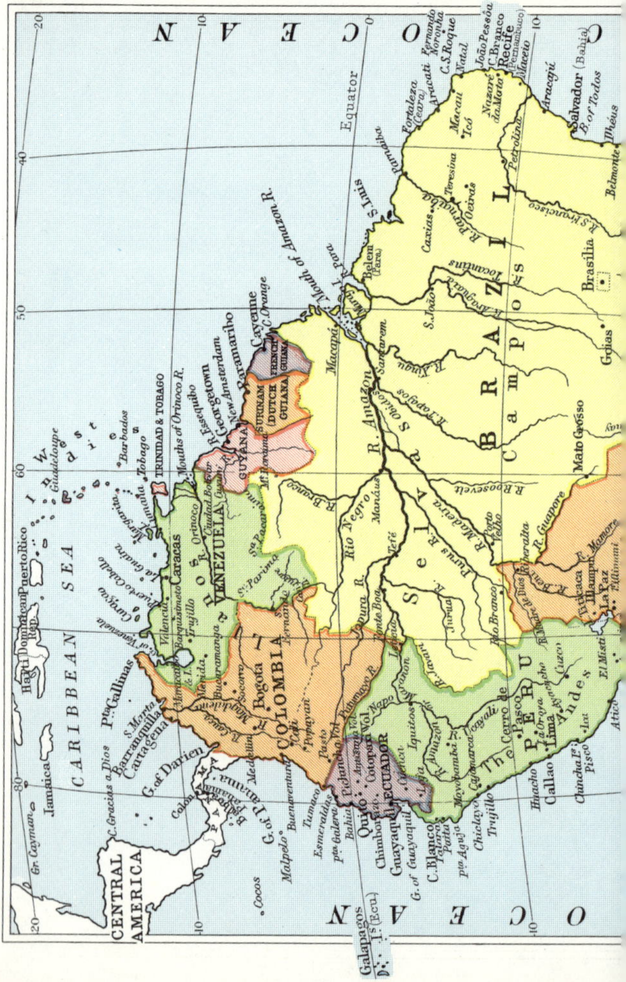

ATLANTIC
PACIFIC
Rio de Janeiro
S. Paulo
Santos
Vitória
Campos
C. Frio
Niteroi
Ouro Preto
Itatiaia
Iguape
Cananéia
Paranaguá
S. Francisco do Sul
Sta. Catarina I.
Florianopolis
Curitiba
R. Paraná
Rio Grande
Pto Alegre
L. Patos
Posadas
Corrientes
Asunción
Concepcion
PARAGUAY
R. Pilcomayo
URUGUAY
Paysandú
Fray Bentos
Colonia
Maldonado
Montevideo
Rio de la Plata
C. S. Antonio
Mar del Plata
C. Corrientes
Buenos Aires
La Plata
Azul
Bahia Blanca
Rosario
Chivilcoy
Santa Fé
Paraná
Gualeguaychu
Formosa
R. Bermejo
R. Salado
Oran
Jujuy
Salta
S. Miguel de Tucuman
Catamarca
La Rioja
Cordoba
S. Juan
Uspallata Pass
Mendoza
San Luis
ARGENTINA
Colorado
R. Negro
Carmen de Patagones
G. of S. Matias
Chubut R.
Rawson
R. Chico
G. San Jorge
Deseado
Santa Cruz
Patagonia
Strait of Magellan
Tierra del Fuego
Staten I.
Cape Horn
Falkland Is (UK)
Stanley
S. Georgia (UK)
Statute Miles
0
500
1000
Tropic of Capricorn
Atacama Desert
Andes
CHILE
Iquique
R. Loa
Tocopilla
Mejillones
Antofagasta
Taltal
Chañaral
Caldera
Copiapó
La Serena
Coquimbo
Mt. Aconcagua
Valparaiso
Santiago
Chillan
Talca
Talcahuano
Concepcion
Lebu
Valdivia
Corral
Puerto Montt
Chiloé I.
Chonos Archo.
G. of Peñas
Wellington I.
Str. of Magellan
Juan Fernandez Is. (Chile)
S. Ambrosio
S. Felix
Calama
Chuquicamata
20
30
40
50
60
70
80
90
100

VENEZUELA, COLOMBIA, GUIANA

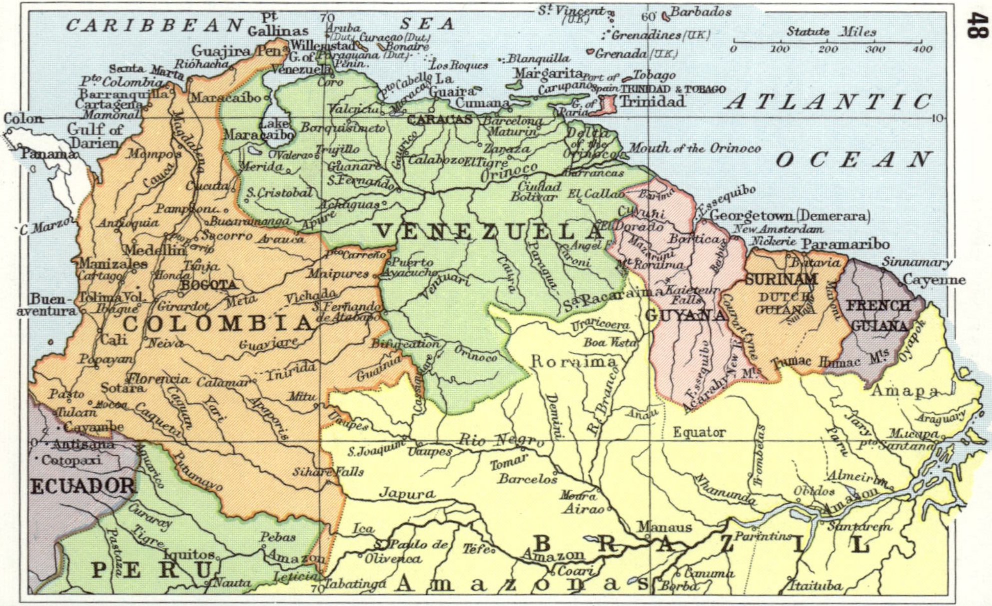

VENEZUELA
COLOMBIA
BOGOTA
Buenaventura
Cali
Popayan
Sotara
Pasto
Tulcan
Tumaco
Esmeraldas
S.Francisco
Pedernales
Ibarra
Cayambe
QUITO
Cotopaxi
Chimborazo
ECUADOR
Riobamba
Guayaquil
Salinas
Cuenca
Loja
Tumbes
C.Blanco
Talara
Pariña
Piura
Sechura
C.Aguja
Lambayeque
Chiclayo
Pacasmayo
Trujillo
Chimbote
Casma
Huacho
LIMA
Callao
Chorillos
Huancayo
Ayacucho
Cuzco
(Cusco)
Chincha Is.
Pisco
Ica
Nazca
Acari R.
Arequipa
Misti
Mollendo
Moquegua
Ilo
Tacna
Arica
Pisagua
Iquique
Rio Loa
Tocopilla
Mejillones
CHILE
Calama
Atacama
Lagunas
Tarapaca
Puno
Lake Titicaca
LA PAZ
Illimani
Ancohuma
Cochabamba
Sahama
Oruro
Poopo
SUCRE
Potosi
Huanchaca
Tupiza
Quiaca
BOLIVIA
Reyes
Riberalta
Beni
Mamore
Madre de Dios
P.to Maldonado
Apolobamba
Ayaviri
Juliaca
PERU
Cerro de Pasco
La Oroya
Huanuco
Huaraz
Uchiza
Pucallpa
Iquitos
Nauta
Marañon
Ucayali
Huallaga
Moyobamba
Chachapoyas
Cajamarca
Jaen
Barranca
Pastaza
Curaray
Tigre
Napo
Putumayo
Caqueta
Pebas
Amazon
Leticia
Tabatinga
BRAZIL
Japura
Ica
S.Paulo de Olivença
Tefe
Jurua
Javari
Acre
Purus
Rio Branco
Abuna
Equator
S.Joaquim
Orinoco
Guaviare
Florencia
Neiva
PACIFIC
OCEAN
Statute Miles
0 100 200 300 400
80
70
10
20

COLOMBIA
PERU
BOLIVIA
CHILE
ARGENTINA
Gran PARAGUAY
B R A
PACIFIC OCEAN
Amazonas
Rondonia
Mato Gro
Acre
Chaco
Amazon
Manaus
Airao
Obidos
Parintins
Pebas
Ica
Fonte Boa
S. Paulo de Olivença
Tefé
Coari
Leticia
Tabatinga
Jurua
Purus
Borba
Abacaxis
Itaituba
R. Tapauá
Tarauaca
Tapajos
S. Manuel
Crato
Humaita
Madeira
Pto. Velho
Roosevelt
Rio Branco
Abuna
Girau Falls
Barracão do Barreto
Teles Pires
Vila Murtinho
Guajara Mirim
Principe da Beira
Riberalta
Cobija
R. Madre de Dios
Beni
Arinos
Pto. Maldonado
Madidi
Mamore
Baures
Guapore
Cuzco (Cusco)
Sta. Rosa
Apolo
Trinidad
S. Miguel
Grande
Mato Grosso
Diamantino
Paraguai
Lampa
Lake Titicaca
Puno
Ancohuma
Illimani
LA PAZ
Arequipa
Misti
Matarani
Mollendo
Moquegua
Ilo
Sajama
Cochabamba
Oruro
S. Javier
S. Ignacio
Cuiabá
Cáceres
S. Lourenço
Santa Cruz
S. Juan
Robore
Tacna
Arica
L. Poopo
SUCRE
Corumba
Taquari
Pisagua
Potosi
Coimbra
Pto. Esperança
Iquique
Tarapaca
Uyuni
Huanchaca
Camargo
Miranda
Lagunas
Villa Montes
Olimpo
Rio Loa
Tocopilla
Chuquicamata
Calama
Tupiza
Tarija
La Quiaca
Apa
Bella Vista
Mejillones
Atacama
Humahuaca
Oran
Concepcion
Antofagasta
S. Salvador de Jujuy
San Martin
R. Teuco
Pilcomayo
Cachinal
Paposo
Llullaillaco Vol.
Salta
San Pedro
Guaira Falls
Taltal
Las Lomitas
ASUNCION
Paraguari
Santa Maria
Metan
S. Miguel de Tucuman
Villarrica
Chañaral
Avia Teria
Paraguay
Formosa
Caldera
Copiapo
Copiapo Vol.
Tintina
Pilar
Parana
Belen
Andalgala
Resistencia
Posadas
Juan Godoy
Santiago del Estero
La Sabana
Corrientes
Tinogasta
Bella Vista
São Borja
Huasco
Vallenar
Catamarca
Mazan
Añatuya
Reconquista
El Toto
Chilecito
Goya
Uruguaiana
La Serena
Rio
do
60
10
20
70

BRAZIL, BOLIVIA, PARAGUAY
Statute Miles
0 100 200 300 400
ATLANTIC
OCEAN
Tropic of Capricorn
Marajo I.
Belem (Para)
Bragança
I. S. João
S. Luis
Parnaiba
Camocim
Fortaleza (Ceara)
Aracati
R. Piranhas
C. S. Roque
Natal
Rio Grande do Norte
João Pessôa
Paraiba
Campina Grande
C. Branco
Recife (Pernambuco)
Pernambuco
Alagoas
Maceio
Penedo
Sergipe
Aracaju
S. Cristovão
Salvador (Bahia)
Bahia
Para
Maranhao
Ceara
Piaui
Teresina
Floriano
Oeiras
Caxias
Tutoia
Brejo
Viana
Sobral
Baturite
Crateus
Crato
Ico
Carolina
Pedro Afonso
Tocantinia
Porto Nacional
Parnagua
Barra
Juazeiro
Jacobina
Itapicuru
São Francisco
Paratinga
Cachoeira
Contas
Itacare
Ilheus
Canavieiros
Belmonte
Porto Seguro
Caravelas
Abrolhos
Goias
BRASILIA
Anapolis
Goiânia
Pirenopolis
Aruanã
Catalão
Montes Claros
Januaria
Rio Pardo
Jequitinhonha
Minas Novas
Teofilo Otoni
Diamantina
Pirapora
Paracatu
Minas Gerais
Serro
Araguari
Uberlândia
Uberaba
Prata
Belo Horizonte
Ouro Preto
S. Joao del Rei
Juiz de Fora
Espirito Santo
S. Mateus
Rio Doce
Vitória
Cachoeira
Itapemirim
R. Paraiba
C. São Tomé
Macaé
Niteroi
C. Frio
Rio de Janeiro
RIO DE JANEIRO
São Paulo
S. Paulo
Campinas
Ribeirao Preto
Araraquara
Franca
Lavras
Itajuba
Santos
S. Sebastião
Sorocaba
Castro
Iguape
Ponta Grossa
Curitiba
Paranagua
São Francisco do Sul
Joinville
Catarina
Blumenau
Florianopolis
Lajes
Laguna
Lagoa Vermelha
Torres
Porto Alegre
Lagoa dos Patos
R. Araguaia
R. Tocantins
Ilha do Bananal

ARGENTINA
CHILE
URUGUAY
BRAZIL
ATLANTIC OCEAN
Andes
Pampas
Patagonia
Copiapo
Juan Godoy
Huasco
Vallenar
El Toro
La Serena
Coquimbo
Ovalle
Illapel
Los Vilos
Viña del Mar
Valparaiso
SANTIAGO
S. Antonio
Pichilemu
Rancagua
Curico
Constitucion
Talca
Linares
Talcahuano
Tomé
Concepcion
Chillan
Lota
Arauco
Los Angeles
Lebu
Angol
Mocha I.
Temuco
Valdivia
Corral
Osorno
L. Llanquihue
Puerto Montt
Ancud
I. of Chiloë
Guafo I.
G. of Corcovado
Chonos Archipelago
Taitao Peninsula
G. of Peñas
Great Wellington Island
Madre de Dios Archipelago
Hanover I.
Pto Natales
Q. Adelaide Ar.
Str. of Magellan
Desolation I.
Santa Ines I.
Cockburn Chan.
Londonderry I.
Hoste I.
Navarino I.
Cape Horn
Belen
Andalgala
Tinogasta
Santiago del Estero
Catamarca
Añatuya
Mazan
Chilecito
La Rioja
Jachal
Dean Funes
S. Juan
Cruz del Eje
Cordoba
Aconcagua
V. Dolores
Mendoza
S. Luis
S. Rafael
Villa Mercedes
Rufino
Realico
Sierra Nevado
Sta Rosa de Toay
Salado
Resistencia
La Sabana
Corrientes
Bella Vista
Reconquista
Goya
Mercedes
Parana
L. Chiquita
Santa Fe
Villa Maria
Concordia
Concepcion
Rosario
Pergamino
BUENOS AIRES
Junin
Chivilcoy
Trenque Lauquen
9 de Julio
General Acha
Ensenada
La Plata
Chascomus
Azul
Olavarria
Tandil
Dolores
C. San Antonio
Tres Arroyos
Mar del Plata
C. Corrientes
Necochea
Bahia Blanca
Colorado
Callaqui Vol.
Zapala
Rio Neuquen
Neuquen
Villarrica Vol.
Luro
Rio Negro
Pto S. Antonio
Viedma
Carmen de Patagones
L. Nahuel-Huapi
San Carlos de Bariloche
G. of San Matias
Minchinmavida Vol.
Esquel
Pto Madryn
Peninsula of S. Jose
Trelew
Rawson
Bahia Nueva
R. Chubut
Senguerr
Camarones B.
Comodoro Rivadavia
Dos Bahias C.
Pto Aisen
Sarmiento
G. San Jorge
Mt S. Valentin
Colonia Las Heras
L. Buenos Aires
R. Deseado
C. Blanco
Deseado
L. S. Martin
Chico
L. Viedma
Port S. Julian
S. Cruz
L. Argentino
Port Santa Cruz
Mt Stokes
Rio Gallegos
Coy Inlet
L. Turbio
C. Virgenes
Str. of Magellan
Punta Arenas
C. Froward
Tierra del Fuego
Mt Darwin
Ushuaia
C. S. Diego
Staten I.
Falkland Islands (U.K.)
Jason Is
West Falkland
Stanley
East Falkland
Falkland Sd
Posados
San Borja
Uruguaiana
Porto A
Livramento
Rivera
Bage
Pelotas
Salto
Paysandu
Melo
Fray Bentos
Durazno
Treinta y Tres
Fray Bentos
Colonia
Lavalleja
Canelones
Rocha
Maldonado
MONTEVIDEO
Rio de la Plata
Statute Miles
0 100 200 300 400
30
40
50
60
80

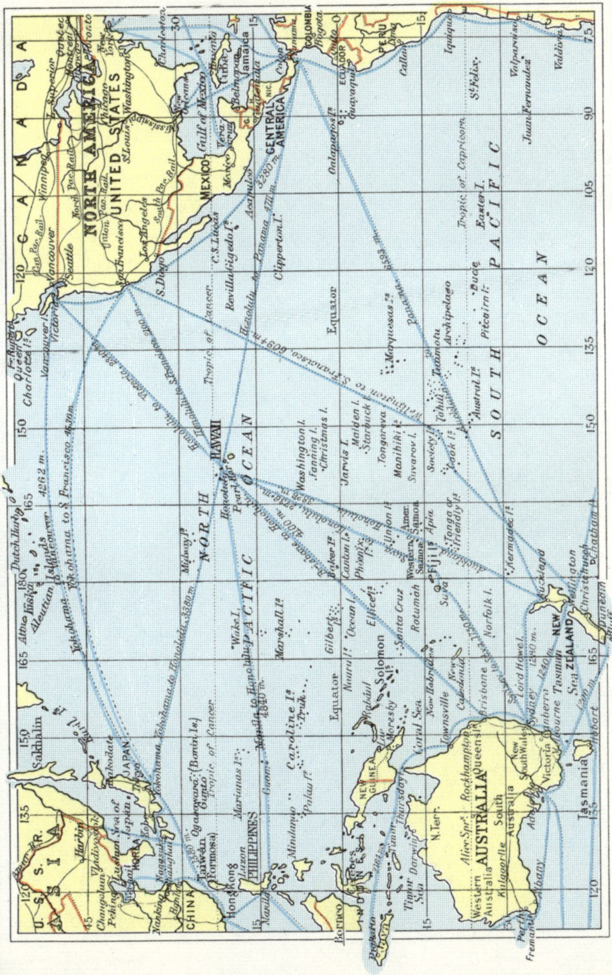

Mercator's Projection

BAFFIN BAY
GREENLAND
Baffin Island
Foxe Basin
Melville Peninsula
Gulf of Boothia
Boothia Pena
Davis Strait
Disko I.
Godhaven
Christianshaab
Jakobshavn
Holsteinsborg
Söndre Strömfjord
Godthaab
Frederikshaab
Julianehaab
C. Farewell
King Frederick VI Ld.
King Christian IX
Angmagsalik
Southampton I.
Foxe Pen.
L. Amadjuak
L. Nettilling
Hudson Strait
Baker L.
Chesterfield Inlet
KEEWATIN
HUDSON BAY
Churchill
C. Chidley
Hebron
Nain
Hopedale
COAST OF LABRADOR
Hamilton Inlet
Goose Bay
Battle Harb.
Str. of Belle Isle
Churchill to Liverpool 2930 m.
Liverpool to Quebec
York Factory
Nelson
Belcher Is.
James Bay
CANADA
MANITOBA
L. Winnipeg
Winnipeg
NTH. AMERICA
ONTARIO
QUEBEC
Thunder Bay
Quebec
Montreal
Ottawa
Toronto
Sudbury
Duluth
St. Paul
Bismarck
Minneapolis
NEW BRUNSWICK
Fredericton
Saint John
NOVA SCOTIA
Halifax
Sable I.
Anticosti
Gulf of St. Lawrence
NEWFOUNDLAND
Gander
St. Johns
Cape Breton I.
Sydney
Westward Track 15th August to 14th January
Eastward Track
Augusta
Portland
Boston
C. Cod
Boston to Gibraltar
New York
Baltimore
Flores
Milwaukee
Detroit
Chicago
Buffalo
Albany
Niagara
Omaha
Lincoln
Kansas City
St. Louis
Cleveland
Pittsburgh
Cincinnati
New York
Philadelphia
Baltimore
Washington
Richmond
Newport News
UNITED STATES
Memphis
Nashville
Atlanta
Mobile
Wilmington
Charleston
Savannah
ATLANTIC OCEAN
New York to Genoa 4055 m.
St. Thomas to Liverpool 3560 m.
Southampton 4060 m.
Bermudas
San Antonio
Galveston
New Orleans
Tampa
Florida
Miami
New Orleans to Liverpool 4530 m.
Kingston to Liverpool 4030 m.
London to Georgetown (Demerara)
Gulf of Mexico
Matamoras
MEXICO
Tampico
Veracruz
Mexico
Merida
Campeche
Key West
Havana
Cuba
Bahamas
Nassau
Calcos Is.
WEST INDIES
Southampton to Barbados 3622 m.
Colon to Marseilles
Jamaica
Hispaniola
Kingston
St. Thomas
Barbuda
Antigua
Nevis
Montserrat
Dominica
St. Lucia
Barbados
Grenada
Trinidad
& Tobago
New York to Capetown
Belmopan
BRIT. HONDURAS
HONDURAS
Trujillo
Acajutla
NICARAGUA
CENTRAL AMERICA
COSTA RICA
Bluefields
S. Juan
Colon
Punta Arenas
CARIBBEAN SEA
Curaçao
La Guaira
Caracas
Orinoco
VENEZUELA
Georgetown (Demerara)
Paramaribo
Cayenne
New Amsterdam
GUYANA
SURINAM
FR. GUIANA
PACIFIC OCEAN
Panama
& Balboa
COLOMBIA
Bogota
Buenaventura
Tumaco
STH. AMERICA

Liverpool Coast
Scoresby Sound
Jan Mayen
North Cape
Hammerfest
Vardo
Tromsø
Polyarnyy
Murmansk
Lofoten Is.
Narvik
Moskenstraumen
Bodø
Arctic Circle
ICELAND
Gällivare
Tornio
White Sea
Oulu
Archangel
Trondheim
Kristiansund
Molde
Ålesund
Umeå
Vaasa
Gulf of Bothnia
FINLAND
NORWAY
SWEDEN
Faeroerne
510 m.
L. Onega
Gävle
Turku
Helsinki
L. Ladoga
Shetland Is.
Bergen
Oslo
Leningrad
Orkney Is.
Uppsala
Stockholm
Tallinn
ESTONIA
Vologda
Stavanger
Norrköping
Pskov
Rockall.
Inverness
Kristiansand S.
Göteborg
Riga
LATVIA
Aberdeen
SCOTLAND
Glasgow
North Sea
DENMARK
Baltic Sea
Memel
Moscow
Edinburgh
Copenhagen
LITHUANIA
Kaunas
Vilna
Londonderry
BRITISH ISLES
Belfast
Gdansk
Kaliningrad
Minsk
Mogilev
Tula
Dublin
Hull
Hamburg
Szczecin
WHITE RUSSIA
Orel
IRELAND
ENGLAND
LONDON
Amsterdam
Hanover
Berlin
Warsaw
Cork
Rotterdam
GERMANY
POLAND
Kursk
Queenstown (Cobh)
Southampton
Antwerp
Leipzig
Prague
Lvov
Kiev
Kharkov
Plymouth
Brussels
Cologne
Cracow
Channel Is.
Paris
CZECHO-SLOVAKIA
EUROPE
Donetsk
Brest
Orleans
Munich
Vienna
UKRAINE
Rostov
St. Nazaire
Loire
FRANCE
Berne
AUSTRIA
HUNGARY
Kishinev
Odessa
La Rochelle
SWITZERLAND
Budapest
Lyons
Trieste
ROMANIA
Galati
Bordeaux
Venice
Fiume
Bucharest
Santander
Genoa
Turin
YUGOSLAVIA
Belgrade
Danube
Sevastopol
Toulouse
Black Sea
Corunna
Vigo
Bilbao
Marseilles
BULGARIA
Plovdiv
Varna
Poti
Saragossa
Rome
ITALY
Adriatic Sea
Istanbul
Batumi
Oporto
Madrid
Corsica
Naples
Brindisi
Üskudar
Ankara
Trabzon
PORTUGAL
Barcelona
Sardinia
ALBANIA
Thessaloniki
Lisbon
Valencia
SPAIN
Baleares
Palermo
Messina
GREECE
Aegean Sea
TURKEY
Erzurum
St. Michael
Seville
Mediterranean Sea
ANATOLIA
Izmir
Konia
Cadiz
Gibraltar
Algiers
Tunis
Sicily
Athens
Aleppo
Tangier
Rabat
Oran
TUNISIA
Malta
Cyprus
SYRIA
Euphrates
Casablanca
Fez
Gabes
Beirut
Damascus
Madeira
Safi
MOROCCO
ALGERIA
Touggourt
Tripoli
Benghazi
Haifa
Tel Aviv-Yafo
IRAQ
Mogador
Marrakech
Figig
El Golea
Ghadames
Al Bayda
Alexandria
Pt. Said
Jerusalem
JORDAN
Canary Is.
Cairo
Suez
Tenerife
Las Palmas
El Aaiún
SPANISH SAHARA
In Salah
LIBYA
FEZZAN
Asyut
EGYPT
SAUDI ARABIA
Villa Cisneros
Murzuq
Aswan
HEJAZ
Medina
Nile
Wadi Halfa
Red Sea
Jidda
C. Blanco
MAURITANIA
SAHARA
Port Sudan
Suakin
Mecca
Nouakchott
St. Louis
Timbuktu
Niger
NIGER
CHAD
Dongola
Berber
Dakar
MALI
Omdurman
Massawa
YEMEN
C. Verde
SENEGAL
UPPER VOLTA
Niamey
Sokoto
L. Chad
Ft. Lamy
Asmara
Khartoum
Aden
Banjul
Bissau
Bamako
Kukawa
Kano
SUDAN
Gondar
Djibouti
Bissagos Is.
GUINEA
Kaduna
ETHIOPIA
Conakry
SIERRA LEONE
IVORY COAST
GHANA
TOGO
DAHOMEY
NIGERIA
Yola
CENTRAL AFRICAN REP.
AFRICA
Addis Ababa
Harar
Freetown
Kumasi
Lagos
Monrovia
LIBERIA
Abidjan
Porto Novo
P. Harcourt
Juba
C. Palmas
Bassam
Takoradi
Sekondi
Accra
Cape Coast
Buea
CAMEROUN
Bangui
L. Rudolf
Fernando Po
Yaoundé
Congo
ZAIRE
KENYA
Gulf of Guinea
Equat. Guinea
RIO MUNI

ojection

ATLANTIC OCEAN
Reykjavik
ICELAND
Hekla
Arctic Circle
Lofoten Is.
Hamm
Faerøerne
Trondheim
Shetland Is.
Rockall
St. Kilda
C. Wrath
Orkney Is.
Bergen
NORWAY
SWEDEN
Oslo
Stavanger
The Naze
Skagerrak
Kattegat
Vänern
Vättern
Göteborg
Kalmar
Gt. BRITAIN & N. IRELAND
SCOTLAND
REP. OF IRELAND
N.I.
Belfast
Glasgow
Edinburgh
Dublin
Cork
C. Clear
Irish Sea
NORTH SEA
Newcastle
Liverpool
Wales
ENGLAND
St. Georges Ch.
Lands End
London
Thames
Portsmouth
Amsterdam
Helgoland
DENMARK
Kiel
BALTIC
Hamburg
Gdansk
Berlin
Poznan
English Channel
C. la Hague
Str. of Dover
BELGIUM
Bruxelles
GERMANY
E.
W.
Leipzig
Dresden
Köln
Bonn
Frankfurt
Wroclaw
Praha
Brno
Brest
Amiens
Paris
Strasbourg
Nantes
Loire
Orleans
FRANCE
Vichy
Lyon
St. Etienne
Bay of Biscay
Bordeaux
Bayonne
Toulouse
Pyrenees
Garonne
Rhone
Marseille
G. of Lions
München
Boden See
Wien
AUSTRIA
Danube
Bern
SWITZERLAND
Geneva
Mt. Blanc
The Alps
Trieste
Milano
Torino
Genova
Venezia
Bologna
G. of Genova
Firenze
ITALY
Roma
Napoli
Brindisi
Zagreb
Zadar
Sava
YUGOSLAVIA
HUNGARY
Adriatic Sea
Durrës
Str. of Otranto
C. Leuca
C. Ortegal
C. Finisterre
La Coruña
Porto
Burgos
Douro
Bilbao
Zaragoza
SPAIN
Madrid
Tagus
Guadiana
PORTUGAL
Lisboa
C. Roca
C. St. Vincent
Valencia
Guadalquivir R.
Ebro R.
Barcelona
Cadiz
Sevilla
Granada
Strait of Gibraltar
Tangier
Gibraltar
Tarifa Pt.
Balearic Is.
Corsica
Elba
Sardinia
MEDITERRANEAN
Palermo
Sicily
C. Spartivento
C. Passero
MALTA
Alger
Tunis
Morocco
Algeria
AFRICA
Tripoli
Benghazi
Statute Miles
0 100 200 300 400 500
60
50
40
30
20
10
0

C. Nordkyn
Kolguyev I.
Cheshskaya B.
Murmansk
White Sea
Mezen
Timan Hills
Pechora
Arkhangelsk
Kem
Oulu
Onega
Dvina
Ural Mounts
Ob
Tobolsk
Sverdlovsk
Perm
L. Onega
L. Saimaa
L. Ladoga
Kronshtadt
Finland
Leningrad
Vologda
Rybinsk Res.r
Volga
Chudskoye Oz. (L. Peipsi)
Valdai Hills
Gorkiy
Kazan
Kama
R.
S.
U.
Riga
Moskva (Moscow)
Ulyanovsk
Kuybyshev
Orenburg
Orsk
Dvina
Kaunas
Vilnius
Minsk
Mogilev
Tula
Saratov
Volga
Ural
Kursk
Pripet R.
Kharkov
Don
Volgograd
Aral Sea
Kiyev
Lvov
Dnieper
Donetsk
Astrakhan
Bug
Dniester
Taganrog
Azov
Rostov
Odessa
Prut
Iasi
Sea of Azov
Crimea
Stavropol
CASPIAN SEA
Galati
Sevastopol
Caucasus Mts
Mt. Elbrus
Tbilisi
Baku
Bucuresti
BULGARIA
Sofiya
Balkan Mts
Varna
BLACK SEA
Bosporus
Sinop
Batumi
Kars
Yerevan
Trabzon
Istanbul
Sea of Marmara
Erzurum
Mt. Ararat
Tabriz
Tehran
Ankara
Dardanelles
R K E Y
Izmir
Archipelago
Mosul
IRAN
Aleppo (Haleb)
Baghdad
Tigris
SYRIA
Euphrates
Rodhos
Crete
CYPRUS
Damascus
IRAQ
Basra
The Gulf
SEA
Haifa
ISRAEL
Port Said
Alexandria
R. Nile
Jerusalem
JORDAN
SAUDI ARABIA
Suez Canal
A S I A
40
60
70
80
50
40
30
40
50

UNITED KINGDOM

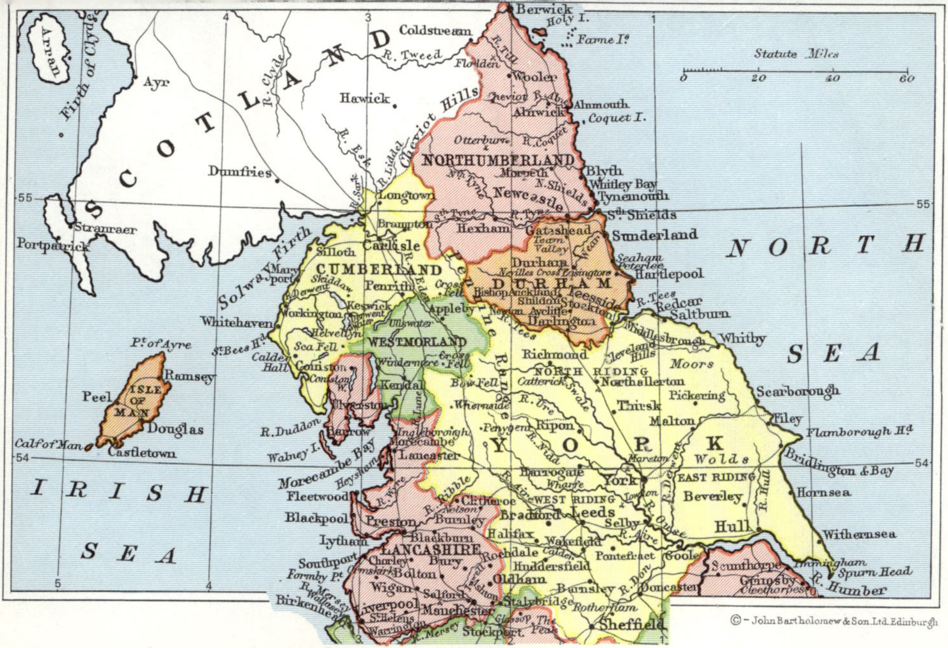
SCOTLAND
NORTH SEA
IRISH SEA
Statute Miles
0 20 40 60
NORTHUMBERLAND
CUMBERLAND
WESTMORLAND
DURHAM
YORK
NORTH RIDING
EAST RIDING
WEST RIDING
LANCASHIRE
ISLE OF MAN
Pennine Range
Cheviot Hills
Cleveland Hills
Moors
Wolds
Berwick
Holy I.
Farne Is
Coldstream
R. Tweed
Flodden
R. Till
Wooler
Alnwick
Alnmouth
Coquet I.
Otterburn
R. Coquet
Morpeth
Blyth
Whitley Bay
Tynemouth
N. Shields
Newcastle
Hexham
Gateshead
St. Shields
Sunderland
Durham
Seaham
Peterlee
Hartlepool
Bishop Auckland
Shildon
Teesside
Stockton
Newton Aycliffe
Darlington
R. Tees
Redcar
Saltburn
Middlesbrough
Whitby
Richmond
Northallerton
Catterick
Pickering
Thirsk
Malton
Scarborough
Filey
Flamborough Hd
Bridlington & Bay
Ripon
Harrogate
York
Beverley
Hornsea
Hull
Withernsea
Immingham
Spurn Head
R. Humber
Scunthorpe
Grimsby
Cleethorpes
Goole
Selby
Leeds
Bradford
Halifax
Wakefield
Pontefract
Huddersfield
Barnsley
Doncaster
Rotherham
Sheffield
Stalybridge
Glossop
The Peak
Stockport
Manchester
Salford
Oldham
Rochdale
Bury
Bolton
Wigan
Liverpool
St. Helens
Warrington
R. Mersey
Wallasey
Birkenhead
Formby Pt
Southport
Ormskirk
Chorley
Blackburn
Burnley
Nelson
Clitheroe
Preston
Lytham
Blackpool
Fleetwood
Heysham
Morecambe Bay
Morecambe
Lancaster
Ingleborough
Penyghent
Whernside
Bow Fell
Kendal
Windermere
Ulverston
Barrow
Walney I.
R. Duddon
Coniston
Calder Hall
St. Bees Hd
Sea Fell
Helvellyn
Whitehaven
Workington
Keswick
Ullswater
Appleby
Cross Fell
Penrith
Skiddaw
Maryport
Silloth
Solway Firth
Carlisle
Brampton
Longtown
R. Liddel
R. Esk
R. Sark
Hawick
R. Clyde
Dumfries
Ayr
Firth of Clyde
Arran
Stranraer
Portpatrick
Pt. of Ayre
Ramsey
Peel
Douglas
Castletown
Calf of Man

Holyhead
ANGLESEY
Holy I.
Beaumaris
Amlwch
Menai St.
Gt. Ormes Hd.
Llandudno
Colwyn Bay
Birkenhead
R. Mersey
Wallasey
Liverpool
St. Helens
Warrington
Manchester
Stockport
Rhyl
St. Asaph
Conway
Bangor
Denbigh
Flint
FLINT
R. Dee
Ellesmere Port
Chester
CHESHIRE
Macclesfield
Mold
DENBIGH
Congleton
Crewe
Nantwich
Caernarvon Bay
Caernarvon
Snowdon
Wrexham
Ruabon
Newcastle under Lyme
CAERNARVON
Ffestiniog
Portmadoc
Pwllheli
Criccieth
Tremadoc Bay
Bala
Llangollen
To Flint
Mt. Drayton
Oswestry
Braich-y-pwll
Bardsey I.
MERIONETH
L. Vyrnwy
STAF
Stafford
Barmouth
Dolgellau
R. Mawddach
Cader Idris
Shrewsbury
Welshpool
Wellington
Wrekin
R. Severn
MONTGOMERY
SHROPSHIRE
Montgomery
Much Wenlock
Bridgnorth
Bilston
Dudley
Cardigan
Bay
Aberystwyth
Plynlimon
Newtown
Llanidloes
Clee Hs.
Ludlow
R. Teme
Mortimers Cross
WORCESTER
RADNOR
Presteigne
Leominster
Aberaeron
CARDIGAN
Builth Wells
New Radnor
Gt. Malvern
HEREFORD
Cardigan
R. Teifi
Hay
Hereford
Goodwick
Strumble Hd.
Fishguard
Newcastle Emlyn
BRECKNOCK
Ledbury
St. Davids Hd.
PEMBROKE
Llandovery
Brecon
Ross
Ramsey I.
CARMARTHEN
Carmarthen
Brecknock Beacons
R. Usk
Monmouth
St. Brides B.
Haverfordwest
R. Towy
R. Wye
Milford
Pembroke
Llanelli
Merthyr Tydfil
Aberdare
Abergavenny
Ebbw Vale
GLOUCES
Milford Haven
Tenby
Rhondda
Mountain Ash
Pontypool
MONMOUTH
Cwmbran
Chepstow
Carmarthen Bay
Swansea
Neath
Pontypridd
Newport
St. Gowens Hd.
GLAMORGAN
Swansea B.
Port Talbot
Margam
Llandaff
Cardiff
Worms Hd.
Porthcawl
Bridgend
R. Severn
Bristol
Malmesbury
Barry
Weston s. Mare
R. Avon
Bath
Bristol Channel
Mendip Hills
Bradford
Frome
Ilfracombe
Lynton
R. Axe
Wells
Lundy
Morte Pt.
Minehead
Exmoor
SOMERSET
Bridgwater
Bideford Bay
Barnstaple
Taunton
R. Tone
R. Parret
Hartland Pt.
Bideford
Wellington
R. Taw
Tiverton
R. Exe
Chard
Yeovil
Blandford Forum
Bude
Torridge
DEVON
Honiton
DORSET
R. Tamar
R. Axe
Bridport
R. Frome
Okehampton
Exeter
Dartmoor
Lyme Regis
Dorchester
Chesil Bank
Padstow B.
Launceston
Teignmouth
Exmouth
Weymouth
Newton Abbot
Wadebridge
Bodmin
Tavistock
Paignton
Torquay
Portland
Newquay
CORNWALL
Saltash
Devonport
Torbay
Portland
Camborne
Plymouth
C. Cornwall
St. Ives
Truro
St. Austell
Plymouth Sound
Dartmouth
Start B.
Start Pt.
Penzance
Falmouth
Kingsbridge
Eddystone Lt. Ho.
Lands End
Mounts B.
Falmouth Har.
ENGLISH
The Lizard
WALES
St. George's Channel
Cambrian Mts.
5
4
3
53
52
51

Statute Miles
0
20
40
53
52
51
50
0
1
2
LINCOLN
LINDSEY
KESTEVEN
HOLLAND
NOTTINGHAM
LEICESTER
RUTLAND
NORTHAMPTON
HUNTS
AND
PETERB
CAMBRIDGE
ISLE OF ELY
BEDFORD
BUCKINGHAM
HERTFORD
OXFORD
BERKSHIRE
LONDON
SURREY
HAMPSHIRE
NORFOLK
SUFFOLK
WEST
EAST
ESSEX
KENT
SUSSEX
WEST
EAST
FRANCE
C H A N N E L
The Wash
Mouth of the Thames
Strait of Dover
Rotherham
Sheffield
E.Retford
Mansfield
Alfreton
Newark
Southwell
Nottingham
Gainsborough
Louth
Mablethorpe
Sutton-on-Sea
Horncastle
Lincoln
Skegness
Boston
Grantham
Spalding
Melton Mowbray
Oakham
Stamford
Leicester
Hinckley
Rugby
Naseby
Corby
Kettering
Daventry
Northampton
Royal Leamington Spa
Wisbech
Peterborough
March
Ely
St. Ives
Huntingdon
St. Neots
Bedford
Cambridge
Newmarket
Gog Magog Hills
Wells
Sheringham
Cromer
Hunstanton
N. Walsham
Kings Lynn
Swaffham
Norwich
Great Yarmouth
Thetford
Lowestoft
Southwold
Bury St. Edmunds
Aldeburgh
Sudbury
Ipswich
Orfordness
Felixstowe
Harwich
The Naze
Walton on the Naze
Clacton on Sea
Saffron Walden
Colchester
Braintree
Stortford
Harlow
Chelmsford
Maldon
Epping
Romford
Southend on Sea
Shoeburyness
Foulness
Basildon
Tilbury
Hitchin
Stevenage
Welwyn G.C.
Ware
Hertford
St. Albans
Hatfield
Watford
Dunstable
Leighton Linslade
Buckingham
Aylesbury
Oxford
H.Wycombe
Marlow
Henley
Slough
Eton
Windsor
Reading
Newbury
Abingdon
Harwell
Woodstock
Chertsey
Weybridge
Epsom
Kingston
Croydon
Woolwich
Greenwich
Gravesend
Rochester
Chatham
Gillingham
Sheerness
Sheppey I.
Margate
Nth. Foreland
Thanet
Ramsgate
Canterbury
Maidstone
Deal
Goodwin Sands
The Downs
Sth. Foreland
Dover
Folkestone
Hythe
Ashford
Royal Tunbridge Wells
Tonbridge
New Romney
Dunge Ness
Rye
Winchelsea
Hastings
St. Leonards
Battle
Lewes
Eastbourne
Beachy Head
Herstmonceux
Newhaven
Brighton
Shoreham-by-Sea
Worthing
Littlehampton
Bognor Regis
Selsey Bill
Chichester
South Downs
Crawley
Horsham
Reigate
Guildford
Godalming
Aldershot
Basingstoke
Andover
Winchester
Eastleigh
Southampton
Southampton Water
Fawley
Portsmouth
Gosport
Solent
Cowes
Ryde
Newport
Shanklin
Ventnor
Sandown
Isle of Wight
St. Catherines Pt.
Calais
Boulogne
R. Somme
Dieppe
R. Trent
R. Witham
R. Welland
R. Nene
Gt. Ouse
R. Wensum
R. Yare
R. Waveney
R. Lark
R. Cam
R. Stour
R. Colne
R. Chelmer
Mersea I.
Blackwater R.
R. Medway
R. Rother
R. Thames
Chiltern Hills
North Downs

SCOTLAND

ZETLAND (SHETLAND)
Yell
Lerwick
Foula
Fair I.
ORKNEY
Kirkwall
Pentland Firth
CAITHNESS
Statute Miles
ORKNEY
Stromness
Scapa Flow
Kirkwall
Pentland Firth
Dunnet Hd.
Duncansby Hd.
Thurso
Wick
CAITHNESS
Helmsdale
Dounreay
SUTHERLAND
Loch Shin
Dornoch
Dornoch Firth
Moray Firth
Lossiemouth
Kinnaird Hd.
Fraserburgh
Peterhead
Buchan Ness
Banff
Portsoy
Cullen
Buckie
Fochabers
Keith
Turriff
Huntly
ABERDEEN
R. Don
Inverurie
Aberdeen
Girdle Ness
Stonehaven
KINCARDINE
R. Dee
Banchory
Ballater
Balmoral Cas.
Braemar
Ben Macdui
BANFF
Grantown-on-Spey
R. Spey
Elgin
Forres
MORAY
Nairn
NAIRN
Inverness
R. Findhorn
Aviemore
Kingussie
INVERNESS
Caledonian Canal
L. Ness
L. Lochy
Tain
Cromarty
Dingwall
Fortrose
Beauly
ROSS & CROMARTY
Loch Maree
Ullapool
Loch Broom
L. Assynt
Lochinver
Cape Wrath
Gairloch
Stromeferry
Kyle of Lochalsh
Ben Attow
Mallaig
Sound of Sleat
The Minch
Little Minch
Butt of Lewis
Stornoway
Lewis
Harris
N. Uist
Benbecula
South Uist
Barra
OUTER HEBRIDES
Skye
Portree
Rum
Eigg
Canna

NORTH
ATLANTIC OCEAN
INNER HEBRIDES
IRISH SEA
North Channel
Firth of Clyde
Firth of Forth
Firth of Tay
Solway Firth
ENGLAND
IRELAND
PERTH
FIFE
KINROSS
CLACKMANNAN
STIRLING
DUNBARTON
ARGYLL
RENFREW
LANARK
WEST LOTHIAN
MIDLOTHIAN
EAST LOTHIAN
BERWICK
PEEBLES
SELKIRK
ROXBURGH
DUMFRIES
KIRKCUDBRIGHT
WIGTOWN
AYR
Arbroath
Dundee
Blairgowrie
Perth
Crieff
Comrie
Dunblane
Ochil Hills
St. Andrews
Cupar
Fife Ness
Methil
North Berwick
Dunbar
St. Abbs Hd.
Berwick upon Tweed
R. Tweed
Duns
Coldstream
Kelso
Jedburgh
Hawick
Melrose
Galashiels
Selkirk
Dalkeith
Leith
Musselburgh
Haddington
Lammermuir Hills
Cheviot Hills
R. Eden
Carlisle
Annan
Dumfries
Langholm
Moffat
Esk
R. Nith
Sanquhar
Lead Hills
Lanark
Motherwell
Hamilton
Glasgow
Airdrie
Paisley
Renfrew
Greenock
Kilmarnock
Irvine
Ardrossan
Saltcoats
Troon
Ayr
Girvan
Dalmellington
New Galloway
R. Dee
Wigtown
Wigtown B.
Luce Bay
Mull of Galloway
Stranraer
Portpatrick
Stirling
Bannockburn
Falkirk
L. Earn
L. Katrine
Killin
R. Forth
Loch Lomond
Loch Long
Loch Fyne
Inveraray
Oban
L. Etive
Awe
Crinan Can.
Tarbert
Kintyre
Campbeltown
Mull of Kintyre
Bute
Rothesay
Arran
Brodick
Lamlash
Ailsa Craig
Sound of Jura
Jura
Islay
Port Ellen
Colonsay
Mull
Iona
Staffa
Tiree
Belfast
Londonderry

IRELAND

Statute Miles
0 10 20 30 40 50
10
9
8
7
6
5
55
54
OCEAN
North Channel
IRISH
SCOTLAND
Kintyre
Mull of Kintyre
Rathlin I.
Fair Hd.
Giants' Causeway
Portrush
Malin Hd.
Lough Swilly
Lough Foyle
Bloody Foreland
Moville
Donegal Mts
DONEGAL
Aran I.
Burtonport
Lifford
Ardara
Rossan Pt.
Donegal
Ballyshannon
Donegal Bay
R. Erne
Killala Bay
Sligo Bay
Downpatrick Hd.
Erris Hd.
Belmullet
Killala
Ballina
Mt. Nephin
Lough Conn
Achil I.
Newport
MAYO
Castlebar
Clew Bay
Clare I.
Westport
Croagh Patrick
L. Carra
Claremorris
Ballinrobe
SLIGO
Sligo
Collooney
Tobercurry
Lough Allen
LEITRIM
Shannon
Carrick on Shannon
Boyle
Elphin
ROSCOMMON
Longford
LONGFORD
REPUBLIC
Ballymahon
FERMANAGH
Lough Erne
Enniskillen
Upper L. Erne
Monaghan
Clones
MONAGHAN
Ulster Canal
CAVAN
Cavan
Kingscourt
Kells
(Ceanannus Mor)
Navan
(An Uaimh)
R. Blackwater
R. Boyne
MEATH
Dundalk
Dun Dealgan
LOUTH
Ardee
Drogheda
Balbriggan
Skerries
Dundalk Bay
Carlingford L.
Ballycastle
Coleraine
Ballymoney
R. Bann
ANTRIM
Ballymena
Larne
Carrickfergus
Antrim
Belfast Lough
Belfast
Londonderry
(Derry)
LONDONDERRY
R. Foyle
Strabane
Castle Dawson
NORTHERN IRELAND
TYRONE
Cookstown
Lough Neagh
Omagh
Dungannon
Lurgan
Portadown
Armagh
ARMAGH
Newry
Newry Canal
Bangor
Donaghadee
Newtownards
Lisburn
Strangford Lough
Dromore
DOWN
Downpatrick
Mourne Mts
Dundrum B.

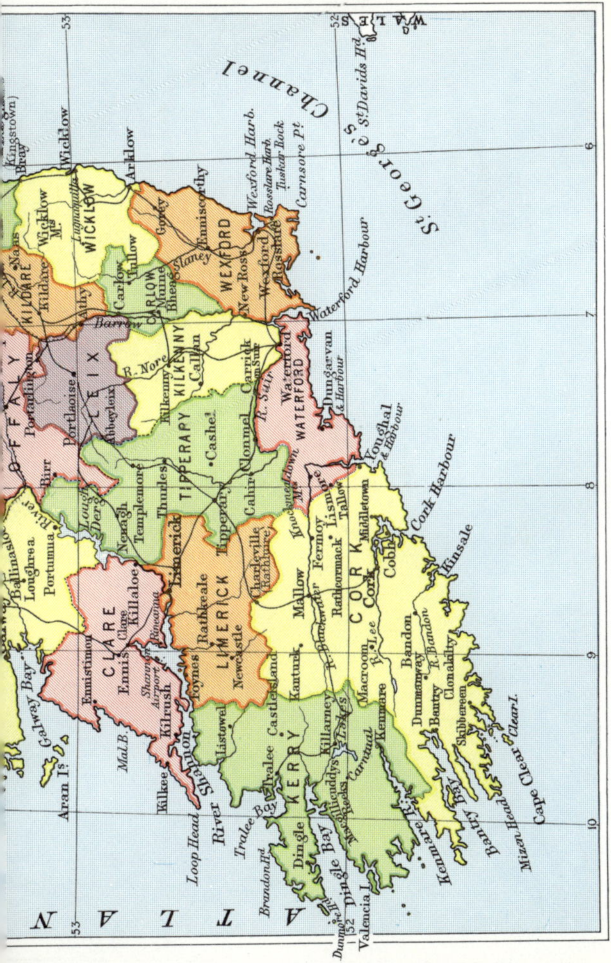
WALES
St Davids Hd.
St George's Channel
Kingstown
Bray
Wicklow
Arklow
Wexford Harb.
Rosslare Harb.
Tuskar Rock
Carnsore Pt.
Waterford Harbour
WICKLOW
Wicklow Mts.
Gorey
Enniscorthy
WEXFORD
Wexford
Rosslare
New Ross
Slaney
Tullow
CARLOW
Carlow
Muine Bheag
KILDARE
Kildare
Naas
Athy
Barrow
OFFALY
LEIX
Portarlington
Portlaoise
Abbeyleix
Birr
R. Nore
KILKENNY
Kilkenny
Callan
Carrick on Suir
R. Suir
Waterford
WATERFORD
Dungarvan & Harbour
Youghal & Harbour
Cork Harbour
Kinsale
TIPPERARY
Cashel
Clonmel
Thurles
Templemore
Tipperary
Cahir
Nenagh
Lough Derg
Knockmealdown Mts.
Lismore
Tallow
Fermoy
Rathcormack
Middletown
Cobh
CORK
Cork
Mallow
Charleville (Rathluirc)
R. Blackwater
Limerick
LIMERICK
Rathkeale
Newcastle
Foynes
Killaloe
CLARE
Clare
Ennis
Ennistimon
Shannon Airport
Kilrush
Kilkee
Loop Head
River Shannon
Mal B.
Galway Bay
Aran Is.
Ballinasloe
Loughrea
Portumna
Castleisland
Listowel
Tralee
Tralee Bay
KERRY
Kanturk
Killarney
Lakes
Macroom
R. Lee
Bandon
R. Bandon
Dunmanway
Clonakilty
Skibbereen
Bantry
Bantry Bay
Kenmare
Kenmare R.
Carrantual
Macgillicuddys Reeks
Dingle
Dingle Bay
Brandon Hd.
Dunmore Hd.
Valencia I.
Cape Clear
Clear I.
Mizen Head
ATLAN
53
52
6
7
8
9
10

SCANDINAVIA

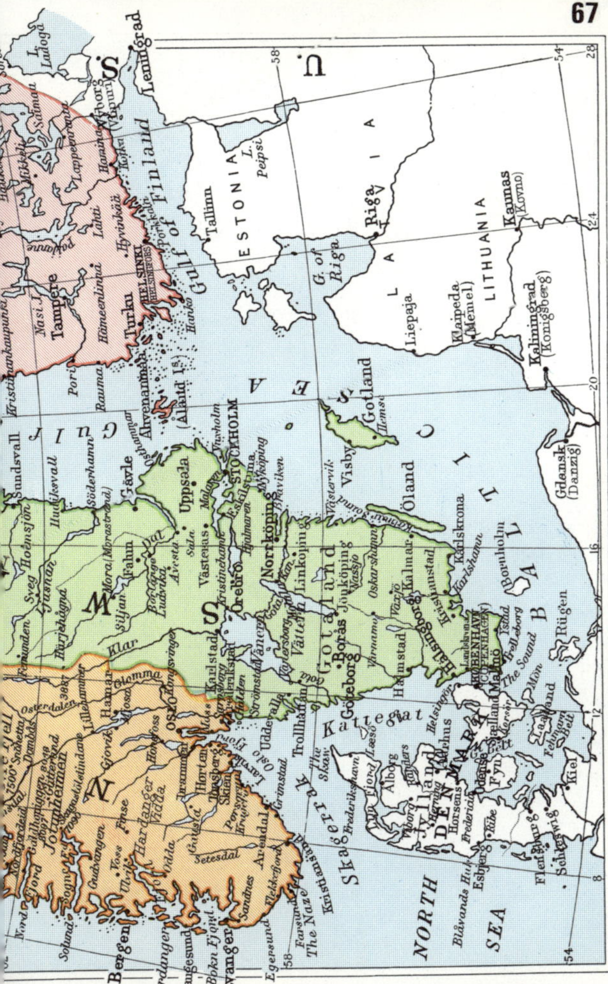

© – John Bartholomew & Son, Ltd, Edinburgh

SOUTH NORWAY

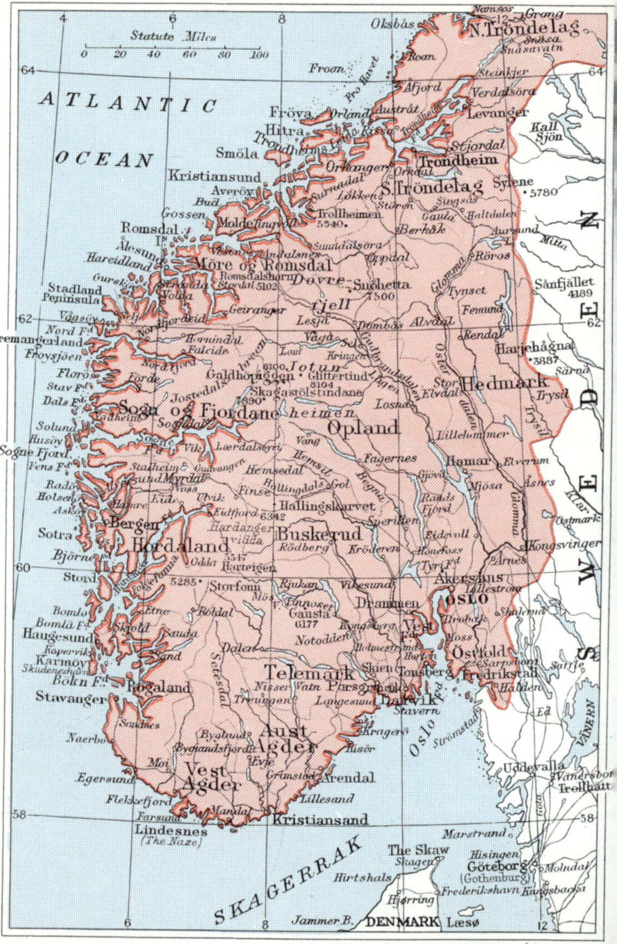

Statute Miles
0 20 40 60
NORWAY
SWEDEN
SKAGERRAK
KATTEGAT
JYLLAND
JUTLAND
SJÆLLAND
(ZEALAND)
FYN
FUNEN
GERMANY
WEST
EAST
VÄNERN
Kragerö
Risör
Tvedestrand
Arendal
Tromöy
Grimstad
Lillesand
Kristiansand
Mandal
Stjernöy
Evje
Otra
Strömstad
Ed
Mellerud
Lidköping
Uddevalla
Vänersborg
Skara
Lysekil
Orust
Trollhättan
Herrljunga
Tjörn
Göta
Alingsås
Marstrand
Kungalv
Göteborg
(Gothenburg)
Borås
Styrsö
Kungsbacka
Svenljunga
Kungsbacka F.
Ätran
Varberg
Falkenberg
Torup
Halmstad
Laholm B.
Lagan
Torekov
Skälder Bay
Ängelholm
Kullen Lt
Höganäs
Gilleleje
Hälsingborg
Helsingør
Landskrona
Malmö
Skanör
Falsterbo
Trelleborg
Östratorp
The Skaw
Skagen
Hirtshals
Ugerby
Hjørring
Hirsholmene
Frederikshavn
Læsø
Læsø Rende
Lokken
Vendsyssel
Jammer Bay
Sæby
Hanstholm
Nørresundby
Aby
Hals
Thisted
Alborg
Lim Fjord
Aars
Agger
Nykøbing
Hadsund
Mariager Fd
Randers Fd
Anholt
Skive
Hobro
Lemvig
Struer
Viborg
Randers
Fornæs
Grenå
Holstebro
Rönde
Herning
Silkeborg
Ebeltoft
Hesselø
Ringkøbing
Ringkøbing Fjord
Himmel B.
482
Århus
Hjelm
Skern
Skanderborg
Sejerø
Tarm
Brande
Gudenå
Tunø
Samsø
Frederikssund
Hillerød
Give
Horsens
Endelave
Samsø Belt
Kalundborg
Lyngby
KØBENHAVN
COPENHAGEN
Grindsted
Vejle
Holbæk
Roskilde
Kastrup
Amager
Saltholm
Blåvands Huk
Varde
Esbjerg
Fredericia
Køge
Køge B.
Bramminge
Kolding
Middelfart
Slagelse
Fanø
Vamdrup
Odense
Nyborg
Soro
Ringsted
Ribe
Gt. Belt
Mandø
Vojens
Lit. Belt
Korsör
Næstved
Haderslev
Assens
Fåborg
Svendborg
Skælskør
Præstø
Fakse B.
Rømø
Åbenrå
Vordingborg
Tönder
Tåsinge
Orehoved
Møn
Stege
Sylt
Westerland
Dybbøl
Als
Sønderborg
Langeland
Nakskov
Maribo
Stubbekøbing
Nykøbing
Flensburg
Ærø
Lolland
(Laaland)
Falster
Nth. Frisian Islands
Rødby
Rødbyhavn
Gedser
Husum
Schlei
Friedrichsort
Femarn Belt
Schleswig
Kiel Bay
Puttgarden
Fehmarn
Tönning
Warnemünde
Kiel
Grossenbrode
Lübeck B.
Stralsund
Helgoland
Rendsburg
Kanal
Heide
Neustadt
Rostock
Neumünster
Eutin
Itzehoe
Elbe
Wismar
Neuwerk
Glückstadt
Lübeck
Cuxhaven
HAMBURG
Rønne
Hammeren Lt.
Sandvig
Christiansø Lt.
BORNHOLM
(to Denmark)
Neksø
same scale

NETHERLANDS, BELGIUM, LUXEMBOURG

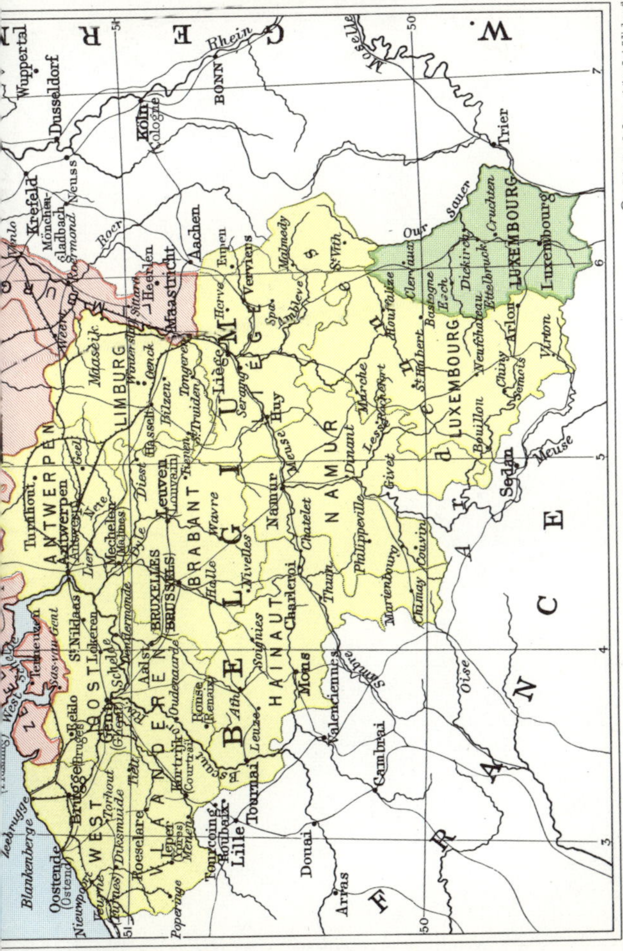
B E L G I U M
F R A N C E
LUXEMBOURG
WEST VLAANDEREN
OOST VLAANDEREN
ANTWERPEN
LIMBURG
BRABANT
HAINAUT
NAMUR
LIÈGE
LUXEMBOURG
Oostende
Blankenberge
Zeebrugge
Brugge
Gent
Eeklo
Kortrijk
Roeselare
Ieper
Torhout
Diksmuide
Poperinge
Nieuwpoort
Aalst
Dendermonde
St. Niklaas
Lokeren
Terneuzen
Sas-van-Gent
Antwerpen
Turnhout
Mechelen
Lier
Geel
Leuven
Diest
Hasselt
Genk
Maaseik
Tongeren
St. Truiden
Bilzen
BRUXELLES
BRUSSEL
Halle
Nivelles
Wavre
Ath
Soignies
Mons
Charleroi
Tournai
Leuze
Thuin
Chimay
Couvin
Marienbourg
Philippeville
Namur
Dinant
Givet
Huy
Liège
Seraing
Herve
Verviers
Eupen
Spa
Malmédy
St. Vith
Bastogne
Marche
St. Hubert
Neufchâteau
Bouillon
Arlon
Virton
Chiny
Semois
Houffalize
Clervaux
Dickirch
Ettelbruck
Luxembourg
Our
Sauer
Meuse
Sedan
Sambre
Oise
Escaut
Schelde
Lille
Roubaix
Tourcoing
Douai
Arras
Cambrai
Valenciennes
Maastricht
Heerlen
Roermond
Venlo
Weert
Aachen
Köln
(Cologne)
Bonn
Düsseldorf
Wuppertal
Krefeld
Neuss
Mönchen-gladbach
Trier
Rhein
Moselle
Roer

ENGLAND
ENGLISH CHANNEL
Plymouth
Falmouth
Lands End
Isles of Scilly
Portsmouth
Dover
Calai
Boulogne
Montreuil
St Valery
Dieppe
Fécamp
Rouen
Le Havre
Cherbourg
C. de la Hague
Alderney
Channel Islands
Guernsey
Sark
Jersey
Pt de Talbert
Granville
St Malo
Dinard
St Servan
St Brieuc
Morlaix
Brest
I. de Ouessant (Ushant I.)
Pt St Mathieu
I. de Sein
Quimper
Brittany
Pontivy
Rennes
Lorient
Vannes
Vilaine
Belle Ile
St Nazaire
R. Loire
Nantes
I. Noirmoutier
I. d'Yeu
Les Sables d'Olonne
La Roche s-Yon
Poitou
Normandy
St Lo
Caen
Elbeuf
Evreux
Argentan
Avranches
Fougères
Mayenne
Alençon
Maine
Laval
Le Mans
Chartres
Versail
Mantes
Seine
Châteaubriant
Angers
Anjou
Saumur
Loir
Tours
Loire
Blois
Orle
Chinon
R. Cher
Vierzon
Bou
Châtellerault
Poitiers
Vienne
Châte
Niort
Civray
La Rochelle
I. de Ré
I. d'Oléron
Rochefort
Saintes
Angoumois
St Junien
Limoge
Limousin
Marche
Gueret
Mon
Royan
Cognac
Saintonge
Angoulême
Perigueux
Tulle
Brive
Pauillac
Blaye
Libourne
Dordogne
Bordeaux
Bergerac
Arcachon
Landes
Guyenne
Garonne
Villeneuve s-Lot
Bazas
Cahors
Figea
Agen
Ville de
Monta
BAY OF BISCAY
Statute Miles
0
50
100
Santander
Bilbao
San Sebastian
Bayonne
Biarritz
Dax
Mont de Marsan
Gascony
Adour
Orthez
Auch
Muret
Toulo
Pau
Oloron
Tarbes
Lourdes
Carcasso
Foix
St Girons
Luz
Pyrenees
Perdido
Maladeta
Andorra
Pamplona
Ebro
SPAIN
6
4
2
0
50
48
46
44
F

BELGIUM
BRUXELLES
WEST GERMANY
SWITZERLAND
ITALY
CORSICA (CORSE)
MEDITERRANEAN SEA
Gulf of Lions
Gulf of Genoa
Côte d'Azur
Champagne
Lorraine
Alsace
Bourgogne
Franche Comté
Nivernais
Bourbonnais
Lyonnais
Dauphiné
Provence
Alps
Liége
BONN
Koblenz
Frankfurt am M
Luxembourg
Mannheim
Saarbrücken
Karlsruhe
Stuttgart
Ulm
Strasbourg
Metz
Nancy
Verdun
Thionville
Sedan
Reims
Laon
St Quentin
Mézières
Tourcoing
Roubaix
Mons
Douai
Valenciennes
Cambrai
Soissons
Epernay
Châlons sur Marne
Bar le Duc
PARIS
Melun
Troyes
Sens
Joigny
Auxerre
Chaumont
Langres
Epinal
Remiremont
Luneville
Saverne
Sarreguemines
Colmar
Mulhouse
Belfort
Basel
Zürich
Luzern
BERN
Biel
Neuchâtel
Boden See (L. of Constance)
Rhein
Aare
Dijon
Besançon
Salins
Lons-le-Saunier
Le Creusot
Chalon sur Saone
Mâcon
Bourg
Clamecy
Nevers
Moulins
Vichy
Roanne
Lyon (Lyons)
Vienne
St Etienne
Issoire
Le Puy
Mt Mezenc
Lausanne
L. Leman (L. of Geneva)
Genève (Geneva)
R. Rhône
Annecy
Aix les Bains
Chambéry
Mont Blanc
Mte Rosa
Lugano
Milano
Mt Cenis
Torino
Po
Voiron
Grenoble
Briançon
Valence
Privas
Gap
Embrun
Mt Viso
Cuneo
Genova (Genoa)
Montelimar
Orange
Digne
Avignon
Nîmes
Alès
Florac
Millau
Mende
Montpellier
Arles
Aix
Draguignan
Marseille (Marseilles)
Toulon
Nice
Monte Carlo
Monaco
Cannes
St Tropez
Is d'Hyères
Sète
Narbonne
Port Vendres
Bastia
Mt Cinto
Mte Rotondo
Ajaccio
Sartene
Bonifacio
R. Meuse
Marne
Seine
Saône
R. Ain
Rhône
Loire
R. Isère
R. Durance
Main
Rhein (Rhine)
50
48
46
42
6
8
10
9

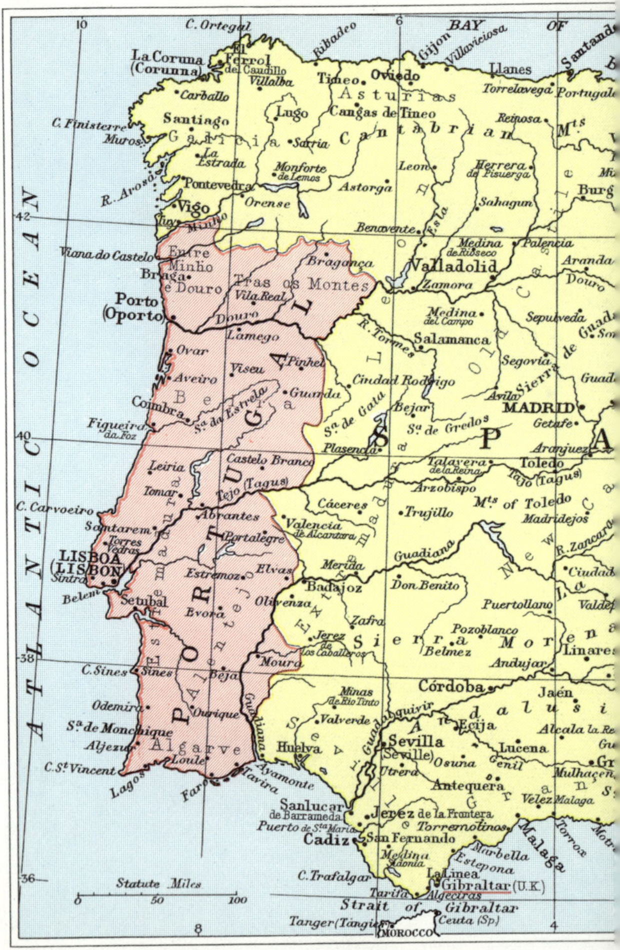
ATLANTIC OCEAN
BAY OF
C. Ortegal
La Coruna (Corunna)
El Ferrol del Caudillo
Villalba
Ribadeo
Gijon
Villaviciosa
Oviedo
Tineo
Llanes
Santander
Torrelavega
Portugalete
Asturias
Carballo
Lugo
Cangas de Tineo
Santiago
C. Finisterre
Muros
Galicia
Sarria
Cantabrian Mts
Reinosa
La Estrada
Monforte de Lemos
Leon
Herrera de Pisuerga
R. Arosa
Pontevedra
Astorga
Burgos
Vigo
Orense
Sahagun
Tuy
Minho
Benavente
Esla
Viana do Castelo
Entre Minho e Douro
Braga
Bragança
Tras os Montes
Medina de Rioseco
Palencia
Valladolid
Aranda
Douro
Zamora
Vila Real
Porto (Oporto)
Lamego
Medina del Campo
Sepulveda
R. Tormes
Salamanca
Ovar
Pinhel
Segovia
Aveiro
Viseu
Guarda
Beira
Ciudad Rodrigo
Avila
Sierra de Guadarrama
Coimbra
Sa da Estrela
Bejar
MADRID
Figueira da Foz
Sa de Gata
Sa de Gredos
Getafe
Leon
Old Castile
Plasencia
SPAIN
Aranjuez
Castelo Branco
Talavera de la Reina
Toledo
Leiria
Tejo (Tagus)
Tajo (Tagus)
Tomar
Arzobispo
C. Carvoeiro
Abrantes
Cáceres
Trujillo
Mts of Toledo
Madridejos
Santarem
Valencia de Alcantara
Portalegre
Extremadura
Torres Vedras
Guadiana
LISBOA (LISBON)
Sintra
Merida
New Castile
R. Zancara
Ciudad
Estremoz
Elvas
Belem
Badajoz
Don Benito
Setubal
Olivenza
Puertollano
La Mancha
Valdepeñas
Evora
Zafra
Alentejo
Jerez de los Caballeros
Pozoblanco
Sierra Morena
Belmez
Linares
Moura
C. Sines
Sines
Beja
Andujar
Córdoba
Jaén
Minas de Rio Tinto
PORTUGAL
Odemira
Valverde
Guadalquivir
Andalusia
Ourique
Ecija
Alcala la Real
Sa de Monchique
Guadiana
Sevilla (Seville)
Lucena
Aljezur
Algarve
Huelva
Osuna
Genil
Loulé
Utrera
Mulhacén
C. St Vincent
Lagos
Faro
Tavira
Ayamonte
Antequera
Velez Malaga
Granada
Sanlucar de Barrameda
Jerez de la Frontera
Puerto de Sta Maria
Torremolinos
Malaga
Torrox
Cadiz
San Fernando
Marbella
Medina Sidonia
Estepona
C. Trafalgar
La Linea
Gibraltar (U.K.)
Tarifa
Algeciras
Statute Miles
0
50
100
Strait of Gibraltar
Tanger (Tangier)
Ceuta (Sp)
MOROCCO
10
8
6
4
42
40
38
36

FRANCE
Bayonne
Dax
Adour
Toulouse
Carcassonne
Gulf of Lions
Perpignan
Irun
Tolosa
Pamplona
Navarra
Pyrenees
Mt Perdido
Mt Maladeta
Andorra
Port Bou
C. Creus
Jaca
Tafalla
Seo de Urgel
Figueras
Rosas
Huesca
Barbastro
Berga
Gerona
Tudela
Ebro
Balaguer
Vich
Manresa
Zaragoza (Saragossa)
Lerida
Segre
Igualada
Mataro
Blanes
Catalonia
Costa Brava
Sabadell
Badalona
Barcelona
Calatayud
Aragon
Reus
Tarragona
Alcañiz
Molina
Tajo (Tagus)
Montalban
Tortosa
R. Ebro
Morella
Albarracin
Teruel
Vinaroz
Alcala
Menorca (Minorca)
Mahon
Balearic Isles
Cuenca
Castellon de la Plana
Pollensa
Alcudia
Burriana
Palma
Manacor
Mallorca (Majorca)
Utiel
Sagunto
Valencia
Requena
Cabrera
La Roda
Cullera
Ibiza (Iviza)
Jucar
Alcira
Albacete
Almansa
Jativa
Denia
Ibiza
Villena
C. Nao
Formentera
Murcia
Alcoy
Hellin
Elche
Alicante
Segura
Cieza
Orihuela
Murcia
SEA
Totana
Mar Menor
C. de Palos
Lorca
La Union
Cartagena
Aguilas
Cuevas de Vera
Dellys
Alger (Algiers)
C. Gata
Almeria
MEDITERRANEAN
Wadi Sheliff
Oran
AFRICA
42
40
38
36
2
0
2
4

SWITZERLAND

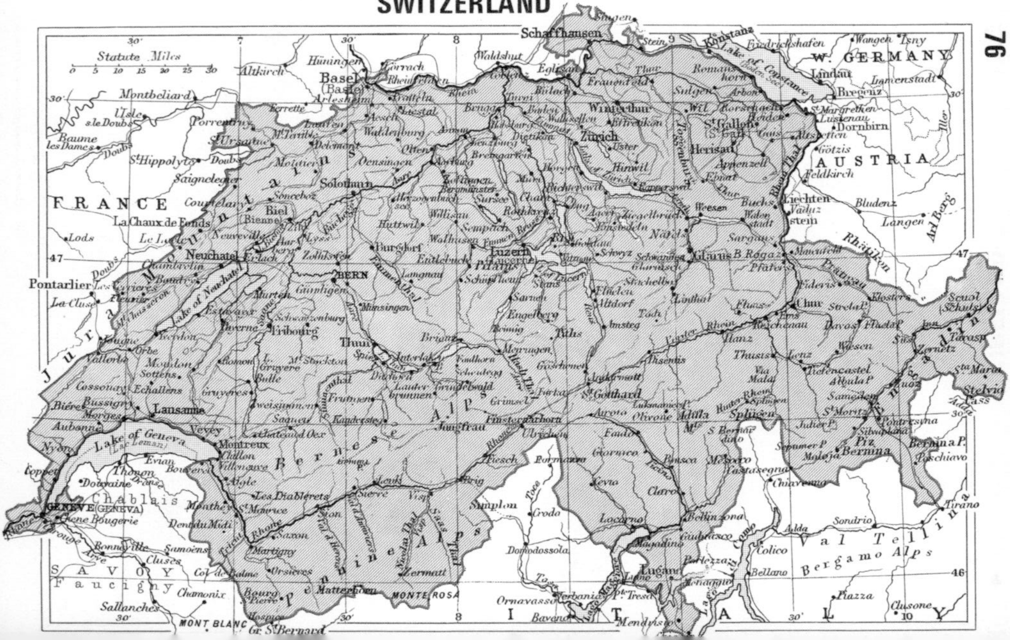

Münster
Warendorf
Gütersloh
Detmold
Bocholt
Nijmegen
Borken
NORDRHEIN-
WESTFALEN
Lippstadt
Holzminden
Höxter
Paderborn
Wesel
Hamm
Gelsenkirchen
Essen
Dortmund
Soest
Warburg
Oberhausen
Duisburg
Krefeld
Bochum
Witten
Warstein
Arnsberg
Arolsen
Iserlohn
Hagen
Düsseldorf
Wuppertal
Remscheid
Solingen
Korbach
Kassel
Sauerland
Rothaar G.
Fritzlar
Frankenberg
KÖLN
(COLOGNE)
Kalk
Siegburg
Siegen
HESSEN
Hersfeld
Marburg
Alsfeld
Aachen
Aix-la-Chapelle
BONN
Bad Godesberg
Linz
Giessen
Vogels Berg
Fulda
Westerwald
Wetzlar
Neuwied
Schlüchtern
Koblenz
Ems
Bad Nauheim
Limburg
Nassau
Homburg
Friedberg
Eifel
WEST
Cochem
Hunsruck
Wiesbaden
Taunus
Offenbach
Spessart
RHEINLAND
Zell
Bingen
FRANKFURT AM M.
Mainz
Bitburg
Wittlich
Bernkastel
Kreuznach
Aschaffenburg
Würzburg
LUXEMBOURG
Luxembourg
Trier
(Treves)
PFALZ
Alzey
Darmstadt
Worms
Bensheim
Odenwald
Saarburg
Birkenfeld
Ludwigshafen
Mannheim
Eberbach
St. Wendel
Kaiserslautern
Hardt Geb.
Merzig
SAAR
Neunkirchen
Homburg
Heidelberg
Saarlouis
Saarbrücken
Zweibrücken
Speyer
Landau
GERMANY
Germersheim
Pirmasens
Bruchsal
Karlsruhe
Heilbronn
Schwäbisch Hall
Metz
LORRAINE
Pforzheim
Ludwigsburg
BADEN
Esslingen
Nancy
Wildbad
Baden-Baden
STUTTGART
Göppingen
STRASBOURG
Kehl
WÜRTTEMBERG
Tübingen
Reutlingen
Offenburg
Freudenstadt
Hechingen
Hohenzollern
Swabian Alps
Ulm
St. Dié
Vosges
ALSACE
Epinal
Colmar
Sigmaringen
Biberach
FRANCE
Villingen
Breisach
Freiburg
Feld Berg
Stockach
Singen
Überlingen
Ravensburg
Mülhouse
Badenweiler
Schaffhausen
Friedrichshafen
Lörrach
Waldshut
Konstanz
Boden See
Lindau
Statute Miles
0 20 40 60
Basel
Rhein
SWITZERLAND
AUSTRIA
E. GERMANY
BAYERN

Statute Miles
0
20
40
60
100
NORTH SEA
Helgoland
Cuxhaven
Wilhelmshaven
West & East Frisian Is
Nh Frisian Is
Westerland
Flensburg
Schleswig
Kiel B.
Fehmarn
Kiel
Holstein
Lübeck B.
Lübeck
Stralsund
Warnemünde
Greifswald
Rostock
Wismar
Bremerhaven
Hamburg
Altona
Wilhelmsburg
Harburg
Schwerin
Elbe
Emden
Groningen
Leeuwarden
Oldenburg
Bremen
Lüneburg
Neustrelitz
Nieder
sachsen
Weser
Verden
Celle
Wittenberge
Fehrbellin
Spandau
EAST
Havel
Zwolle
AMSTERDAM
Utrecht
Enschede
Zutphen
Arnhem
NETHERLANDS
R. Ems
Lingen
Osnabrück
Minden
Aller
Hannover
Wolfburg
Braunschweig
(Brunswick)
Brandenburg
Potsdam
Magdeburg
Hildesheim
Salzgitter
Nordrhein
Bielefeld
Münster
WEST
Westfalen
Wesel
Gelsenkirchen
Hamm
Rhine
Krefeld
Mönchengladbach
Essen
Dortmund
Duisburg
Wuppertal
Ruhr
Düsseldorf
Maas
Harz Mts
Dessau
Wittenberg
GERMANY
Göttingen
Nordhausen
Halle
Kassel
Mühlhausen
Leipzig
Altenburg
Köln
Cologne
GERMANY
Siegen
Eisenach
Hessen
Erfurt
Weimar
Gotha
Gera
Maastricht
Aachen
BONN
Marburg
Giessen
Taufstein M.
Fulda
Werra
Meiningen
Karl-Marx
Zwickau
Plauen
Koblenz
Rheinland
Rhein
Wiesbaden
Frankfurt am M.
Hanau
Offenbach
Darmstadt
Bingen
Mainz
Coburg
Bamberg
Schweinfurt
Schnee Berg
Fichtel Geb.
Erz Geb.
Karlovy Vary
(Karlsbad)
Trier
Luxembourg
Pfalz
Mosel
Worms
Main
Würzburg
Bayreuth
Böhmer Wald
Plzen
Pilsen
Saar-
land
Kaiserslautern
Ludwigshafen
Mannheim
Saarbrücken
Speyer
Heidelberg
Rothenburg
Nürnberg
Fürth
Ansbach
Metz
LORRAINE
Haguenau
Heilbronn
Bayern
Karlsruhe
Regensburg
Bayrischer W.
Nancy
Baden-Baden
Baden-
Stuttgart
Nördlingen
(Danube)
Straubing
Strasbourg
Kehl
Tübingen
Württemberg
Ulm
Donau
Ingolstadt
Isar
Passau
Vosges Mts
ALSACE
Schwarzwald
Augsburg
Landshut
Colmar
Danube
München
(Munich)
Sigmaringen
Tuttlingen
Inn
Freiburg
Mulhouse
Feld B.
Schaffhausen
Bodensee
L. Constance
Rosenheim
Traunstein
Salzburg
Kempten
Oberammergau
Berchtesgaden
Doubs
Basel
Rhein
Konstanz
Kufstein
Aare
Zurich
Dornbirn
Schwaz
Neuchâtel
Liechtenstein
Landeck
Innsbruck
Zell
Luzern
Glarus
Rhein
BERN
Gr. Glockner
SWITZERLAND
Chur
Brenner Pass
Drava
Villach
FRANCE
BELGIUM
6
10
12
54
52

POLAND
Klaipeda (Memel)
Neman
Sovetsk
Kaunas (Kovno)
Kaliningrad (Königsberg)
Chernyakhovsk (Insterburg)
Pregolya
Bornholm (Den.)
SEA
Gulf of Danzig
Gdynia
Słupsk
Gdańsk (Danzig)
Kołobrzeg
Koszalin
Elbląg
Malbork (Marienburg)
Olsztyn (Allenstein)
Śniardwy
Goldap
Suwałki
Giżycko (Lötzen)
Grodno
Kwidzyn (Marienwerder)
Szczecinek
Nidzica
Łomza
Białystok
Wisła (Vistula)
Piła
Bydgoszcz
Toruń
Notec
Ostrołęka
Narew
Ostrow Maz.
Włocławek
Płock
Modlin
Warta
Gniezno
Poznan
Siedlce
Bug
WARSZAWA (WARSAW)
Brest (Brest Litovsk)
Warta
Leszno
Kalisz
P O L A N D
Łodz
Dęblin
Odra
Bober
Głogów
R. Bartsch
Pilica
Radom
Piotrków
Chełm
Lublin
Wrocław (Breslau)
Görlitz
Legnica
Silesia
Kielce
Zamość
Brzeg
Opole (Oppeln)
Częstochowa
Świdnica
Wałbrzych
Riesen Gebirge
Tomaszow
Bytom (Beuthen)
Nysa
Gliwice (Gleiwitz)
Sosnowiec
Katowice
Vistula
San
Sudeten Geb.
Raciborz
Tarnów
Jarosław
Kraków (Cracow)
Pardubice
Opava
Ostrava
Cieszyn (Teschen)
Nowy Sacz
Przemysl
Olomouc
High Tatra
Jihlava
Brno
Zilina
Spisska Nova Ves
Presov
Vah
S L O V A K I A
Morava
Trencin
Uzhgorod
Kosice (Kassa)
Piestany
Hron
Banska Stiavnica
Mukachevo
Krems
Bratislava (Pressburg)
Danube
St. Polten
WIEN (VIENNA)
Miskolc
Nyiregyhaza
Wiener Neustadt
Neusiedler See
Komarno
Vac
Gyor
BUDAPEST
Tisza
Sopron
Raba
Debrecen
Bruck
Szombalhely
H U N G A R Y
Oradea (Grosswardein)
Graz
Balaton
Kecskemet
Leibnitz
18
20
22
16
54
50
48

E. GERMANY
Erfurt
Dresden
Karl Marx Stadt (Chemnitz)
Zwickau
Plauen
Coburg
Main
Bamberg
Würzburg
Nürnberg
Amberg
Ansbach
W. GERMANY
Regensburg
Ingolstadt
Straubing
Danube
Ulm
Augsburg
Landshut
Passau
München (Munich)
Inn
Lech
Kempten
Boden S. (L. Constance)
Rosenheim
Erz Geb.
Ústí nad Labem
Most
Chomutov
Decin
Liberec
Litoměřice
Ml. Boleslav
Riesen Geb.
Silesia
Wrocław (Breslau)
Glatz
Sudeten Mts
Karlovy Vary (Karlsbad)
Cheb (Eger)
Ohre
PRAHA PRAGUE
Elbe
Kolin
Hradec Králové
Pardubice
Opava (Troppau)
Šumperk
Sternberk
BOHEMIA
CZECHOSLOVAKIA
ČESKÉ ZEMĚ
Plzen (Pilsen)
Bohmer Wald
Vltava
Písek
Tabor
Jihlava (Iglau)
Moravian Mts
Prostejov
Olomouc (Olmütz)
Prerov
MORAVIA
Brno (Brünn)
České Budějovice (Budweis)
Znojmo
Morava
White Carpathians
Gmünd
Breclav
Freistadt
Krems
LOWER AUSTRIA
UPPER AUSTRIA
Linz
Danube
St Polten
WIEN VIENNA
Bratislava (Pressburg)
Wels
Steyr
Baden
Wiener Neustadt
Salzach
Salzburg
Ischl
Enns
Neusiedler See
Leitha
Neunkirchen
Sopron
AUSTRIA
SALZBURG
Chain
Leoben
Bruck
BURGENLAND
Szombathely
HUNGARY
Papa
Bakony
Veszprem
Raba
Dornbirn
VORARLBERG
Solbad Hall
Kitzbühel
Inn
Landeck
Innsbruck
Liechtenstein
TIROL
Brenner P.
Tauern
STYRIA
Tamsweg
Graz
Körmend
Gr. Glockner
Lienz
CARINTHIA
Leibnitz
Villach
Klagenfurt
Karawanken
Maribor
Drava
Mur
Balaton
Nagykanizsa
Kaposvar
Rhaetian Alps
Ortles
Adige
Bolzano
Carnic Alps
Julian Alps
Mt Adamello
Trento
Dolomites
Udine
Sava
Celje
Varaždin
Riva
Rovereto
Belluno
Ljubljana (Laibach)
L. d'Iseo
L. di Garda
Gorizia
Postumia
Zagreb (Agram)
Virovitica
Brescia
Verona
Treviso
Trieste
Karlovac
Sisak
Cremona
Padova (Padua)
Adige
Venezia (Venice)
Istra
Rijeka (Fiume)
Sava
Mantua
Po
Krk
Kapela Mts
Una
Bos. Novi
Vrbas
Parma
Ferrara
Pula
Velebit
Banja Luka
Modena
Bologna
Ravenna
ADRIATIC SEA
Pag
Bihac
Dinaric Alps
YUGOSLAVIA
Travnik
San Marino
Rimini
Dugi Otok
Zadar
Lucca
Firenze (Florence)
Arno
Knin
Livorno (Leghorn)
Split (Spalato)
Sibenik
Arezzo
Ancona
Imotski
Perugia
Brac
ITALY
Hvar

Statute Miles
0 50 100
POLAND
Kielce
Czestochowa
Katowice
Krakow
Vistula
Zamosc
Bug
Sokal
Rovno
Horyn
Brody
San
Jaroslaw
Rzeszów
Tarnów
Bochnia
Przemysl
Lvov (Lemberg)
U. S. S. R.
Cieszyn
Nowy Sącz
Galicia
Sambor
Drogobych
Stryy
Ternopol
Carpathian Mountains
Dniester
Buczacz
Zbrucz
Kamenets Podolskiy
High Tatra
Žilina
Ružomberok
Prešov
Ondava
Ivano-Frankovsk (Stanislav)
Kolomyya
Uzhgorod (Ungvar)
Kosice (Kassa)
Banská Bystrica
Latorica
Mukachevo
Chernovtsy
Yasinya
Khust
Hernad
Miskolc
Tokaj
Tisza
Satu Mare
Sighet
Eger
Nyiregyhaza
Vac
Szamos
Baia Mare
Cimpulung
Botosani
Debrecen
PEST
Jászberény
HUNGARY
Tasnad
Bistrita
Piatra Neamt
Cegled
Oradea
Dej
Szolnok
Dunaujvaros
Cluj (Kolozsvár)
Kecskemét
Transylvania
Bekes
Szentes
T.Mures
Kiskunfelegyhaza
Bekescaba
Gyula
Bihor Mts
Aiud
Mures
Danube
Szeged
Hodmezovasarhely
Mako
Arad
Alba Julia
Sighisoara
Olt
Subotica
Sombor
Senta
Timisoara
Lugoj
Sibiu
Brasov
Tisa
ROMANIA
Timis
Transylvanian Alps
Novi Sad
Zrenjanin
Tirgu Jiu
Pitesti
Ploiesti
Vršac
Sava
Pancevo
Iron Gate
Bazias
Zemun
Orsova
Turnu Severin
Olt
BUCURESTI (BUCHAREST)
Sabac
BEOGRAD (BELGRADE)
Slatina
Arges
Drina
Valjevo
Craiova
YUGOSLAVIA
Morava
Kragujevac
Vidin
Giurgiu
Ruse
Zajecar
Dunarea (Danube)
Lom
Dunav
Užice
Krusevac
BULGARIA
Foca
Niš (Nish)
Pirot
Vratsa
Pleven
Veliko Turnovo
Pljevlja
Novi Pazar
Isker
20 22 24 26
50 48 46 44

Boden See
Zurich
Rhein
Bern
SWITZERLAND
Lausanne
Rhône
Geneve
Mt Blanc
Mte. Rosa
Valle d'Aosta
L. Maggiore
L. di Como
L. di Garda
FRANCE
ALPS
Salzburg
WIEN (VIENNA)
Wiener Neustadt
AUSTRIA
Inn
Innsbruck
Mur
Graz
Gyor
Balaton L.
Trentino
Alto Adige
Bolzano
Trento
Carnic Alps
Friuli
Venezia Giulia
Udine
Belluno
Klagenfurt
Maribor
Kranj
Varazdin
Drava
Lombardia
Milano (Milan)
Brescia
Cremona
Mantova
Veneto
Verona
Padova
Adige
Venezia (Venice)
Gorizia
Ljubljana (Laibach)
Trieste
Zagreb (Agram)
Karlovac
Sisak
Torino (Turin)
Pavia
Piemonte
Po
Alessandria
Parma
Emilia Romagna
Ferrara
Bologna
Adria
Opatija
Rijeka (Fiume)
Cuneo
Savona
Liguria
Genova (Genoa)
Apennine
Ravenna
Forli
Pula
Cres
Senj
Una
Bas Novi
Bihac
Gospic
Kljuc
YUGO
44
Nice
La Spezia
Carrara
San Remo
Ligurian Sea
Lucca
Pisa
Livorno (Leghorn)
Firenze (Florence)
Arno
Arezzo
Rimini
SAN MARINO
Pesaro
Marche
Dugi Otok
Kornat
Zadar
Knin
Travnik
Sibenik (Sebenico)
Trogir
Split (Spalato)
Ancona
ADRIATIC SEA
Toscana
Siena
Piombino
Elba
Perugia
Umbria
Spoleto
Macerata
Ascoli Piceno
Brac
Hvar
Vis
Korcula
Mljet
Grosseto
S. Stefano
Viterbo
Rieti
Mte. Corno (Gran Sasso)
Pescara
Chieti
Aquila
Corsica (Corse)
Ajaccio
Civitavecchia
Lazio
Tiber
ROMA (Rome)
Fiumicino
Abruzzo
Molise
Termoli
Palagruza
Dubro
ITALY
Velletri
Apennines
Anzio
Latina
Cassino
Gargano
M. Foggia
Str. of Bonifacio
Caprera I.
Porto Torres
Sassari
Olbia
Alghero
Orosei
Gaeta
Ponzini
Napoli (Naples)
Ischia
Capri
Bay of Naples
Vesuvius
Sorrento
Salerno
Campania
Barletta
Bari
Puglia
Potenza
Taranto
Basilicata
40
Sardinia
Sardegna
Oristano
M. Gennargentu
Muravera
Iglesias
Carloforte
Cagliari
Carbonia
C. Spartivento
TYRRHENIAN SEA
C. Licosa
Camerota
G. of Policastro
Lauria
Gulf of Taranto
Carigliano
Belvedere
Cosenza
Calabria
Crotone
C. Colo
Stromboli
Lipari Is.
Pizzo
Catanzaro
G. of Squilla
Castellammare
Palermo
Trapani
Cefalu
Messina
Palmi
Cittanova
Reggio Calabria
Marsala
Mazara
Alcamo
Taormina
Etna
Adrano
C. Spartivento
Str. of Messina
Sicily (Sicilia)
Caltanissetta
Catania
C. Bon
Agrigento
Licata
Ragusa
Siracusa (Syracuse)
Noto
Modica
C. Passero
TUNIS
Pantelleria
AFRICA
MEDITERRANEAN
36
Statute Miles
0 50 100 150
Gozo
Valletta
MALTA
8
12
16

Chernovtsy
(Cernauti)
Bukovina
Botosani
U. S. S. R.
Dniester
(Dnestr)
Beltsy
Kishinev
Bendery
Odessa
Miskolc
Tisza
Satu Mare
Suceava
Debrecen
BUDAPEST
G A R Y
Oradea
Maramures
Bistrita
Piatra Neamt
Iasi
Roman
Kecskemet
Crisana
Dej
Cluj
(Kolozsvár)
Tirgu Mures
Bacau
Moldavia
Prut
Belgorod Dnestrovskiy
Hódmezővásárhely
Transylvania
Carpathian Mts
Birlad
Szeged
Arad
ROMANIA
Focşani
Siretul
Galati
Deva
R. Mures
Sibiu
Brasov
Braila
Izmail
Subotica
Senta
Timisoara
Caransebes
Transylvanian Alps
Buzau
Tulcea
Sulina
Sombor
Zrenjanin
Novi Sad
Banat
Ploiesti
Vršac
Pančevo
Tirgu Jiu
Pitesti
Dobruja
Zemun
Iron Gate
Turnu Severin
Walachia
BUCURESTI
(BUCHAREST)
Arges
Sabac
BEOGRAD
(BELGRADE)
Smederevo
Požarevac
Craiova
Jiu
Olt
Danube
Constanta
Mangalia
Kragujevac
Calafat
Caracal
Giurgiu
Dunarea
Silistra
Vidin
Ruse (Ruschuk)
Tolbukhin
Titovo Užice
Lom
Mikhaylovgrad
Pleven
Svishtov
Razgrad
Kruševac
Aleksinac
Shumen
Varna
Pljevlja
Niš
(Nish)
Veliko Turnovo
(Kolarovgrad)
Novi Pazar
Vratsa
Lovech
Balkan Mts
Shipka
Sliven
Pirot
Yambol
Burgas
Leskovac
Iskur
Stara Zagora
BLACK SEA
Peć
SOFIYA
(SOFIA)
Samokov
BULGARIA
Priština
Maritsa
Cetinje
Titograd
Prizren
Pazardzhik
Plovdiv
(Philippopolis)
Kirklareli
Shkodër
(Scutari)
Blagoevgrad
Skopje
(Üskub)
Rhodope Mts
Haskovo
Kurdzhali
Edirne (Adrianople)
Bosporus
Titov Veles
Stip
Struma
Smolyan
TURKEY
Istanbul
(Constantinople)
Üskudar
TIRANË
Drin
Petrich
Xanthi
Komotini
Tekirdag
Sea of Marmara
Elbasan
Bitola
(Monastir)
Drama
Thrace
ALBANIA
Vardar
Serrai
Kavalla
Alexandroupolis
Edhessa
Macedonia
Thasos
Bursa
Vlorë
(Valona)
Korçe
Veroia
Thessaloniki
(Salonica)
Samothraki
Gelibolu
Kozani
Olympus
(Olimbos)
Mt Athos
Epirus
G. of Thermai
Limnos
Balikesir
Ioannina
Thessaly
C. Dhrepanon
Dardanelles
ASIA
Larisa
Kerkira
(Corfu)
Trikkala
Volos
Nth Sporades
Lesvos
(Mitilini)
Kardhitsa
Pindus Mts
MINOR
Arta
Lamia
Evvoia
(Euboea)
AEGEAN SEA
Preveza
Levkas
Agrinion
Parnassos
Khios
Izmir
(Smyrna)
GREECE
G. of Corinth
Thivai
(Thebes)
Khalkis
ATHINAI (ATHENS)
Andros
Samos
Kefallinia
Mesolongion
Patrai
Korinthos
Canal
Piraievs
(Piraeus)
Tinos
Ikaria
Peloponnisos
(Morea)
Argos
Saronic Gulf
Kea
Zakinthos
Pirgos
Tripolis
Archipelago
Naxos
Ionian Islands
Idra
Paros
Sporades
Kalamai
Sparti
G. of Argolis
Cyclades
Pilos
Githion
Milos
Rodhos
C. Malea
Thira
Kithira
Dodecanese
Karpathos
(Scarpanto)
Khania
(Canea)
Suda B.
Crete
Rethimnon
Iraklion
(Candia)
C. Sideron
Mt Ida
C. Matapan
SEA
20
24
28
44
40
36

NORTH ITALY

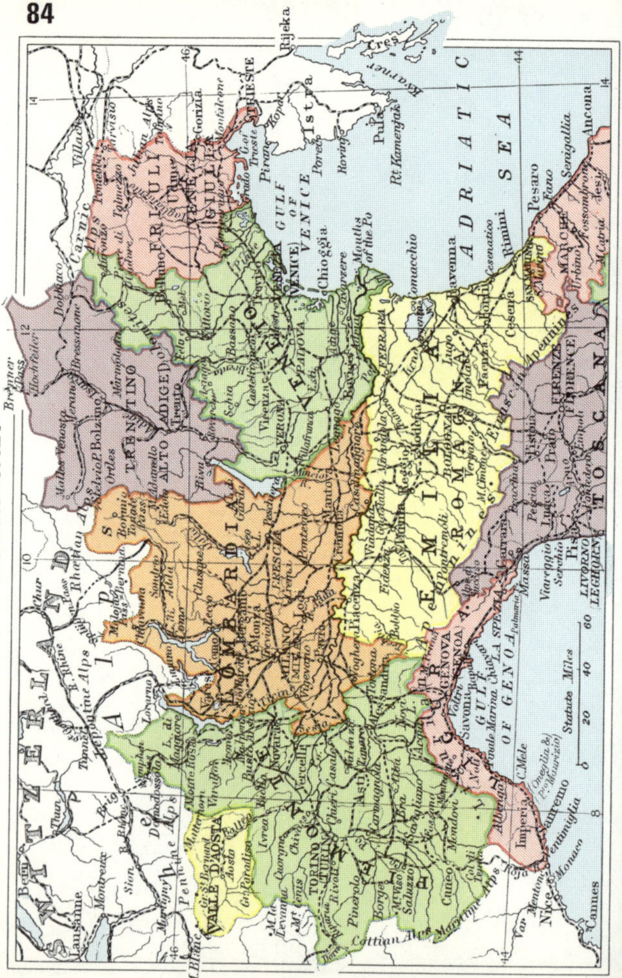
SWITZERLAND
ADRIATIC SEA
GULF OF GENOA
GULF OF VENICE
LOMBARDIA
VENETO
EMILIA ROMAGNA
TOSCANA
PIEMONTE
LIGURIA
TRENTINO ALTO ADIGE
FRIULI VENEZIA GIULIA
VALLE D'AOSTA
MARCHE
MILANO (MILAN)
TORINO (TURIN)
GENOVA (GENOA)
VENEZIA (VENICE)
FIRENZE (FLORENCE)
LIVORNO (LEGHORN)
BOLOGNA
TRIESTE
PADOVA
VERONA
BRESCIA
FERRARA
LA SPEZIA
Ravenna
Rimini
Pesaro
Ancona
Rijeka
Cres
Pula
Istra
Nice
Cannes
Monaco
Lausanne
Bern
Chur
Brenner Pass
Pennine Alps
Lepontine Alps
Rhaetian Alps
Carnic Alps
Julian Alps
Cottian Alps
Maritime Alps
Dolomites
Apennines
Mouths of the Po
Statute Miles
0 20 40 60

YUGOSLAVIA
ALBANIA
Debar
Prilep
Struga
Ohrid
Elbasan
Resan
Bitola
(Monastir)
Prespa
Devoli
Berat
Petrich
Rupel Pass
L. Dojran
Gevgelija
Vardar
Drama
Sidhirokastron
Serrai
Kavalla
Amfipolis
Pella
Kilkis
Monastir Gap
Florina
Edhessa
Yiannitsa
Thessaloniki
L. Volvi
THESSALONIKI
(SALONICA)
CHALCIDICE
Polygyros
Stavros
G. of Strimon
Ierissos
Athos Peninsula
Mt. Athos
Singitic G.
Sithonia
Sykia
G. of Kassandra
Kassandra
Valta
C. Kalogeros
Kastoria
Voion Mts.
Ptolemais
Veroia
Imathia
Kozani
Pieria
Katerini
G. of Thermai
Servia
Mt. Olympus
Gjinokaster
(Argyrokastron)
Leskovik
Konitsa
Grevena
Khasia
Elasson
Mts. Tsaritsani
Pinios
(Salamvria)
Ampelakia
Mt. Ossa
Agyia
Metsovon
Ioannina
Kerkira
Corfu
Filiates
Kalamas
Ioannina (Yannina)
EPIRUS
Trikkala
Kalambaka
Tirnavos
Larisa
THESSALY
Polidendri
Mt. Pilion
Thesprotia
Paramythia
Margariton
Pindus Mts.
Kardhitsa
Karditsa
Volos
Magnisia
Gioura
C. Aspro
Parga
Preveza
Arta
Farsala
G. of Volos
Skiathos
Pelagonisi
Paxoi
Kastrosikia
Domokos
Almyros
Othrys
Skopelos
Ndrn. Sporades
Rendina
Phthiotis
Sperkhios
Lamia
Istiaea
Preveza
G. of Arta
Evritania
Karpenision
Pass of Thermopylae
Ch. of Evvoia
Evvoia
Levkas
Vonitsa
Amfilokhia
Acarnania & Ætolia
CENTRAL GREECE
Atalandi
Kimi
Levkas
C. Doukato
Agrinion
Mt. Giona
Parnassus
Amfissa
Phocis
Levadia
Khalkis
Euboea
Ithaka
Mesolongion
Navpaktos
Boeotia
Mt. Elikon
Thivai (Thebes)
Oropos
Kefallinia
Argostolion
C. Skrofa
G. of Patras
Patrai (Patras)
Aiyion
G. of Corinth
Villia
Elevsis
Marathon
C. Pápas
Achaia
Sikion
Korinthos (Corinth)
Corinth Canal
Megara
Attica
ATHINAI (ATHENS)
C. Monda
Mt. Erimanthos
Mt. Killini
Isthmus
Piraievs
Mt. Imittos
Saronic G.
Elis
Zakinthos
Amalias
Pirgos
PELOPONNISOS
(MOREA)
Argos
Argolis
Aiyina
Lavrion
Makronision
Kea
C. Katakolon
Olympia
R. Alfios
Nafplion
Tripolis
Poros
G. of Kiparissia
Megalopolis
Arcadia
Messenia
G. Kranidion
Idhra
G. of Argolis
Spetsai
Kiparissia
Meligala
Malevo Mts.
Evrotas
Leonidhion
Strophades
Messini
Sparti (Sparta)
Kalamai
Anavrion
Pilos
Laconia
Sapientza
Yithion
(Marathonisi)
Monemvasia
Korone
Gulf of Messenia
G. of Laconia
Areopolis
C. Akhritas
C. Malea
Kithira (Cerigo)
C. Matapan
Capsali
Statute Miles
0
20
40
60
80
20
22
24
40
38

WESTERN U.S.S.R.

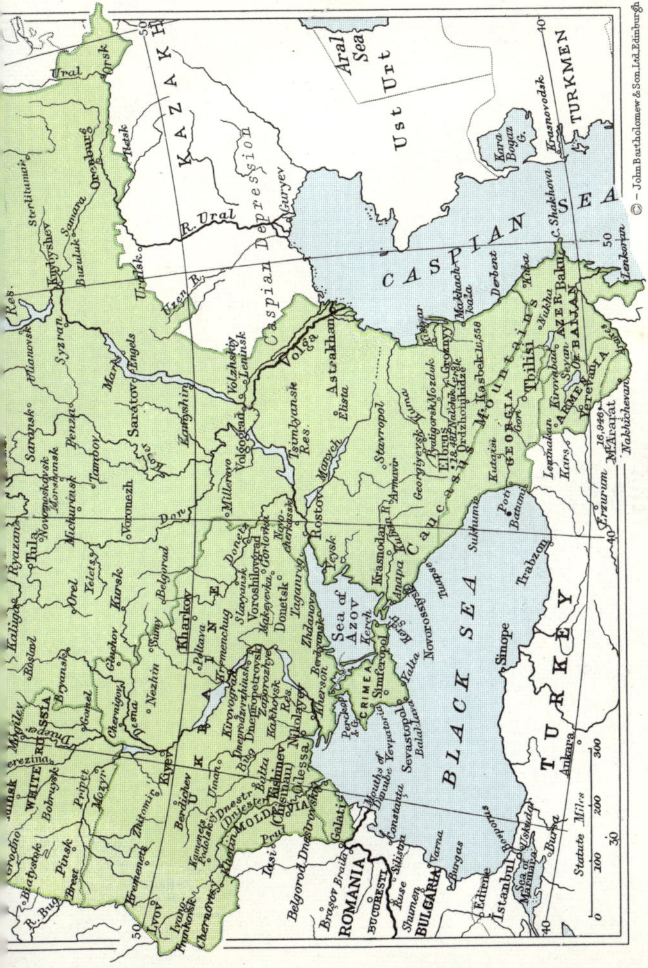

KAZAKH
TURKMEN
Aral Sea
Ust Urt
Caspian Depression
CASPIAN SEA
Kara Bogaz G.
Krasnovodsk
BLACK SEA
Sea of Azov
CRIMEA
UKRAINE
WHITE RUSSIA
MOLDAVIA
GEORGIA
ARMENIA
AZERBAIJAN
TURKEY
ROMANIA
BULGARIA
Caucasus Mountains
R. Ural
Ural
Orsk
Orenburg
Guryev
Uralsk
Kuybyshev
Syzran
Saratov
Engels
Volgograd
Astrakhan
Volga
Elista
Rostov
Tsimlyansk Res.
Stavropol
Krasnodar
Grozny
Makhach-kala
Derbent
Baku
Tbilisi
Yerevan
M. Ararat
Elbrus
M. Kasbek
Batumi
Poti
Sukhumi
Novorossiysk
Kerch
Simferopol
Sevastopol
Yalta
Odessa
Nikolayev
Kherson
Zaporozhye
Dnepropetrovsk
Donetsk
Zhdanov
Taganrog
Voroshilovgrad
Kharkov
Poltava
Kremenchug
Kirovograd
Kiyev
Zhitomir
Berdichev
Vinnitsa
Kishinev (Chişinău)
Lvov
Brest
Pinsk
Gomel
Mogilev
Bryansk
Orel
Kursk
Belgorod
Voronezh
Tula
Ryazan
Tambov
Penza
Saransk
Don
Donets
Dnepr
Dnestr
Pripyat
Desna
Trabzon
Erzurum
Kars
Sinope
Ankara
Istanbul
Bursa
Edirne
Varna
Burgas
Constanta
Galati
Braila
Bucureşti
Ruse
Shumen
Sea of Marmara
Statute Miles
© – John Bartholomew & Son, Ltd. Edinburgh

UKRAINE

UKRAINE
SEA OF AZOV
BLACK SEA
Crimea
KIEV
KHARKOV
DONETSK
DNEPROPETROVSK
ODESSA
ROSTOV
VOLGOGRAD
MOLDAVIA
Statute Miles

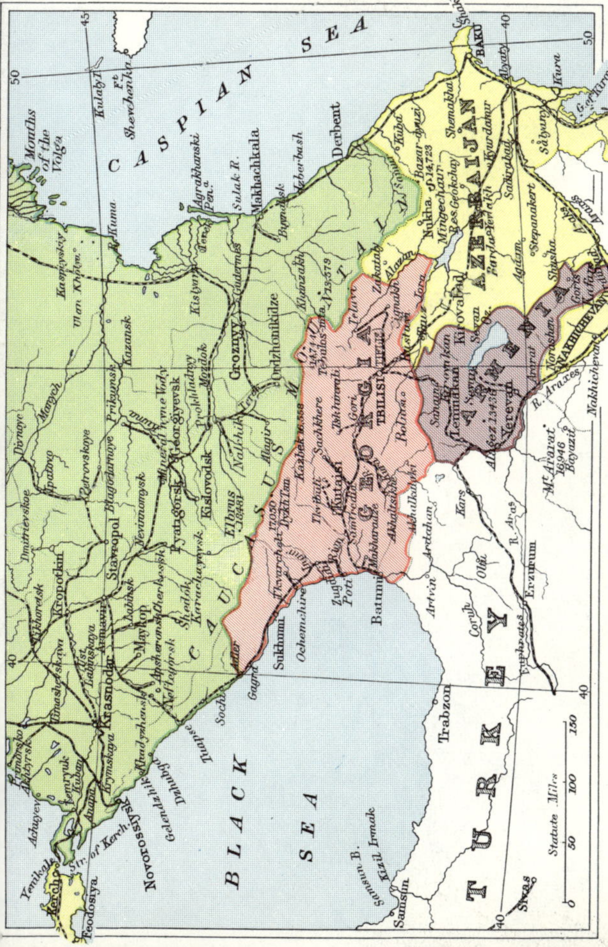
CASPIAN SEA
BLACK SEA
CAUCASUS MTS.
GEORGIA
ARMENIA
AZERBAIJAN
TURKEY
NAKHICHEVAN
TBILISI
BAKU
Yerevan
Baku
Derbent
Makhachkala
Groznyy
Ordzhonikidze
Mozdok
Kizlyar
Gudermes
Khasavyurt
Buynaksk
Kislovodsk
Pyatigorsk
Georgiyevsk
Mineral'nyye Vody
Prokhladnyy
Nal'chik
Elbrus 18481
Stavropol
Nevinnomyssk
Cherkessk
Karachayevsk
Krasnodar
Maykop
Armavir
Kropotkin
Tikhoretsk
Novorossiysk
Tuapse
Sochi
Gagra
Sukhumi
Ochemchire
Zugdidi
Poti
Batumi
Kutaisi
Gori
Telavi
Rustavi
Akhaltsikhe
Akhalkalaki
Zakataly
Nukha
Mingechaur Res.
Kirovabad
Yevlakh
Stepanakert
Shusha
Agdam
Shemakha
Kurdamir
Sabirabad
Kuba
Lenkoran
Ali-Bayramly
Kura
Araks
Dzhulfa
Nakhichevan
Leninakan
Kirovakan
Sevan
Alagez 13438
Mt Ararat 16946
Bayazit
Kars
Ardahan
Artvin
Erzurum
Trabzon
Samsun
Sivas
Kizil Irmak
Euphrates
Coruh
R. Aras
R. Araxes
Kerch
Feodosiya
Str. of Kerch
Anapa
Temryuk
Kuban
Yeysk
Mouths of the Volga
Kuma
Terek
Sulak R.
Agrakhanski Pen.
Ft Shevchenko
Kulaly I.
Manych
Statute Miles
0 50 100 150

SOVIET CENTRAL ASIA

Bakhta
Mirnoye
Zotina
Yeniseysk
Maklakovo
Mariinsk
Bogotol
Achinsk
Tom
Yenisey
Novokuznetsk
Abakan
Teletsk Oz.
Upper Tunguska
Angara
Boguchany
Kansk
Krasnoyarsk
Bratsk
Nizhneudinsk
Sayan Mounts.
Kyzyl
Oka
Irkutsk
Mirnyy
Vilyuysk
Yakutsk
Olekminsk
Lena
Nuya
Mirn
Kirensk
Ust' Kut
Lena
Kirenga
Nizhne Angarsk
R. Angara
Baikal Mts
Oz. Baikal
Bodaybo
Vitim
Barguzin
Ulan-Ude
Chita
Yablonovyy Mts
Mugocha
Nerchinsk
Shilka
Karymskoye
Borzya
Argun
R. Onon
Kyakhta
Gusinoozersk
Selenga
R. Olekma
Skovorodino
Stanovoi Mts.
Udskoye
Magdagachi
Amga
Ust' Maya
Aldan
Uchur
Khandyga
Kolyma Mts.
Magadan
Tauysk B.
Okhotsk
Maia R.
Dzhugdzhur Mts.
Ayan
St. John I.
Shantar Is.
G. of Sakhalin
Nikolayevsk
Sakhalin
Amgun
Mariinsk
Zeya
Svobodnyy
Belogorsk
Blagoveshchensk
Amur
Komsomolsk
Sovetskaya Gavan
Khabarovsk
Birobidzhan
Gulf of Tatarskiy
Yuzhno Sakhalinsk
La Perouse Str.
Wakkanai
Sikhota
Tetyukhe
Olga
Oz. Khanka
Ussuriysk
Vladivostok
Peter the Great B.
Hakodate
Ubsa Nur
Altai Mountains
Jirgalanta (Kobdo)
Hobsogol Dalay
Jibhalanta (Uliassutai)
Dzabhan
Karakorum
Orhon
Ulaanbaatar
Chaybalsan
Kerulen
Hulun Nor
Hailar
Buyr Nur
MONGOLIA
Gobi
Hami
Khingan Mounts.
Nonni
Nunkiang
Manchuria
Tsitsihar
Sungari
Harbin (Haerhpin)
Fuyu
Kirin
Changchun
CHINA
Statute Miles
0 100 200 300 400 500 600

ARCTIC
BRITISH ISLES
London
North Sea
SCANDINAVIA
North Cape
Novaya Zemlya
Kara Sea
Paris
EUROPE
Berlin
Baltic Sea
Arkhangelsk
Leningrad
UNION OF SOVIET
Salekhard
Wien (Vienna)
Moskva (Moscow)
Ural Mts
Ob
Surgut
Tobolsk
Roma
Sicily
Volga
Sverdlovsk
Petropavlovsk
Omsk
Istanbul
Mediterranean Sea
GREECE
Black Sea
Astrakhan
R. Ural
Orsk
Tobol
Ishim
R. Irtysh
Kirghiz Steppes
Karaganda
Trabzon
Ankara
Izmir
TURKEY
Erzurum
Caucasus Mts
Tbilisi
Caspian Sea
Oz. Balkhash
KAZAKH
Rodhos
Taurus M
CYPRUS
Aleppo
SYRIA
Ararat
Aral Sea
Syr Darya
Khiva
UZBEK
Tashkent
KIRGIZ
Kokand
Jerusalem
Cairo
Suez
JORDAN
Damascus
Mosul
Elburz Mt
TURKMEN
Ashkhabad
Amu Darya
Bukhara
Samarkand
Kashgar
Mashhad
Merv
Dushanbe
TADZHIK
Pamirs
Yarkan
SINK
EGYPT
Mt Sinai
Babylon
Baghdad
Tehran
Herat
Hindu Kush
Basra
Esfahan
IRAN (PERSIA)
Shiraz
Kabul
AFGHANISTAN
Srinagar
KASHMIR
Peshawar
Rawalpindi
Medina
Hejaz
SAUDI ARABIA
Hasa
Riyadh
Nejd
The Gulf
Bushehr (Bushire)
Kandahar
Kalat
PAKISTAN
R. Indus
Lahore
Multan
Simla
Himalaya
Jiddah
Mecca
Red Sea
R. Nile
Muscat
G. of Oman
Karachi
Delhi
Agra
Kanpur
Allahabad
Lucknow
OMAN
Ras al Junaiz
G. of Kutch
Baroda
INDIA
YEMEN
Mocha
DEM. REP. YEMEN
Narbada
Surat
Nagpur
Kuria Muria Is
G. of Cambay
Aden
G. of Aden
Str. of Babel Mandeb
Bombay
Godavari
Hyderabad
Krishna
Arabian Sea
Socotra I. (Yemen)
Panjim
C. Guardafui
Laccadive (Ind.) Is
Bangalore
Calicut
Mysore
Madr
AFRICA
L. Victoria
Cape Comorin
Palk S
Trinco
G. of Mannar
Colombo
Galle
SRI LA
Maldive Is
INDIAN OCE
Zanzibar
Statute Miles
0
500
1000
Gan
40
60
80
20
0

Bering Str.
Wrangel I.
New Siberian Is
Anadyr G.
St Matthew I.
Bering Sea
Aleutian Is.
Tiksi
Bulun
R. Lena
Arctic Circle
Kolyma Mts
Magadan
Kamchatka
Petropavlovsk Kamchatskiy
C. Lopatka
Okhotsk
Sea of Okhotsk
Yakutsk
Sakhalin
Kuril Is.
REPUBLICS
IALIST
Nikolayevsk
Blagoveshchensk
Amur
Stanovoy Mts
Oz. Baikal
Irkutsk
Chita
Hokkaido
Hakodate
Khabarovsk
Vladivostok
Manchuria
Harbin
Sea of Japan
JAPAN
Honshu
Tokyo
Yokohama
Ulaanbaatar
Karakorum
MONGOLIA
Gobi
INNER MONGOLIA
Changchun
Kirin
Shenyang (Mukden)
Korea
Seoul
Peking
Tientsin
Kyoto
Shikoku
Kyushu
Yellow Sea
Korea Str.
Nagasaki
Ogasawara Jima
Nan Shan
Hwang Ho
Tsingtao
Shanghai
Nanking
CHINA PEOPLE'S REP.
Wuhan (Hankow)
Hangchow
Ningpo
Wuchang
Cheng-tu
Lhasa
Yangtze Kiang
Chungking
Chang-sha
Ryukyu Is.
Foochow
Taipei
Tropic of Cancer
Nan-ling Mts
Amoy
Taiwan (Formosa I.) (Chin. Nat. Rep.)
Kunming
Canton
Si-kiang
Hong Kong
Macao
Bhamo
Lashio
Mandalay
BURMA
LAOS
Tongking
Hanoi
Hainan I.
Luzon I.
PHILIPPINES
Yap
G. of Tongking
Prome
Hue
VIETNAM
R. Mekong
Manila
Moulmein
INDO CHINA
China Sea
Palawan I.
Mindanao
Palau Is.
PACIFIC OCEAN
THAILAND
Bangkok (Krung Thep)
KHMER REP.
Phnom Penh
Sulu Sea
Isthmus of Kra
G. of Siam
Cambodia Pt (Ca Mau Pt)
Labuan
Sabah
Celebes Sea
Molucca Is.
Halmahera
MALAYSIA
Brunei
Sarawak
Kuching
Irian Jaya
New Guinea (Papua)
Str. of Malacca
Kuala Lumpur
Malacca
Medan
Singapore
Borneo
INDONESIA
Celebes
Seram
Buru
Sumatra
Padang
Banjarmasin
Makassar Str.
Makasar
Banda Sea
Palembang
Sunda Str.
Djakarta
Java Sea
Timor (Port.)
Java
Surabaja
Darwin
AUSTRALIA

U. S. S.
Semipalatinsk
Sayansk Mounts.
Irkutsk
Kyzyl
Munku Sardyk
Tannu-ola Mts.
Belukha Mt.
Hobsogol Dalay
N. Selenginsk
Balkhash Ozero
Ayaguz
Zaysan Oz.
Altai
Khangai
Tarbagatay
Zaisan
Jirgalanta (Kobdo)
Selenga
Orhon
Mts
Hara Usa
Jibhalanta (Uliassutai)
Dzabhan
Ili
Ala Tau
Karamai
DZUNGARIA
Kuldja
MONGO
Khan Tengri
Urumchi
Kitai
Southern Altai
Tien Shan Mounts
Bogdo-Ula
Sairam
Kara Shahr
Barkol (Chensi)
KASHGAR
Aksu
Kucha
Turfan
Kashgar Daria
Baghrash Kol
Shanshan
Hami
Gobi
Tarim
Yarkand
Takla Makan Desert
Lop Nor
SINKIANG (CHINESE TURKISTAN)
Yarkand
Karakoram
Anst
Charchan
Khotan
Astin Tagh
Kiuchuan
Changyeh
Ala Shan
Nan Shan
Yinchuan
Kunlun Mountains
Ching Hai
NINGSIA HUI
Bulamangua Ra.
Karakoram Ra.
TSINGHAI
Sining
Lanchow
Indus
KAN-SU
Alin Kangri
Tangla Range
Lungsi
Paoki
Hwang Ho
TIBET
Dangra Tso
Zilling Tso
CH
Nam Tso
Chamdo
CHAMDO
PEOPLE
NEPAL
Shigatse
Lhasa
Tsangpo
Cheng-tu
Kathmandu
Mt. Everest
Yamdrok Tso
Yangtze Kiang
Paan (Batang)
SZE-CHWAN
Chungking
Kangchenjunga
Darjeeling
Chamalhari
Bhutan
Ipin
Ning-yuan
Patna
Brahmaputra
Ganges
ASSAM
Myitkyina
BANGLA-DESH
Tali
KWEI-CH
Kweiya
INDIA
Calcutta
Irrawaddy
Teng-Yueh
Kunming
Bhamo
Kutsing
YUN-NAN
Mahanadi
Lashio
BURMA
Meng-tsz
Chittagong
Pu-erh
Mandalay
Szemao (Sumao)
Song-ka
N. VIETNAM
Lang-son
Sontay
Hanoi
Akyab
BAY OF BENGAL
LAOS
Luang Prabang
80
90
100
30
20

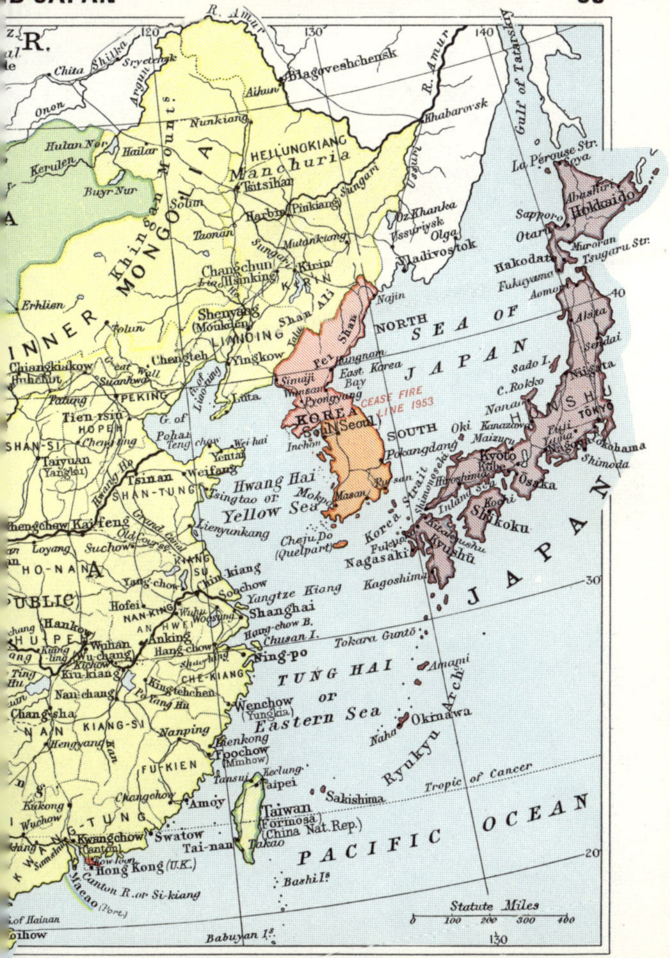
Manchuria
HEILUNGKIANG
MONGOLIA
INNER
Khingan Mounts.
KIRIN
LIAONING
R. Amur
Blagoveshchensk
Khabarovsk
Vladivostok
Harbin
Tsitsihar
Changchun (Hsinking)
Shenyang (Moukden)
Yingkow
Chengteh
PEKING
Tien-tsin
HOPEH
SHAN-SI
Taiyuan (Yangku)
Tsinan
SHAN-TUNG
Tsingtao or
Weifang
Yentai
Hwang Hai or Yellow Sea
KOREA
NORTH
SOUTH
Seoul
Pyongyang
Inchon
Wonsan
Hungnam
East Korea Bay
Najin
Pusan
Masan
Mokpo
Pohangdang
CEASE FIRE LINE 1953
Cheju Do (Quelpart)
Korea Strait
SEA OF JAPAN
JAPAN
Hokkaido
Sapporo
Otaru
Muroran
Hakodate
Tsugaru Str.
La Pérouse Str.
Soya
Abashiri
Aomori
Akita
Sendai
Niigata
Sado I.
C. Rokko
HONSHU
TOKYO
Yokohama
Shimoda
Nagoya
Kyoto
Kobe
Osaka
Maizuru
Kanazawa
Oki
Hiroshima
Inland Sea
Shimonoseki
Shikoku
Kochi
Kyushu
Kitakyushu
Fukuoka
Nagasaki
Kagoshima
Gulf of Tatarsky
Tokara Guntō
Amami
Okinawa
Naha
Ryukyu Arch.
TUNG HAI or Eastern Sea
Shanghai
Hang-chow B.
Chusan I.
Ning-po
Hang-chow
CHE-KIANG
Wenchow (Yungkia)
Foochow (Mmhow)
FU-KIEN
Nanping
Amoy
Swatow
Kwangchow (Canton)
Hong Kong (U.K.)
Macao (Port.)
Canton R. or Si-kiang
Taiwan Formosa (China Nat. Rep.)
Taipei
Keelung
Tai-nan
Takao
Sakishima
Bashi Is
Babuyan Is
Tropic of Cancer
PACIFIC OCEAN
Statute Miles
0 100 200 300 400
Yangtze Kiang
Nanking
Wuhan
Hankow
Wu-chang
Kiu-kiang
Nan-chang
Chang-sha
KIANG-SI
Hofei
Anking
Soochow
Lienyunkang
Kaifeng
Loyang
Suchow
Chita
Hailar
Hulun Nor
Kerulen
Buyr Nur
Erhlien
Dolun
Chiangkiakow
Kalgan
Taonan
Solun
Nunkiang
Aihun
Ussuri
Oz. Khanka
Olga
Ussuriysk
Mutankiang
Kirin
Lü-ta
Tengchow
Wei hai
Sungari
Chiangkiakow
Great Wall
120
130
140
40
30
20

JAPAN

SEA OF JAPAN
PACIFIC OCEAN
HONSHU
SHIKOKU
KYŪSHŪ
SOUTH KOREA
TOKYO
Yokohama
Nagoya
Kyoto
Osaka
Kobe
Hiroshima
Nagasaki
Kagoshima
Fukuoka
Sapporo
Pusan
Tsushima
Oki guntō
Sado
Izu Shichi to
Goto Retto
Statute Miles

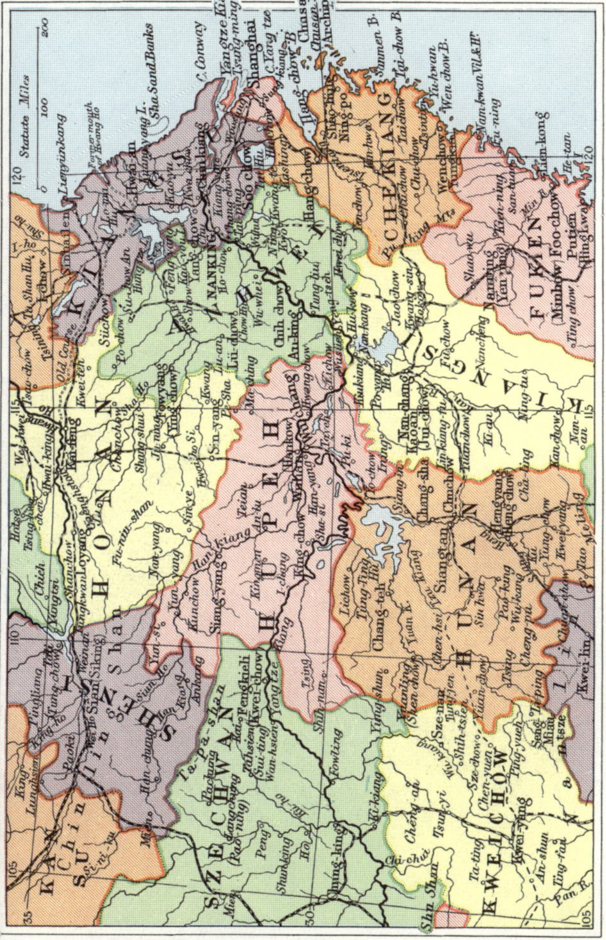
Statute Miles
0
100
200
HONAN
HUPEH
HUNAN
KIANGSI
KIANGSU
CHEKIANG
FUKIEN
SHENSI
SZECHWAN
KWEICHOW
Shanghai
NANKING
Hankow
Wuchang
Ichang
Chang-sha
Siangtan
Nan-chang
Foo-chow
Wenchow
Ning-po
Hangchow
Soochow
Chinkiang
Yangtze Kiang
Chusan
Archipelago
Kai-feng
Loyang
Chung-king
Kwei-yang
Kwei-lin
Sha Sand Banks
C. Yang tze
Old Course
Han kiang

INDO-CHINA

Statute Miles
0 100 200 300 400 500
TIBET
C H I N A
INDIA
BURMA
THAILAND
(SIAM)
LAOS
VIETNAM
NORTH
SOUTH
KHMER REP. (CAMBODIA)
MALAYA
SUMATRA
BORNEO
Hainan I.
Brahmaputra
Sadiya
Putao
Gauhati
Shillong
Silchar
Imphal
Myitkyina
Mogaung
Irrawaddy
Pao-shan
Bhamo
Katha
Mawlaik
Kalewa
Yeu
Mogok
Namtu
Lashio
Chittagong
Monywa
Mandalay
Maymyo
Sagaing
Amarapura
Ava
Pakokku
Myingyan
Meiktila
Yun-chinghung
Kengtung
Akyab
Minbu
Arakan
R. Salween
Irrawaddy
Karenni
Prome
Sandoway
Myanaung
Henzada
Pegu
Rangoon
Bassein
C. Negrais
Preparis
G. of Martaban
Martaban
Moulmein
Amherst
Ye
Tavoy
Mergui
Mergui Archipelago
Andaman Islands
(To India)
Port Blair
Nicobar Is
(To India)
Tali
Kunming
Kweilin
Mekong
Tropic of Cancer
Nan-ning
Hong Ha (Red R.)
Lao Cai
Dai Black R.
Ha Giang
Tuyen Quang
Son Tay
Bac Ninh
Hanoi
Haiphong
Nam Dinh
Vinh
Gulf of Tongking
CEASE FIRE LINE 1954
Dong Hoi
Quang Tri
Hue
Da Nang (Tourane)
Quang Ngai
Qui Nhon
Ban Me Thuot
Nha Trang
Phan Thiet
Vung Tau
Saigon
My Tho
Vinh Long
Vinh Loi
COCHIN CHINA
Con Son
M. Sing
Luang Prabang
Xieng Khouang
Vientiane
Nong Khai
Chiang Rai
Chiang Mai
M. Lamphun
M. Nan
M. Phrae
Udon Thani
Phitsanulok
Nakhon Sawan
Menam
Nakhon Ratchasima
Khammarat
Saravane
Muang Ubon
Pakse
Khong
Siem Pang
Stung Treng
Kratie
Nakhon Pathom
Ayutthaya
BANGKOK
Krung Thep
Thonburi
Prachin
Siem Reap
Battambang
Chanthaburi
Tonle Sap
Kompong Chhnang
Phnom Penh
Kampot
Kompong Som
Phet Buri
Tenasserim
Prachuap Khiri Khan
Gulf of Siam
Kra Isthmus
Victoria Pt
Surat Thani
Nakhon Thammarat
Songkhla
MALAY PENINSULA
Pte de Ca Mau
SOUTH CHINA SEA
Bunguran Is (Natuna)
Anambas Is
Banda Atjeh
Sabang
Achin
Pulau Langkawi
Georgetown
Pinang
Kota Bharu
Ipoh
Gunung Tahan
Kuala Lipis
Pt Swettenham
Kuala Lumpur
Pekan
MALACCA STRAIT
Malacca
Johor Baharu
SINGAPORE
BAY OF BENGAL
95
100
105
110
25
20
15
10
5

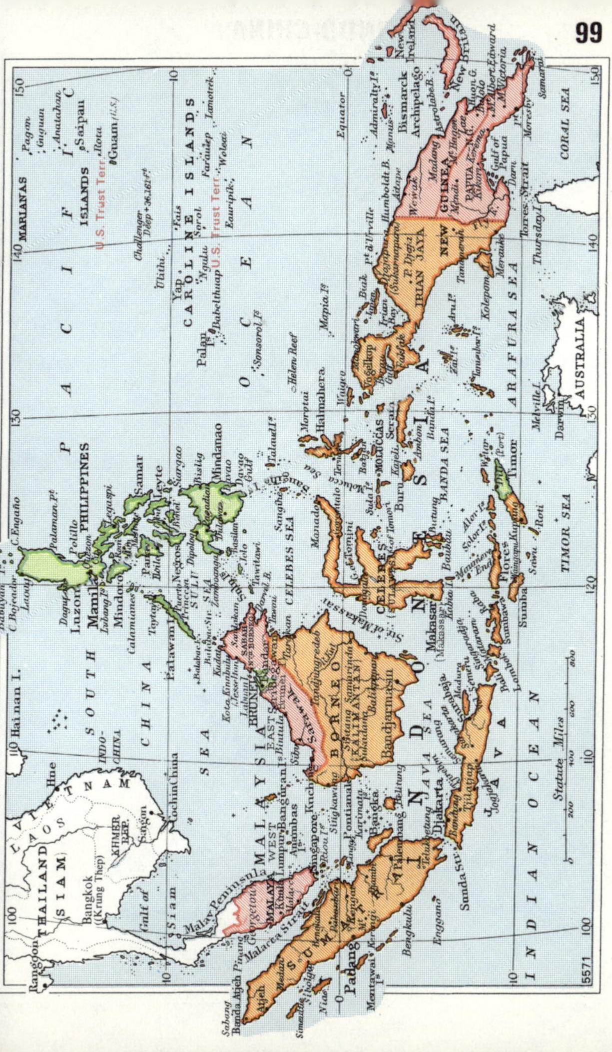

MARIANAS ISLANDS
U.S. Trust Terr.
Guam (U.S.)
Saipan
CAROLINE ISLANDS
P A C I F I C
O C E A N
PHILIPPINES
Luzon
Manila
Mindoro
Samar
Leyte
Mindanao
Palawan
SOUTH CHINA SEA
SULU SEA
CELEBES SEA
Hainan I.
VIETNAM
LAOS
KHMER REP.
THAILAND (SIAM)
Bangkok (Krung Thep)
Gulf of Siam
Malay Peninsula
MALAYSIA
WEST
EAST
Kuala Lumpur
Singapore
BRUNEI
SABAH
BORNEO
KALIMANTAN
Kuching
Pontianak
Bandjarmasin
INDONESIA
SUMATRA
Atjeh
Medan
Padang
Palembang
Bengkulu
JAVA
Djakarta
Bali
Lombok
Sumbawa
Flores
Sumba
Timor
CELEBES
Makasar
Manado
MOLUCCAS
Halmahera
Ceram
Buru
Ambon
BANDA SEA
JAVA SEA
IRIAN JAYA
NEW GUINEA
PAPUA
Port Moresby
Bismarck Archipelago
New Britain
New Ireland
ARAFURA SEA
TIMOR SEA
CORAL SEA
AUSTRALIA
Darwin
Torres Strait
INDIAN OCEAN
Malacca Strait
Sunda Str.
Str. of Makassar
Molucca Sea
Equator
Statute Miles
0 100 200 400 600 800
5571

WEST MALAYSIA

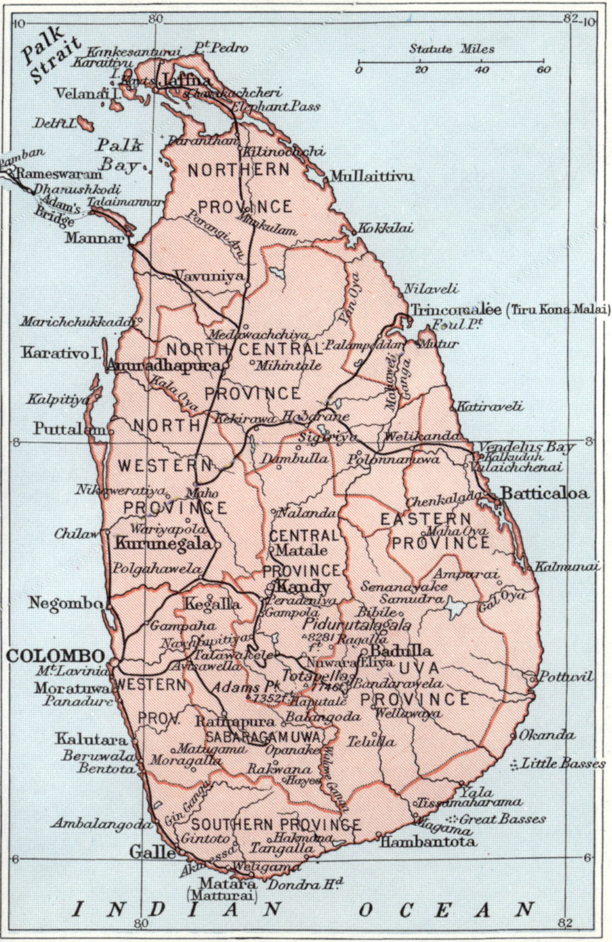
Palk Strait
Kankesanturai
Pt Pedro
Karaitivu I.
Kayts
Jaffna
Velanai I.
Chavakachcheri
Elephant Pass
Delft I.
Statute Miles
0 20 40 60
Palk Bay
Paranthan
Pamban
Rameswaram
Kilinochchi
NORTHERN PROVINCE
Mullaittivu
Dharushkodi
Adam's Bridge
Talaimannar
Mankulam
Parangi Aru
Kokkilai
Mannar
Vavuniya
Nilaveli
Yan Oya
Trincomalee (Tiru Kona Malai)
Foul Pt
Marichchukkaddi
Medawachchiya
NORTH CENTRAL PROVINCE
Palampoddaru
Mutur
Karativo I.
Anuradhapura
Mihintale
Mahaweli Ganga
Kala Oya
Kalpitiya
Katiraveli
Kekirawa
Habarane
Puttalam
NORTH WESTERN PROVINCE
Sigiriya
Welikanda
Vendelus Bay
Kalkudah
Valaichchenai
Dambulla
Polonnaruwa
Batticaloa
Nikaweratiya
Maho
Chenkalady
Nalanda
EASTERN PROVINCE
Chilaw
Wariyapola
Maha Oya
Kurunegala
CENTRAL PROVINCE
Matale
Polgahawela
Kalmunai
Amparai
Kandy
Senanayake Samudra
Negombo
Kegalla
Peradeniya
Gal Oya
Gampola
Bibile
Gampaha
Pidurutalagala
8281 ft
Ragalla
Nawalapitiya
Badulla
COLOMBO
Talawakele
Nuwara Eliya
UVA PROVINCE
Mt Lavinia
Avissawella
Totapella
Pottuvil
Moratuwa
WESTERN PROV.
Adams Pk
7352 ft
7746
Bandarawela
Panadure
Haputale
Wellawaya
Ratnapura
Balangoda
SABARAGAMUWA
Okanda
Kalutara
Telulla
Matugama
Opanake
Beruwala
Little Basses
Bentota
Moragalla
Rakwana
Walawe Ganga
Hayes
Yala
Gin Ganga
Tissamaharama
Great Basses
Ambalangoda
SOUTHERN PROVINCE
Lagama
Gintota
Hakmana
Hambantota
Galle
Tangalla
Akuressa
Weligama
Matara (Matturai)
Dondra Hd
INDIAN OCEAN
80
82
10
8
6

AFGHANISTAN
Herat
Hari-Rud
KABUL
Kabul
Jalalabad
Peshawar
Khyber
Ghazni
Gardez
Thal
Helmand
Farah
Juwain
Kandahar
Ft. Sandeman
Pishin
Quetta
God-i-Zireh
Zahidan
I R A N
Kalat
P A K I S T A N
BALUCHISTAN
Hamun-i-Mashkel
Tump
Dasht R.
Gwadar
Pasni
Bela
Sukkur
SIND
Hyderabad
Karachi
Korangi
N.W. FRONTIER
Islamabad
Rawalpindi
Indus
Jhelum
Chenab
Sialkot
Gujranwala
Dera Ismail Khan
Sulaiman Hills
Lahore
Lyallpur
Multan
THE PUNJAB
Sutlej
Bahawalpur
Mithan Kot
Khanpur
CHITRAL
Chitral
Hindu-Kush
Gilgit
K2
JAMMU AND KASHMIR
Skardu
Srinagar
Leh
Jammu
HIMACHAL PRADESH
H.P.
Amritsar
Jullundur
Simla
Chandigarh
Ludhiana
Ambala
PUNJAB
Dehra Dun
Saharanpur
Hardwar
Meerut
HARYANA
DELHI
Moradabad
Bareilly
UTTAR
Shahja
Mattra
Bharatpur
Agra
PRADE
Bikaner
RAJASTHAN
Thar
Jaisalmer
Jodhpur
Jaipur
Ajmer
Chambal
Kanpur
Cawnpore
Gwalior
Lashkar
Allahabad
Pali
Nimach
Kotah
Udaipur
Saugor
Indore
Bhopal
Vindhya Ra.
Jabalpur
Jubbulpur
Tropic of Cancer
Rann of Kutch
Kutch
Bhuj
Kandla
G. of Kutch
Jamnagar
GUJARAT
Ahmedabad
Wadwan
Rajkot
Bhavnagar
Broach
Baroda
Dhar
I N D
MADHYA
PRAD
Narmada
Satpura Ra.
Tapti
Kamptee
Nagpur
Amravati
Akola
Berar
Yeotmal
Diu I.
GD&D.
G. of Cambay
Daman
Surat
Nasik
Aurangabad
Bassein
Salsette I.
Thana
MAHARASHTRA
Bombay
Nander
Ahmadnagar
Godavari
Poona
Bankot
A R A B I A N
S E A
Western Ghats
Satara
Sholapur
Hyderabad
Golconda
Ratnagiri
Krishna
Kolhapur
Belgaum
Panjim
GOA DAMAN & DIU
Hubli
Kurnool
ANDHRA
Karwar
Bellary
N. Penner
Honawar
Nellore
Cuddapah
KARNATAKA
Kolar
Arcot
Pulicat
Madras
Mangalore
Bangalore
Saidapet
Vellore
Mysore
Laccadive (To India) Archipelago
Amindivi Is.
Cannanore
Tellicherry
Mahe
Nilgiri Hs.
Salem
Cuddalore
Pondicherry
Tranquebar
Coimbatore
Calicut
TAMIL NADU
Karikal
Negapatinam
Trichinopoly
Tanjore
Cochin
KERALA
Madurai
Palk Strait
Jaffna
Alleppey
Quilon
Malabar
Coromandel
Minicoy
Trivandrum
Tuticorin
Nagercoil
Adams Br.
C. Comorin
G. of Mannar
Kandy
Colombo
Galle
65
70
75
80
30
25
20
15
10

Statute Miles
0 100 200 300 400 500
TIBET
CHINA
Tangla Mts
Di-chu
Nag-Chu
Zilling Tso
Dangra Yum
Tengri Nor
Lhasa
Brahmaputra or Tsangpo
Mt. Everest 29028 ft.
Kangchenjunga
Chumalhari
Kathmandu
Thimphu
BHUTAN
SIKKIM
Gangtok
Darjeeling
ARUNACHAL PRADESH
Sadiya
Taipudia
Dibrugarh
Putao
Brahmaputra
Nowgong
Gauhati
Goalpara
Shillong
MEGHALAYA
NAGALAND
Kohima
Myitkyina
Mogaung
KACHINS
Irrawaddy
Tengyueh
Tali
Kunming
Yangtze Kiang
Min
Mekong
Patna
Monghyr
Bhagalpur
Ganges
Gaya
BIHAR
Rajmahal
BANGLADESH
Silchar
MANIPUR
Imphal
Dacca
TRIPURA
MIZORAM
Katha
Shamo
Kunlong Ferry
Murshidabad
Asansol
Durgapur
W. BENGAL
Burdwan
Jamshedpur
Hooghly
Calcutta
Chalna
Chittagong
Kalewa
Yeu
Mogok
Lashio
BURMA
Mandalay
Kani
Sagaing
Amarapura
Ava
Myingyan
Kiang Hung
Lao-kai
Song-bo
M. Sing
Kiang Tung
Rourkela
Balasore
M^ths of Ganges (Ganga)
R. Hooghly
Cuttack
Puri
Chilka L.
Ganjam
Meiktila
Minbu
Akyab
Arakan
Irrawaddy
R. Salween
Chiang Rai
Luang Prabang
Karenni
Chiang Mai
Nan
Prome
Lampun
Sandoway
THAILAND (SIAM)
Pegu
Rangoon
Bassein
C. Negrais
Martaban
Moulmein
Amherst
Ye
Menam
Ayutthaya
BANGKOK (KRUNG THEP)
Prakan
Preparis
G. of Martaban
Tavoy
BAY OF BENGAL
Andaman Islands (To India)
Port Blair
Mergui
Tenasserim
Mergui Archipelago
Gulf of Siam
Kra Isthmus
Victoria Pt.
Phangnga
Songkla
Nicobar I^s
30
25
20
15
10
85
90
95
100
105

UTTAR PRADESH

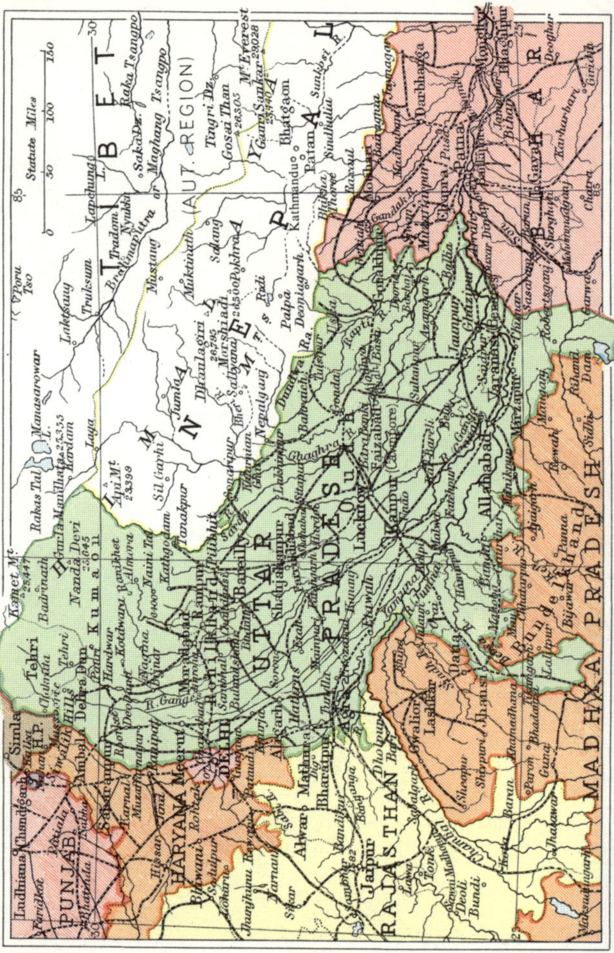

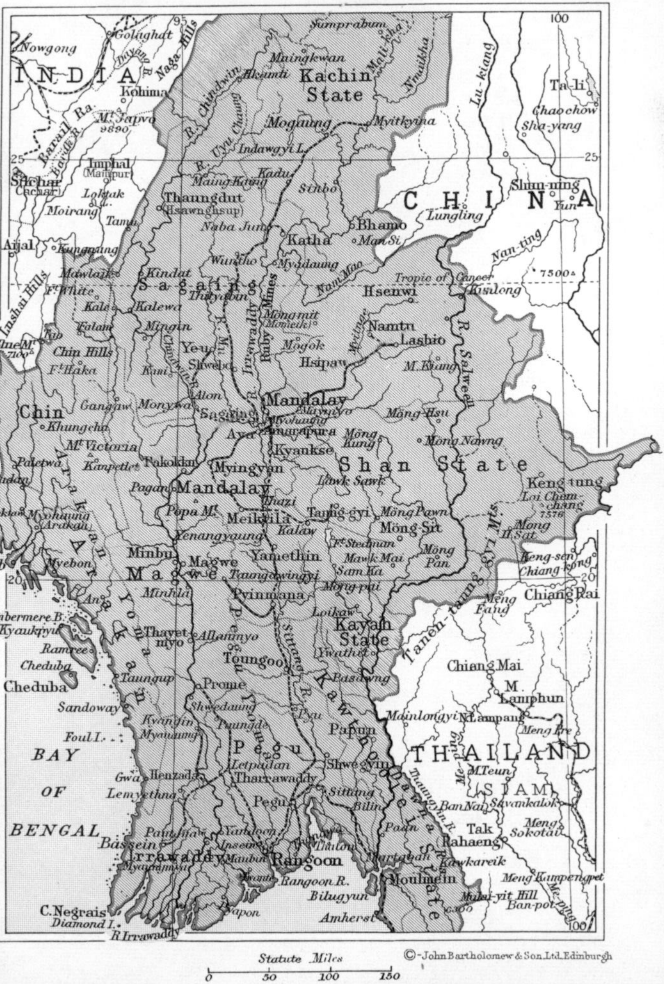
Sumprabum
Golaghat
Nowgong
Naga Hills
Maingkwan
Mali-kha
Nmaikha
INDIA
Kohima
Akumti
Kachin State
Lu-kiang
Ta-li
Chaochow
Sha-yang
Barail Ra.
Mt. Japvo 9890
R. Chindwin
Uyu Chaung
Mogaung
Myitkyina
Indawgyi L.
Imphal (Manipur)
Silchar
Cachar
Loktak
Moirang
Tamu
Kadu
Maing Kaing
Sinbo
Thaungdut (Hsawnghsup)
CHINA
Shun-ning
Yun
Lungling
Bhamo
Man Si
Naba Junc.
Katha
Aijal
Kungaung
Nan-ting
Wuntho
Myadaung
Nam Mao
7500
Mawlaik
Kindat
Sagaing
Tropic of Cancer
Kunlong
Lushai Hills
Ft. White
Thityabin
Hsenwi
Kale
Kalewa
Ruby Mines
Falam
Mingin
Mong mit (Momeik)
Namtu
Lashio
Blue Mt. 7100
Tiddim
Chin Hills
Yeu
Shwebo
Irrawaddy R.
Mogok
Hsipaw
R. Salween
Ft. Haka
Kani
Chindwin R.
M. Kiang
Alon
Mandalay
Gangaw
Monywa
Sagaing
Maymyo
Mong Hsu
Chin
Khungcha
Myohaung
Ava
Amarapura
Mong Kung
Mong Nawng
Mt. Victoria
Kyaukse
Paletwa
Kanpetlet
Pakokku
Myingyan
Shan State
Keng tung
Pagan
Mandalay
Lawk Sawk
Loi Chem-chang 7576
Thazi
Myohaung
Arakan
Popa Mt.
Meiktila
Taunggyi
Mong Pawn
Mong Sit
Mong Hsat
Yenangyaung
Kalaw
Arakan Yoma
Ft. Stedman
Minbu
Magwe
Yamethin
Mawk Mai
Mong Pan
Keng-sen
Chiang-kong
Sam Ka
Magwe
Taungdwingyi
Mong pai
Loi Lem Mts.
Chiang Rai
Minhla
Pyinmana
Meng Fang
Combermere B.
Kyaukpyu
Loikaw
Kayah State
Thayetmyo
Allanmyo
Ramree
Toungoo
Ywathit
Tanen-taung-gyi
Cheduba
Pegu Yoma
Sittang R.
Kawkareik
Chiang Mai
Cheduba
Taungup
Prome
Basawng
M. Lamphun
Sandoway
Shwedaung
Pyu
Mainlongyi
N. Lampang
Kyangin
Tharrawaddy
Papun
Meng Pre
Foul I.
Myanaung
Pegu
THAILAND
Dawna Ra.
BAY OF BENGAL
Letpadan
Shwegyin
Me-ping
M. Teun
Gwa
Henzada
Tharrawaddy
SIAM
Lemyethna
Pegu
Sittang
Bilin
Thaungyin R.
Ban Nai
Savankalok
Paan
Tak
Rahaeng
Meng Sokotai
Bassein
Yandoon
Insein
Thongwa
Thaton
Irrawaddy
Myaungmya
Maubin
Rangoon
Martaban
Kawkareik
Twante
Rangoon R.
Moulmein
Meng Kampengpet
Bilugyun
Mulai-yit Hill 6800
Ban-pot
Me-ping
C. Negrais
Diamond I.
Pyapon
Amherst
Mon State
R. Irrawaddy
95
100
25
20
Statute Miles
0 50 100 150

MEDITERRANEAN SEA
TURKEY
İstanbul
Üsküdar
Zonguldak
Karabuk
Sinop
Samsun
Trabzon
Batumi
Poti
Tbilisi
Kars
Bursa
Balikesir
Eskişehir
ANKARA
Sivas
Erzurum
Manisa
Izmir
Afyon
Kayseri
Konya
Antalya
Taurus Mts
Tarsus
Mersin
Adana
Maraş
Diyarbakir
Urfa
Elâzig
Rezā'iyeh
Tabriz
Rodhos
Nicosia
CYPRUS
Larnaca
İskenderun
Aleppo
Antakya
SYRIA
Hama
Homs
Palmyra
Tripoli
Beirut
Haifa
ISRAEL
Tel Aviv
Yafo
Damascus
Amman
Jerusalem
Dead Sea
JORDAN
Maan
Mosul
Nineveh
Kirkuk
IRAQ
Mesopotamia
BAGHDAD
Babylon
Basra
Abadan
KUWAIT
Kuwait
Alexandria
Port Said
CAIRO
Suez
MIL. ADMIN.
Aqaba
Sinai
Gulf of Aqaba
G. of Suez
Syrian Desert
Jauf
Nafud Desert
Jabal Shammar
Hail
SAUDI ARAB
Anaiza
Najd
Riyadh
Hejaz
Al Wajh
Yanbu' al Bahr
Medina
Jiddah
Mecca
Asir
RED SEA
EGYPT
AFRICA
River Nile
Tropic of Cancer
SUDAN
Port Sudan
Suakin
Khartoum
ETHIOPIA
Farasan Is
Kamaran I.
YEMEN
Sana
Al Hudaydah
Mocha
Perim I.
Aden
DEM. REP.
Hadhra
Caucasus
R. Kura
R. Araxes
Mt Ararat
Van Gölü
Urmia
Hamadan
Kermanshah
Dezful
Ur
Menderes
Kizil Irmak
Euphrates
Tigris
Archipelago
C. Baba
Sea of Marmara
Ru

U. S. S. R.
Tashkent
Kokand
Khiva
Amu Darya (Oxus)
UZBEK
Samarkand
Bukhara
Krasnovodsk
Kara Kum
TADZHIK
Dushanbe
Pamir Plateau
TURKMEN
Chardzhou
Mary (Merv)
Murghab
Ashkhabad
Termez
Kunduz
Hindu Kush
Atrek
Bandar Shah
Gorgan
Babol
Sabzevar
Mashhad
Andkhui
Mazar-i-Sharif
Maimana
Semnan
Kushka
Heri Rud
Herat
KABUL
Khyber Pass
Peshawar
RAWALPINDI
Indus
Great Salt Desert
Khurasan
Kashan
AFGHANISTAN
IRAN (PERSIA)
Gazik
Birjand
Esfahan (Isfahan)
Yazd
R. Helmand
Arghandab
Kandahar
Lut Desert
Hamun-i-Helmand
Quetta
Bolan Pass
Kerman
Persepolis
Zahedan
Kalat
PAKISTAN
Shiraz
INDIA
R. Indus
Bandar Abbas
Hyderabad
Bahrain I.
Qeshm
Hormuz Str.
GULF
Sharjah
Jask
Makran
Gwadar
Karachi
Gulf of Oman
United Arab Emirates
Matrah
Muscat
Sur
Ras al Had
Oman
Masira
Khali
ARABIAN SEA
Kuria Muria Is
YEMEN
Salalah
Statute Miles
0 100 200 300 400 500 600
Socotra (Yemen)

TURKEY

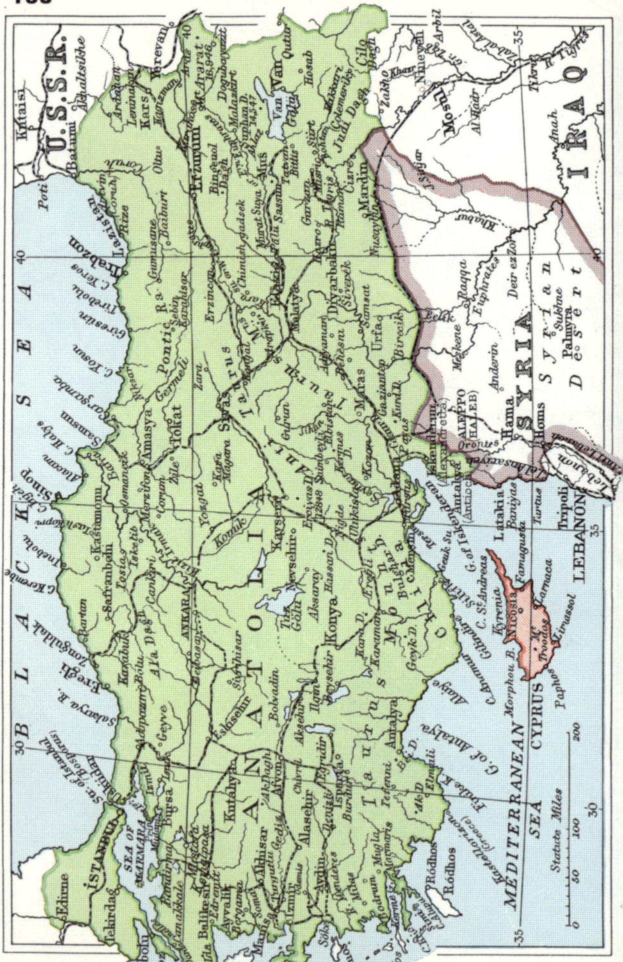
U.S.S.R.
BLACK SEA
ANATOLIA
SYRIA
IRAQ
LEBANON
CYPRUS
MEDITERRANEAN SEA
Syrian Desert
SEA OF MARMARA
ISTANBUL
ANKARA
Statute Miles
0 50 100 200

Statute Miles
0 20 40 60
MEDITERRANEAN SEA
to Port Said 230 m.
J. to B. 120 m.
LEBANON
Anti Lebanon
Lebanon
SYRIA
ISRAEL
JORDAN
PALESTINE
Tel Kalakh
Homs
Homs Bahret
En Nahr el Kebir
El Mina
Tripoli
(Tarabulus)
Ehden
Hermil
El Kaa
Batrun
Bsherri
Ras Baalbek
Sadad
Lebye
El Qaryatein
En Nebk
Juniye
Baalbek
BEIRUT
Zahle
el Hadeth
Riyak
Jerud
Qasr Zigal
Zebdani
Quteife
Sidon
(Saida)
Rasheiya
Es Salihiye
Dumeir
En Nabatiye
DAMASCUS
(DAMAS)
Mt Hermon
Qatana
Kiswe
N. el-Qasimiye
Tyre
(Sur)
Qiryat Shemona
Baniyas
el Quneitra
Bint Jubail
Mesmiye
Nahariyya
Es Sanamein
Acre
(Akko)
CEASE FIRE LINE
El Leja
Safad
(Tsefat)
Nawa
W. el Rarts
B. of Acre
Shefaram
L. of Tiberias
Sheikh Miskin
Haifa
Tiberias
Jebel ed Nemara
Atlit
Es Suweidiya
Druz
Nazareth
Mazerib
JEBEL ED DRUZ
Afula
Dera
Busra
Zikhron Ya'aqov
Beyt Shean
Salkhad
Caesarea
Hadera
Irbid
Nasib
Jenin
Imtan
Natanya
Tulkarm
J. Ajlun
Mafraq
Herzliya
Nablus
Jarash
H-5 Oil Pipe Line
Tel Aviv-Yafo
ISRAEL MIL. ADMIN.
Petah Tiqva
Salt
Zarqa
Jordan R.
GHOR
Ramla
Lydda (Lod)
Suweilih
AMMAN
Qasr el Azraq
Rehovot
Jericho
Naur
El Mawaqqar
Ashdod
EL QUDS ESH SHERIF
JERUSALEM
W. Rajil
Ashqelon
Beyt Bethlehem
Madaba
Jiza
El Hazim
Qiryat Gat
Qal'at ed Dab'a
Hebron
(El Khalil)
Dead Sea
(Bahr Lut)
Dhiban
Gaza
Khan ez Zabib
Khan Yunis
Rafah
Arad
Karak
Beersheba
El Qatrana
Dimona
Sedom
Tarin
W. Bayir
Yeroham
Et Tafila
ISRAEL MIL. ADMIN.
Subeita
Qal'at el Hasa
Bayir
Negev
Jurf ed Darawish
El Qussaima
Araba
Shaubak
Ain Kadeis
Qal'at Uneiza
32
34
36
PETRA

AFRICA

EUROPE
ASIA
ATLANTIC OCEAN
MEDITERRANEAN SEA
RED SEA
Black Sea
Caspian Sea
SAUDI ARABIA
Medina
Mecca
Jerusalem
Ankara
Istanbul
Cyprus
Paris
London
Lisboa
Strait of Gibraltar
Azores I.s (P.)
Madeira (P.) I.
Canary I.s (Sp.)
Tenerife
Cape Verde I.s
MOROCCO
Casablanca
Rabat
Fès
Marrakech
Essaouira
ALGERIA
Alger (Algiers)
Oran
Annaba
Ouargla
TUNISIA
Tunis
LIBYA
Tripoli
Benghazi
Fezzan
Murzuq
Ghat
ARAB REP. OF EGYPT
Alexandria
Cairo
Port Said
Suez
Damietta
Nile
Asyut
Aswān
Libyan Desert
Wadi Halfa
Port Sudan
SUDAN
Khartoum
Omdurman
Dongola
Atbara
Berber
Kassala
El Obeid
El Fasher
Nyala
ERITREA
Massawa
Aden
Djibouti
Berbera
Addis Ababa
Harar
ETHIOPIA
Socotra I.
C. Guardafui
SAHARA
Ahaggar
Tibesti
CHAD
L. Chad
NIGER
Agades
Zinder
Niamey
NIGERIA
Sokoto
Kano
Kaduna
MAURITANIA
Atar
SPANISH SAHARA
Villa Cisneros
MALI
Tombouctou
Segu
SENEGAL
St. Louis
Dakar
Banjul
THE GAMBIA
Bissau
PORT. GUINEA
GUINEA
SIERRA LEONE
IVORY COAST
UPPER VOLTA
TOGO
DAHOMEY
GHANA
Tropic of Cancer

ATLANTIC OCEAN
INDIAN OCEAN
Gulf of Guinea
Equator
Tropic of Capricorn
England to The Cape 5950 Miles
Ascension I. (U.K.)
St. Helena I. (U.K.)
Tristan da Cunha (U.K.)
São Tomé
Annobon
C. Lopez
GABON
Libreville
Franceville
CONGO
Brazzaville
Kinshasa
ZAIRE
Kisangani
Stanley Falls
Mbandaka
Kananga
Lubumbashi
Kasai
ANGOLA
Luanda
Lobito
Benguela
Moçamedes
Nova Lisboa
Malanje
Cubango
Kwando
ZAMBIA
Lusaka
RHODESIA
Salisbury
Bulawayo
Limpopo
BOTSWANA
Kalahari Desert
SOUTH WEST AFRICA (NAMIBIA)
Windhoek
Walvis B.
Swakopmund
Luderitz Bay
Port Nolloth
Orange R.
SOUTH AFRICA
Cape Town
Cape of Good Hope
C. Agulhas
Mossel Bay
Port Elizabeth
Algoa B.
East London
Durban
Pietermaritzburg
NATAL
SWAZILAND
TRANSVAAL
Pretoria
Johannesburg
Kimberley
Vryburg
Bloemfontein
ORANGE FR. STATE
Lourenço Marques
Delagoa B.
C. Correntes
Beira
Sofala
Quelimane
Blantyre
MALAWI
L. Nyasa
Moçambique
Mozambique Channel
TANZANIA
Tabora
Dodoma
Ujiji
Mbeya
Dar es Salaam
Zanzibar
Pemba I.
Kilwa Kivinje
C. Delgado
Mwanza
Arusha
Mt. Kilimanjaro
KENYA
Nairobi
Mombasa
Malindi
Lamu
Kampala
BURUNDI
L. Tanganyika
L. Victoria
Brava
Mogadishu
Comoro Is.
Mayotte I.
Nossi Bé
C. d'Ambre
Amirante Is.
MALAGASY REP. (MADAGASCAR)
Tananarive
Majunga
Tamatave
C. Ste. Marie
Statute Miles
0 100 200 300 400 500 1000

EGYPT, LIBYA

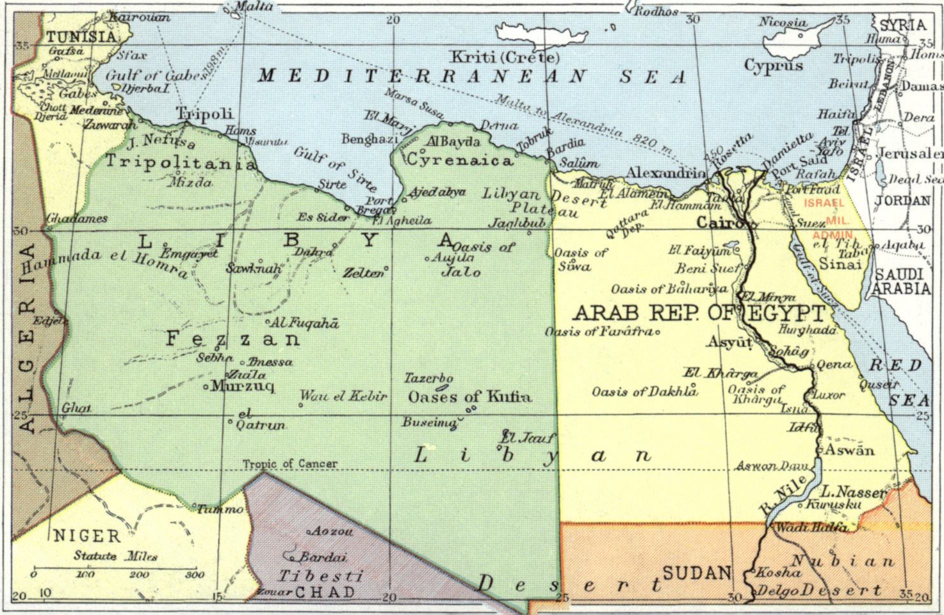
MEDITERRANEAN SEA
Malta
Rodhos
Kriti (Crete)
Cyprus
Nicosia
SYRIA
Hama
Homs
Tripoli
LEBANON
Beirut
Damascus
Haifa
Dera
Tel Aviv Yafo
ISRAEL
Jerusalem
Dead Sea
JORDAN
Aqaba
SAUDI ARABIA
Rafah
Port Said
Port Fuad
ISRAEL MIL. ADMIN.
Suez
el Tih
Taba
Sinai
Gulf of Suez
RED SEA
Quseir
Hurghada
Damietta
Rosetta
Alexandria
Tanta
Cairo
El Hammam
El Alamein
Matruh
Qattara Dep.
Oasis of Siwa
El Faiyum
Beni Suef
Oasis of Bahariya
El Minya
ARAB REP. OF EGYPT
Oasis of Farafra
Asyut
Sohag
Qena
Luxor
Isna
Idfu
Aswan
Aswan Dam
El Kharga
Oasis of Kharga
Oasis of Dakhla
L. Nasser
Kurusku
R. Nile
Wadi Halfa
SUDAN
Kosha
Delgo
Nubian Desert
Libyan Desert
Libyan Plateau
Salûm
Bardia
Tobruk
Derna
Al Bayda
Cyrenaica
El Marj
Marsa Susa
Benghazi
Ajedabya
Jaghbub
Oasis of Aujila
Jalo
Gulf of Sirte
Sirte
Port Brega
El Agheila
Es Sider
Zelten
Dahra
Sawknah
LIBYA
Hammada el Homra
Emgayet
Tripolitania
Mizda
J. Nefusa
Tripoli
Hams
Misurata
Zuwarah
Ghadames
Al Fuqahā
Fezzan
Sebha
Brak
Zuila
Murzuq
Wau el Kebir
Tazerbo
Oases of Kufra
Buseima
El Jauf
el Qatrun
Ghat
Edjele
Tropic of Cancer
Tummo
NIGER
CHAD
Aozou
Bardai
Tibesti
Zouar
ALGERIA
TUNISIA
Kairouan
Sfax
Gafsa
Mellaoui
Gabes
Gulf of Gabes
Djerba I.
Chott Djerid
Medenine
Malta to Alexandria 820 m.
198 m.
450
Statute Miles
0 100 200 300
10
15
20
25
30
35

MEDITERRANEAN SEA
ISRAEL
Ashqelon
Gaza
Rafah
El 'Arish
Qezi'ot
Qiraiya
PORT SAID (BÛR SA'ÎD)
Port Fuad
Sabkhet el Bardawil
PELUSIUM
Români
El Qantara
Suez Canal
Ismâ'ilîya
Bitter Lakes
Fayid
Suez (El Suweis)
Pt. Taufiq
Damietta (Dumyât)
L. Manzala
Mansûra
Zagazig
Bilbeis
El Tell el Kebir
CAIRO (EL QAHIRA)
Heliopolis
Helwân
El Gîza
Pyramids
MEMPHIS
El Badrsheîn
R. Nile
Rosetta (Rashîd)
ALEXANDRIA (El Iskandarîya)
Abuqîr
Ramleh
Max
Burg el 'Arab
Arabs G.
El Hammam
El Alamein
Râs el Daba
El Maghra
Qattara Depression
Wadi el Natrûn
Deir Suriâni
Deir Makaryus
LOWER EGYPT
Shibin el Kom
Tanta
Benha
Qalyûb
El Mahalla el Kubra
Bultîn
L. Burullus
Damanhûr
Libyan Desert
Desert
El Faiyûm
Birket Qârûn
Ibshawai
Sinnûris
Tâmiya
El 'Aiyât
Atfih
Wasta
Beni Suef
Bush
Ihnâsya el Madina
Yusef
W. Muweilih
Aba el Wakf
El Bahnasa
El Fashn
El Hiba
Maghâgha
Abu Girg
Beni Mazâr
Samâlût
Qulûsana
EGYPT
N. Galala Plateau
S. Galala Plateau
Geb. Ataqa
G. Umm Tennâsib
Deir Mar Pablos
Râs Gharib
Gulf of Suez
SINAI PENINSULA
ISRAEL MILITARY ADMINISTRATION
Desert et Tih
Nakhl
Geb. Halal
Geb. Yi'Allag
Sudr
Abu Zenima
Feirân
G. Serbâl
Geb. Kâtherina
Monastery of St. Catherine
G. Mûsa
Geb. el Tih
Ruag
Bawiti
El Harra
Statute Miles
0 20 40 60
30 32 34

NORTH-WEST AFRICA

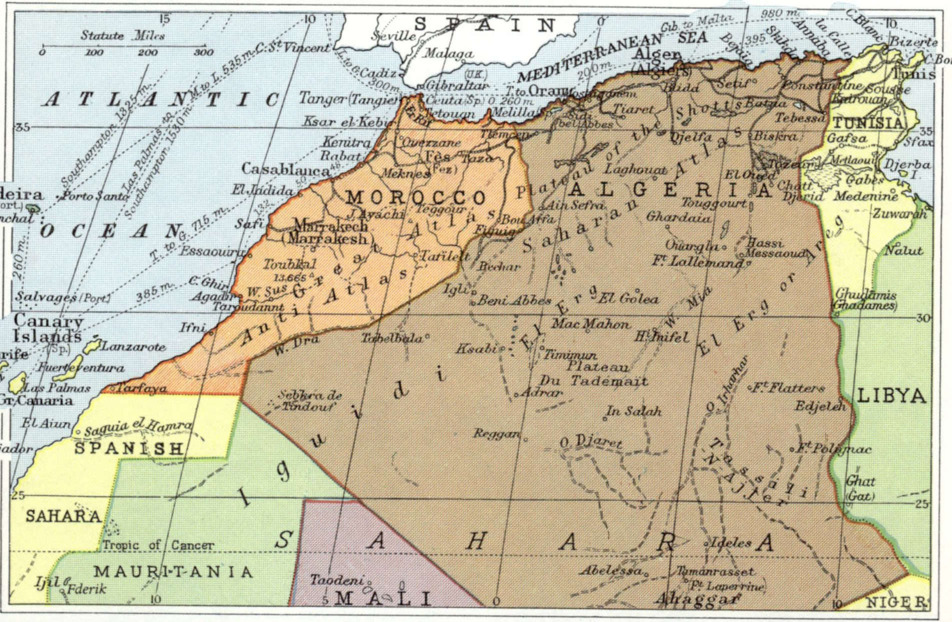

MAURITANIA
Hodh
Nouakchott
Nema
Kiffa
Kaedi
R. Senegal
Tombouctou
(Timbuktu)
R. Niger
Kabara
Bourem
Gao
Hombori
MALI
Sahel
Macina
Mopti
Nioro
Nara
L. Debo
Nyamina
Segou
San
Kita
Bamako
Koulikoro
Koutiala
Sikasso
Siguiri
Kankan
Ouassoulou
St. Louis
Dagana
Matam
Bakel
Kayes
Medine
SENEGAL
Thies
Rufisque
C. Verde
Dakar
Diourbel
Kaolack
Banjul
THE GAMBIA
R. Gambia
Tambacounda
Baloulabe
Ziguinchor
PORTUGUESE GUINEA
Bissau
Bolama
Bissagos Is.
(Bijagos)
Boke
GUINEA
Labe
Mamou
Kindia
Faranah
R. Niger
Daro Mt.
Beyla
Lola
Conakry
Los Is.
(Fr.)
SIERRA LEONE
Kabala
Freetown
Pendembu
Bo
Sherbro I.
N'Zerekore
LIBERIA
Robertsport
Monrovia
Buchanan
R. Cess
Greenville
Harper
R. Kavalli
UPPER VOLTA
Yatenga
Mossi
Dedougou
Koudougou
Ouagadougou
Bobo Dioulosso
IVORY COAST
Kong
Bouna
White Bandama
Sequela
Bouake
Bondoukou
Sassandra
Dimbokro
Baoule
Komoe
Abidjan
Bingerville
Tabou
Gr. Bassam
GHANA
Gambaga
Mango
Tamale
Yendi
Salaga
Black Volta
White Volta
Sunyani
Kumasi
Koforidua
Atakpame
Ho
Oda
Sekondi
Takoradi
Cape Coast
Winneba
Accra
TOGO
Sokode
Palime
Lome
Anecho
R. Volta
DAHOMEY
NIGER
Cape Verde Is.
(Port)
São Antão
São Vicente
Sal
S. Nicolau
Boa Vista
Maio
Fogo
Brava
São Tiago
ATLANTIC
OCEAN
Grain Coast
Ivory Coast
Gold Coast
C. Palmas
C. Three Points
GULF OF GUINEA
S. Dakar to Rio de Oro 580m.
S.T. to F. 720 m.
482 m.
M. to S. 588m.
Statute Miles
0
100
200
300
400

NIGER
Zinder
Niamey
Say
Sokoto
Katsina
Kano
Nguru
Kukawa
Maiduguri
L. Chad
CHAD
Ft. Lamy
UPPER VOLTA
Borgu
Bussa
DAHOMEY
Zaria
Kontagora
Kaduna
Bauchi
Nikki
Parakou
Zungeru
Bida
Bukuru
Kafanchan
Keffi
Yola
Garua
Ilorin
NIGERIA
Baro
Ibi
Benue
Ogbomosho
Lokoja
Ibadan
Abeokuta
Oshogbo
Loko
Wukari
Benin City
Idah
Onitsha
Makurdi
Ogoja
Enugu
Warri
Lagos
Porto Novo
Apapa
Cotonou
Ouidah
Slave Coast
Forcados
Owerri
Bamenda
Tibati
Kounde
Ngaoundere
Mora
Marua
Lai
Lame
Moundou
Mbassai
CAMEROUN
Calabar
Kongsamba
Cameroun Mt.
13,350
P. Harcourt
Bight of Benin
Niger Delta
Akassa
Bonny
Victoria
Buea
Douala
Tiko
Fernando Poo (Sp.)
Sta. Isabel
Sanaga
Dume
Yaoundé
Yokadouma
Ebolowa
Kribi
Lomie
CENT. AFRICAN REP.
Bozum
Buar
Carnot
Barda
Bight of Biafra
EQUATORIAL GUINEA
Bata
RIO MUNI
Principe (Port.)
Benito
Oyem
Mekambo
Uesso
Corisco B.
Mitzic
Kembona
São Tomé (Port.)
Equator
Gabon
Libreville
Boué
GABON
C. Lopez
P. Gentil
Ogooué
Lambaréné
Lastoursville
Franceville
CONGO
Bonga
Gambama
Annobon (Sp.)
ATLANTIC
Sette Cama
Mbigu
M'Banda
Bolobo
480 m.
Makabang
Ngantchu
Mayumba
Brazzaville
Loango
Pt. Noire
Stanley Pool
Kinshasa
Tshela
ZAIRE
OCEAN
Cabinda
Boma
Banana
Matadi
R. Congo
Sto. Antº do Zaire
S. Salvador
Kwango
165 m.
Ambriz
Luanda
ANGOLA (PORT.)
Cuanza
Ambaca
Malanje
Dondo
Statute Miles
0
100
200
300

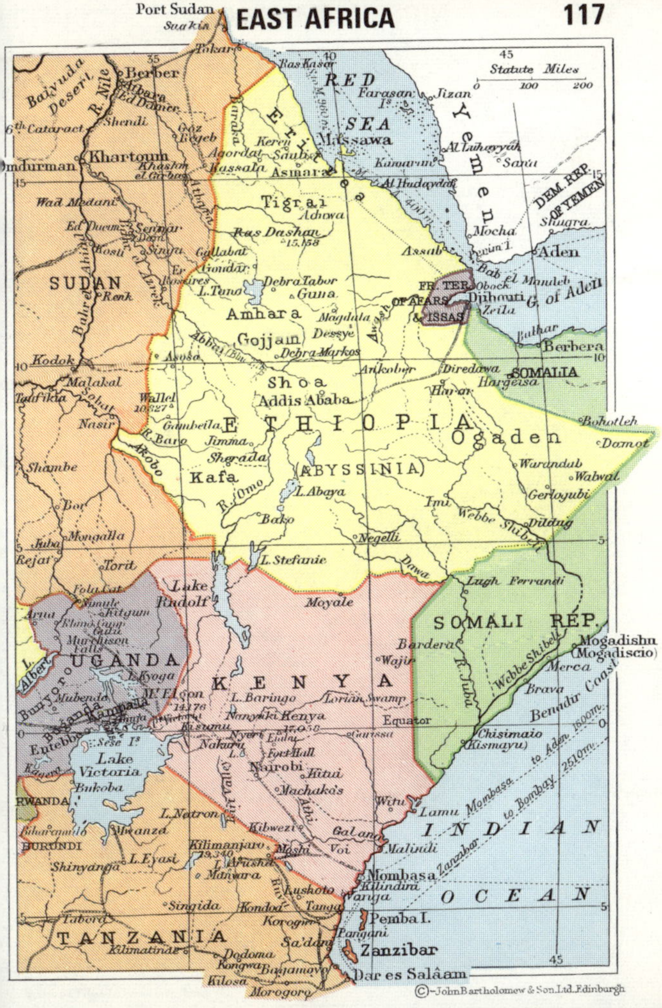

Statute Miles
0 100 200
RED SEA
INDIAN OCEAN
SUDAN
ETHIOPIA
(ABYSSINIA)
Eritrea
Yemen
DEM. REP. OF YEMEN
FR. TER. OF AFARS & ISSAS
SOMALIA
SOMALI REP.
KENYA
UGANDA
TANZANIA
RWANDA
BURUNDI
Port Sudan
Suakin
Tokar
Berber
Atbara
Ed Damer
Shendi
Khartoum
Omdurman
Kassala
Wad Medani
Kosti
Renk
Kodok
Malakal
Nasir
Juba
Mongalla
Torit
Massawa
Keren
Asmara
Tigrai
Adowa
Ras Dashan 15,158
Gondar
L. Tana
Debra Tabor
Amhara
Gojjam
Dessye
Debra Markos
Shoa
Addis Ababa
Kafa
Jimma
Harar
Diredawa
Ogaden
L. Abaya
L. Stefanie
Moyale
Assab
Mocha
Aden
Djibouti
Zeila
Berbera
Hargeisa
Bohotleh
Webbe Shibeli
Mogadishu (Mogadiscio)
Merca
Brava
Benadir Coast
Chisimaio (Kismayu)
R. Juba
Lake Rudolf
L. Kyoga
Kampala
Entebbe
Lake Victoria
L. Baringo
Kenya 17,058
Kisumu
Nairobi
Machakos
Equator
Lamu
Malindi
Mombasa
Tanga
Pemba I.
Zanzibar
Dar es Salâam
Kilimanjaro 19,340
Moshi
Arusha
Mwanza
Bukoba
Tabora
Dodoma
Morogoro
Mombasa to Aden 1600m.
Mombasa to Bombay 2510m.
Zanzibar
©-John Bartholomew & Son.Ltd.Edinburgh

ANGOLA
Pto Amboim
Novo Redondo
Lobito
Benguela
Nova Lisboa
Silva Porto
Malanje
Lunda
Dilolo
ZAIRE
Katanga
Luso
Moxico
Zambezi
Caconda
Benguela
Cangamba
Serpa Pinto
Sada Bandeira
Moçâmedes (Mossamedes)
Mocamedes
Pto Alexandre
Chivemba
Huila
Evale
Kafima
Cuito Cuanavale
Cubango
Bambe
Kwito
Kwando
Tiger Bay
Cunene
Balovale
Kabompo
Barotse
Mongu
Mumbwa
Senanga
Nanzhila
Pemba
Sesheke
Maramba
Victoria Falls
Wankie
Malindi
C. Fria
Kaoko-veld
Namib
Etosha Pan
Tsumeb
Grootfontein
Otavi
Waterberg
Outjo
Damaraland
(NAMIBIA)
Okavango Swamp
Tsau
L. Ngami (dry)
Makarikari Salt Pans
BOTSWANA
Serowe
Palapye Rd.
Swakopmund
Walvis Bay
Windhoek
Gobabis
SOUTH WEST AFRICA
Walvis B.
Rehoboth
Sandfish B.
Tropic of Capricorn
Kalahari
Tsane
Desert
Mariental
Great
Nama Land
Nosob
Gibeon
Molepolole
Gaborone
Zeerust
Mafeking
Pretoria
Bethanie
Keetmanshoop
Molopo
Riet Fontein
Vryburg
Luderitz
Desert
Karasburg
Kuruman
REP.
OF
ATLANTIC
Warmbad
Orange Mouth
Aughrabies Falls
Postmasburg
Kimberley
Orange R.
Alexander Bay
Port Nolloth
Springbok
Bloemfontein
Hopetown
SOUTH AFRICA
De Aar
Orange
Bitterfontein
Carnarvon
Victoria West
Calvinia
OCEAN
Olifants R.
CAPE OF GOOD HOPE
Graafwater
Nieuwveld Ra.
Graaff Reinet
Beaufort W.
St. Helena B.
Great Karroo
Saldanha B.
Oudtshoorn
Worcester
George
Grahamstown
Cape Town
Knysna
Port Elizabeth
Mosselbaai (Mossel Bay)
Cape of Good Hope
C. Agulhas
Southampton 5950 m.
St. Helena 1700 m.
Rio de Janeiro 3270 m.
M. to S. 500 m.
1440 m.
260 m.
200 m.
300 m.
195 m.
90 m.
422 m.
15
20
25
30
35
10

TANZANIA
Njombe
Mtwara
C. Delgado
Masasi
Songea
Rovuma
Livingstone Ra.
Karonga
Kasama
Livingstonia
L. Bangweulu
Mansa
Chinteche
Mzimba
Chitambo
Serenje
Luangwa
Kota-kota
Salima
F.t Jameson
Domira B.
F.t Johnston
Lake Nyasa
MALAWI
Furancungo
Chipawa
Zumbo
Cabora Bassa Dam
Tete
M.t Darwin
Ncheu
Zomba
L. Chilwa
Blantyre
Chiromo
Mlanje
Mokuba
Shire
Kariba
Sinoia
Kildonan
Shamva
P.t Herald
Chemba
Salisbury
Mashona Land
Sena
Rusape
V.a Manica
Umtali
Melsetter
Gwelo
F.t Victoria
Zimbabwe
W. Nicholson
Beitbridge
Limpopo
Kruger Nat. Park
Sabi
Gaza Land
Chibuto
Vila de João Belo
Lourenço Marques
Delagoa Bay
Mbabane
Swazi L.d
Piet Retief
Zulu Land
Drakensberg
S.ta Lucia Bay
NATAL
Pietermaritzburg
Durban
Scottsburgh
P.t Shepstone
Port S.t Johns
INDIAN OCEAN
Statute Miles
0 100 200 300
MOÇAMBIQUE
Vila Cabral
Lugenda
P.to Arroio
Lurio
Nacala
Nampula
Lumbo
Meconta
Antonio Enes
Angoche B.
Quelimane
Chinde
Zambezi
Beira
Nova Sofala
Bazaruto I.
Inhambane
C. Correntes
Ibo
P.to Amelia
Lurio B.
Memba
Moçambique (Mozambique)
G.de Comoro I.
Moheli
Anjouan
Comoro I.s (Fr.)
Mayotte
MOÇAMBIQUE CHANNEL
Bassas da India
S.t Andre C.
Soalala
Maintirano
MALAGASY REP.
C. d'Ambre
Diégo Suarez
Nossi Bé
Vohémar
Narendry B.
Analalava
Antalaha
Majunga
Mananara
Antongil B.
C. S.t Andre
Maevatanana
I. S.te Marie
Alaotra L.
Fénérive
Andreba
Tamatave
Tananarive (Antananarivo)
Ankaratra M.ts
Antsirabe
Andevoranto
Mahanoro
Morondava
MALAGASY REP. (MADAGASCAR)
Ambohibe
Mangoky
Fianarantsoa
Mananjary
Manakara
Farafangana
Tuléar
Vangaindrano
Betroka
Tropic of Capricorn
F.t Dauphin
C. S.te Marie
INDIAN OCEAN
On the same scale
Durban 1345 m.

Sarawak
BORNEO
Samarinda
Bandjarmasin
Laut
Makassar Str.
Mahasar
CELEBES
Bone B.
G. of Tomini
Manado
Ternate
Halmahera
Is.
MOLUCCAS
Sula Is.
Seram
Buru
Ambon
Butung
I N D O N E S I A
Banda Sea
Kai Is.
Aru Is.
Tanimbar Is.
Kolepom I.
Manokwari
Biak
Japen
Irian B.
Pt. d'Urville
Djajapura
IRIAN JAYA
Java Sea
Madura
JAVA
Surabaja
Bali
Lombok
Sumbawa
Flores Sea
Flores
Solor Is.
Alor Is.
Wetar
Dili
Timor
Kupang
Roti
Sumba
Arafura Sea
Torres
Thursday
Van Diemen G.
Cobourg Pen.
Wessel I.
Melville B.
Melville I.
Bathurst I.
Darwin
Rum Jungle
Arnhem Land
Gulf of Carpentaria
Groote Eylandt
Wellesley Is.
Timor Sea
Queens Channel
Cambridge G.
Katherine
Daly R.
Roper
Victoria
Birdum
Barkly Tableland
Burketown
Collier Bay
King Sd.
Wyndham
C. Leveque
Black Rocks
Derby
Broome
Fitzroy R.
Newcastle Waters
NORTHERN
Tennant Creek
TERRITORY
Mount Isa
Georgina R.
Great Sandy Desert
Mt. Wilson
Central Mt. Stuart
Port Hedland
Roebourne
Onslow
Exmouth G.
N. West Cape
L. Mackay
L. Macdonald
Macdonnell Ra.
Alice Springs
L. Amadeus
L. Hopkins
Mt. Bruce
Ashburton
L. Disappointment
Gibson Desert
A U S T R A L
Carnarvon
Shark B.
Meekatharra
Wiluna
Murchison R.
WESTERN
AUSTRALIA
Steep Pt.
L. Austin
Neales R.
Oodnadatta
L. Eyre
Great Victoria Desert
SOUTH AUSTRALIA
Maralinga
L. Torrens
L. Gairdner
Nullarbor Plain
Geraldton
Kalgoorlie
Boulder
Coolgardie
Northam
L. Lefroy
L. Cowan
Eucla
Broken Hill
Port Augusta
Peterborough
Port Pirie
Whyalla
Great Australian Bight
Perth
Fremantle
York
Swan R.
Geographe B.
C. Naturaliste
Bunbury
Albany
C. Leeuwin
Esperance
Recherche Archip.
King George Sd.
Spencer G.
St. Vincent G.
Kangaroo I.
Encounter B.
Adelaide
Warrnambool
INDIAN OCEAN
Statute Miles
0
500
1000
100
110
120
130
140
0
10
20
30
40

Equator
Admiralty Is
Manus
New Hanover
Bismarck Archipelago
New Ireland
Rabaul
Kokopo
Madang
Lae
New Britain
NEW GUINEA
Huon G.
Mt Victoria
G. of Papua
Pt Moresby
York
Samarai
China Str.
Louisiade Archo
Bougainville
Solomon Islands
Choiseul I.
Sta Isabel
New Georgia
Guadalcanal
Malaita
San Cristobal
Bennell
Gilbert Is (UK)
Sta Cruz Is (UK)
Nderi
CORAL SEA
Great Barrier Reef
Cairns
Willis Is
Espiritu Santo
Banks Is
Malekula
New Hebrides (UK & Fr)
Efate
Eromanga
Fiji Is
P A C I F I C
Halifax B.
Townsville
Port Denison
Bowen
Chesterfield Is (Fr)
Mackay
Fitzroy R.
Rockhampton
New Caledonia (Fr)
Noumea
Loyalty Is
Tropic of Capricorn
Hervey B.
Bundaberg
Maryborough
Fraser or Grt Sandy I.
Gt Dividing Ra.
Toowoomba
Moreton Bay
Brisbane
Ipswich
C. Byron
O C E A N
Grafton
Norfolk I. (Aust.)
Bourke
Tamworth
Port Macquarie
New England Ra.
Maitland
Lord Howe I. (Aust.)
Bathurst
Newcastle
Katoomba
Goulburn
Sydney
Wollongong
Canberra
Albury
Mt Kosciusko
Mt Townsend
Kermadec Is (N.Z.)
T A S M A N S E A
Cape Howe
Melbourne
Wilsons Prom.
Bass Strait
Furneaux Is
Launceston
North C.
Auckland
Hamilton
New Plymouth
Mt Egmont
East C.
NEW ZEALAND
North I.
Gisborne
Cook Str.
Napier
Ruapehu
Nelson
Wellington
Hokitika
South I.
Christchurch
Chatham Is
West C.
Mt Cook 12349
Dunedin
Stewart I.
Invercargill
150
160
170
180
0
10
20
30
40

Statute Miles
0 100 200
145
150
15
20
25
C O R A L
S E A
Q U E E N S L A N D
Cape York Peninsula
Thursday I.
C. York
Newcastle B.
Somerset
Shelburne B.
Wenlock R.
Weipa
Lloyd B.
C. Direction
C. Sidmouth
Princess Charlotte B.
C. Melville
C. Flattery
Cooktown
C. Tribulation
Great Barrier Reef
Laura
Palmer R.
Maytown
R. Mitchell
Staaten R.
Port Douglas
Cairns
Gordonvale
C. Grafton
Mt. Bartle Frere
5287
Double Pt.
Innisfail
Chillagoe
R. Lynd
Herberton
Tully
Rockingham B.
Cardwell
Hinchinbrook I.
R. Einasleigh
Croydon
R. Gilbert
Gregory Ra.
Forsayth
Ingham
Halifax B.
Bowling Green B.
Townsville
Mt. Elliot
Ayr
Upstart B.
Port Denison
Burdekin R.
Woolgar
Norman R.
Charters Towers
Ravenswood
Bowen
Whitsunday I.
Proserpine
Cumberland Is.
Richmond
Hughenden
Collinsville
Clarke R.
Repulse B.
Mackay
C. Palmerston
Eton
Sarina
Northumberland Is.
Broad Sound
C. Townshend
Port Clinton
Winton
Collingwood
Bowen Downs
Aramac
Belyando R.
Clermont
St. Lawrence
Yeppoon
Rockhampton
Keppel B.
Curtis I.
Port Curtis
Bustard Hd.
Tropic of Capricorn
Opalton
Longreach
Barcaldine
Jericho
Emerald
Mt. Mudge
Westwood
Mt. Morgan
Gladstone
Springsure
Diamantina R.
Diamantina Lakes
Thomson R.
Isisford
Blackall
Yaraka
Tambo
Baralaba
Biloela
Dawson R.
Bundaberg
Mt. Perry
Burnett R.
Hervey B.
Sandy C.
Fraser or Gt. Sandy I.
Maryborough
Jundah
Barcoo
Welford
Mt. King
Windorah
Beal Ra.
Augathella
Morven
Dawson R.
Taroom
Gayndah
Gympie
Wide B.
Double I. Pt.
Cooroy
Nambour
Kingaroy
Yamma Yamma
Cooper Cr.
Quilpie
Charleville
Mitchell
Surat
Roma
Miles
Chinchilla
Moreton
Eromanga
Bellalie
Warrego R.
Condamine
Dalby
BRISBANE
Grey Ra.
Bulloo
Clifton
Toowoomba
Darling Downs
Ipswich
Cunnamulla
Dirranbandi
St. George
Moonie R.
Warwick
Allora
Boonah
Thargomindah
Paroo
Goondiwindi
Stanthorpe
Lismore
Sturt Desert
Bulloo Downs
Bulloo L.
Hungerford
Thallon
Mungindi
Wallangarra
NEW SOUTH WALES
Samarai
China Str.
Moresby I.
Duperre I.
Misima
Tagula
Willis Group
Lihou Reef

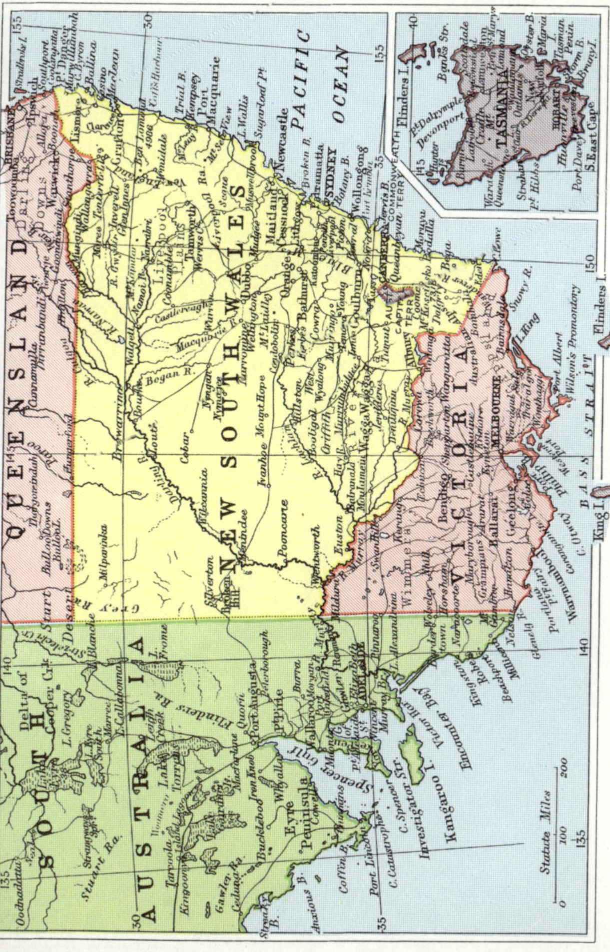
QUEENSLAND
NEW SOUTH WALES
VICTORIA
SOUTH AUSTRALIA
TASMANIA
PACIFIC OCEAN
BASS STRAIT
AUSTRALIAN CAPITAL TERR.
COMMONWEALTH TERRY
BRISBANE
SYDNEY
MELBOURNE
ADELAIDE
HOBART
CANBERRA
Newcastle
Wollongong
Geelong
Ballarat
Bendigo
Broken Hill
Spencer Gulf
Kangaroo I.
King I.
Flinders I.
Wilson's Promontory
Eyre Peninsula
Encounter Bay
Investigator Str.
Statute Miles
0
100
200

WESTERN AUSTRALIA

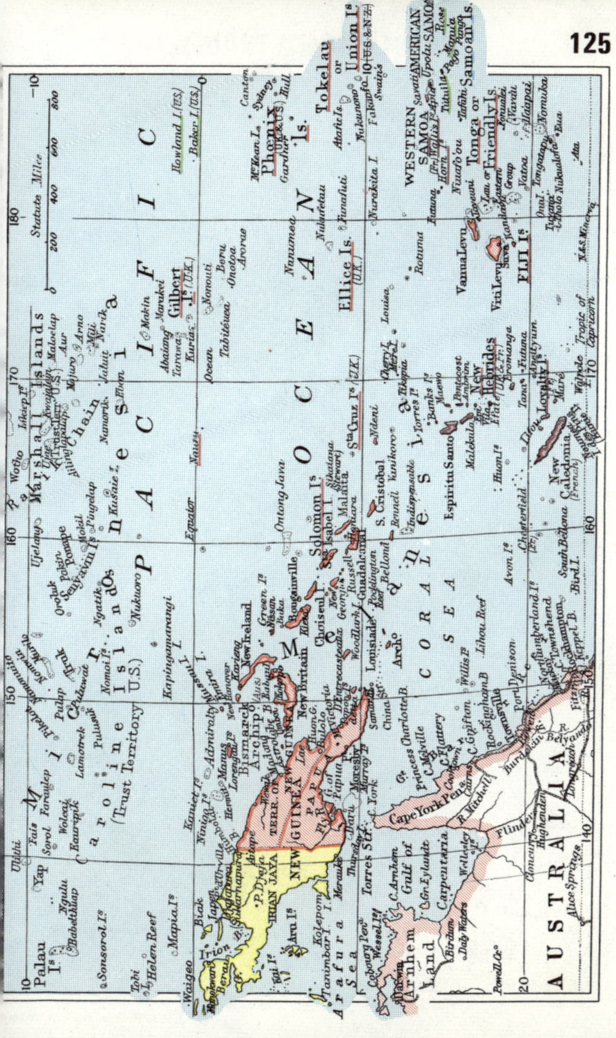
P A C I F I C
O C E A N
M i c r o n e s i a
M e l a n e s i a
Caroline Islands
(Trust Territory U.S.)
Marshall Islands
Gilbert Is. (U.K.)
Ellice Is. (U.K.)
Phoenix Is. (U.K.&U.S.)
Tokelau or Union Is.
WESTERN SAMOA
AMERICAN SAMOA
Samoan Is.
Tonga or Friendly Is.
FIJI Is.
New Hebrides
Loyalty Is.
New Caledonia (French)
Solomon Is.
Sta Cruz Is. (U.K.)
Bismarck Archip.
New Britain
New Ireland
Admiralty Is.
NEW GUINEA
TERR. OF NEW GUINEA
PAPUA
IRIAN JAYA
A r a f u r a S e a
Torres Str.
Gulf of Carpentaria
Arnhem Land
Cape York Pen.
C O R A L S E A
AUSTRALIA
Equator
Tropic of Capricorn
Statute Miles
0 200 400 600 800
180
170
160
150
140
10
20
Nauru
Ocean
Palau Is.
Yap
Guadalcanal
Malaita
Bougainville
Darwin

Statute Miles
0
50
100
174
176
178
36
38
40
42
C. Reinga
C. Maria van Diemen
North C.
Great Exhibition B.
Rangaunu B.
Doubtless B.
Whangaroa Har.
Bay of Islands
C. Brett
Ahipara
Mangonui
Russell
Rawene
Hokianga H.
NORTHLAND
Whangarei
Tutukaka Hd.
Whangarei Har.
Lit. Barrier I.
Gt. Barrier I.
Hauraki Gulf
C. Colville
Gt. Mercury I.
Mercury Is. (Iles d'Haussez)
Mercury B.
Coromandel
Kaipara Harbour
CENTRAL AUCKLAND
Auckland
Manukau Har.
Thames
Mayor I.
Bay of Plenty
Tauranga Har.
Tauranga
Matata
White I.
C. Runaway
Port Waikato
Hamilton
Cambridge
Te Awamutu
Te Puke
Rotorua
Aotea Har.
Kawhia Harb.
Otorohanga
Te Kuiti
Waitomo
STH. AUCKLAND BAY OF PLENTY
EAST COAST
Tokomaru B.
Tolago B.
Gisborne
Poverty B.
Te Karaka
PACIFIC OCEAN
TASMAN SEA
N. Taranaki Bight
Waitara
New Plymouth
Oakura
C. Egmont
Mt. Egmont
Stratford
Eltham
Opunake
Otakeho
Hawera
Patea
TARANAKI
L. Taupo
Taupo
Tokaanu
Mt. Ngauruhoe
Mt. Ruapehu
Ohakune
L. Waikare
Wairoa
Mohaka
Mahia Penin.a
Portland I.
Hawke Bay
HAWKES BAY
Napier
Hastings
Clive
C. Kidnappers
Taihape
Wanganui
Marton
Waipukurau
Dannevirke
Palmerston N.
Porangahau
Woodville
C. Turnagain
Foxton
Levin
Pahiatua
Otaki
Alfredton
Masterton
Castle Pt.
Greytown
Upper Hutt
WELLINGTON
Petone
Martinborough
Pahaoa R.
C. Palliser
Palliser B.
COOK STRAIT
Farewell Spit
Collingwood
Golden B.
Takaka
Tasman Bay
D'Urville I.
Nelson
Richmond
Havelock
Picton
Blenheim
Cloudy B.
Seddon
C. Campbell
MARLBOROUGH
NELSON
Kekerengu
Divisions coloured are statistical areas

Statute Miles
0
50
100
TASMAN SEA
PACIFIC OCEAN
COOK STRAIT
Pegasus Bay
Canterbury Bight
Foveaux Strait
NELSON
MARLBOROUGH
WESTLAND
CANTERBURY
OTAGO
SOUTHLAND
Southern Alps
Foxton
Otaki
WELLINGTON
C. Farewell
Farewell Spit
Whanganui Inlet
Collingwood
Golden B.
Takaka
Tasman Bay
Rocks Pt.
Karamea
Seddonville
Westport
C. Foulwind
Charleston
Nelson
Richmond
Havelock
Picton
Blenheim
C. Campbell
Kaikoura
Parnassus
Cheviot
Greymouth
Hokitika
Ross
Rangiora
Kaiapoi
Oxford
Springfield
Christchurch
Lyttelton
Banks Peninsula
Akaroa
Little River
Ellesmere
Okarito
Bruce B.
Haast
Jackson Bay
Cascade Pt.
Timaru
Waimate
Oamaru
Hampden
Moeraki Pt.
Palmerston
Waikouaiti
Otago Harbour
Port Chalmers
C. Saunders
Dunedin
St. Kilda
Green I.
Milton
Balclutha
Kaitangata
Owaka
Awarua Pt.
Milford Sd.
Pembroke
Sutherland Falls
George Sd.
Arrowtown
Queenstown
Wakatipu L.
Wanaka L.
Cromwell
Clyde
Alexandra
Naseby
Roxburgh
Kingston
Lumsden
Mossburn
Te Anau L.
L. Manapouri
Gore
Clinton
Mataura
Wyndham
Invercargill
Riverton
Bluff
Fortrose
Waikawa
Solander I.
Stewart I.
Paterson Inlet
Port Pegasus
S.W. Cape
Divisions coloured are statistical areas

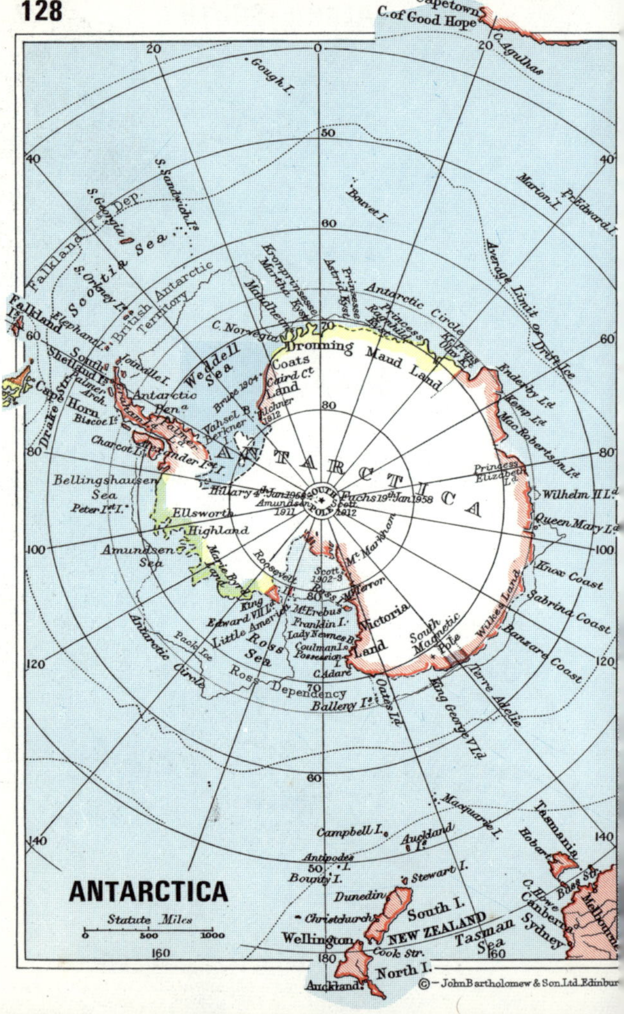

ANTARCTICA

Statute Miles
0 500 1000

Gazetteer

Aberdeen, city and port, N.E. Scotland
Abidjan, port and cap. of Ivory Coast, Africa
Accra, cap. of Ghana, West Africa
Aconcagua, highest peak of Andes; 23,035 ft.
Acre, state, Brazil
Addis Ababa, cap. of Ethiopia
Adelaide, cap. of South Australia
Afghanistan, an independent state on the N.W. frontier of Pakistan; cap. Kabul
Ahmedabad, town and cap. of Gujarat, India
Akron, city, Ohio, S. of Cleveland
Al Bayda', town, Libya
Alabama, state, U.S.A.; cap. Montgomery
Alagoas, state, Brazil
Alaska, state of U.S.A., in N.W. America
Albania, rep., on the Balkan Peninsula; cap. Tiranë
Albany, city and cap. of New York
Alberta, prov., Canada; cap. Edmonton
Albuquerque, town, New Mexico
Alexandria, city and port, U.A.R.
Algeria, rep., on north coast of Africa
Algiers (Alger), cap. of Algeria
Allentown, city, Pennsylvania, N.W. of Philadelphia
Alma Ata, town, Kazak, N.E. of Frunze
Amapá, state, Brazil
Amarillo, town, Texas
Amazonas, state, Brazil
Amazon, river, S. America, 4,000 m. long

American Samoa, prov., Pacific Ocean
Amman, cap. of Jordan
Amsterdam, cap. and port, Netherlands
Amur, river, U.S.S.R., enters Sea of Okhotsk
Anaheim, town, California
Andhra Pradesh, state, India
Andorra, republic, Pyrenees Mts.
Andros Island, Bahamas, W. Indies
Angola, Portuguese col., W. Africa; cap. Luanda
Anguilla, island, Leeward Is., W. Indies
Anhwei, prov., China
Ankara, cap. of Turkey, S.E. of Istanbul
Annapurna, mt. Nepal, 26,504 ft.
Antigua I., Leeward Is., W. Indies
Ararat, Mount, Turkey, 16,946 ft.
Argentina, rep., S. America; cap. Buenos Aires
Arizona, state, W. U.S.A.; cap. Phœnix
Arkansas, state, S. U.S.A.; cap. Little Rock
Armenia, rep., U.S.S.R.; cap. Yerevan
Ascension Island, S. Atlantic Ocean
Assam, state, India; cap. Shillong
Asuncion, port and cap. of Paraguay
Athens (Athínai), city and cap. of Greece
Atlanta, cap. of Georgia, U.S.A.
Auckland, prov. and city, North I., N.Z.
Austin, cap. of Texas, on Colorado River
Australia, state, cap. Canberra, smallest continent
Austria, rep., Cent. Europe; cap. Vienna
Azerbaijan, rep., U.S.S.R.; cap. Baku
Badrinath, mt., India/Tibet; 23,190 ft.
Baghdad, city and cap. of Iraq
Bahama Islands, group in West Indies
Bahia, state, Brazil

Bahrain, island and state, The Gulf
Baikal, Lake, U.S.S.R.; area 13,500 sq. m.
Baku, port and cap. of Azerbaijan
Balearic Isles, group, in Mediterranean
Balkhash, Lake, Kazak, U.S.S.R.
Baltimore, city and port, Maryland
Bamako, cap. of Mali, on R. Niger
Bandar Seri Begawan, town and cap. of Brunei
Bandarpunch, mt., India
Bangalore, town and cap. of Karnataka, India
Bangkok (Krung Thep), city and cap. of Thailand
Bangui, town, cap. of Cent. Afr. Rep.
Banjul, cap. of The Gambia, W. Africa
Barbados, island, W. Indies
Barbuda, island, Leeward Is., W. Indies
Barcelona, city and port, Spain
Basildon, new town, Essex, England
Bata, town and cap. of Equat. Guinea
Baton Rouge, city, cap. of Louisiana
Bear Lake, Great, N.-W. Terr., Canada
Beaumont, town, Texas, S.E. of Dallas
Beirût, city and cap. of Lebanon
Belfast, port and cap. of N. Ireland
Belgium, kingdom, W. Europe; cap. Brussels
Belgrade, Beograd
Belize, state, Cent. Amer., cap. Belmopan
Belmopan, cap. of Belize
Belo Horizonte, city, Brazil, N. of Rio de Janeiro
Benghazi, port, Libya, N. Africa
Benoni, town, S. Africa
Beograd (Belgrade), city, cap. of Yugoslavia
Berkeley, city, California, on San Francisco B.
Berlin, city, Germany, on R. Spree

Bermuda, island group, N. Atlantic
Berne (Bern), cap. of Switzerland
Bhutan, state, in the Himalayas
Bihar, state, India; cap. Patna
Birkenhead, port, Cheshire, England
Birmingham, city, Alabama
Birmingham, city, Warwicks, England
Blackburn, town, Lancs, England
Blackpool, seaside town, Lancs, England
Bloemfontein, cap. of O.F.S., S. Africa
Bogotá, cap. of Colombia, S. America
Bolivia, rep., S. America; cap. Sucre
Bolton, town, Lancs, England
Bombay, city and port, W. India, cap. of Maharashtra
Bonn, city and cap. of W. Germany
Bordeaux, city and port, S.W. France
Boston, city and port, cap. of Mass., U.S.A.
Botswana, rep., S. Africa, cap. Gaborone
Bournemouth, town, Hants, England
Bradford, city, Yorks, England
Brahmaputra, river, Asia, flows into Bay of Bengal, 1800 m. long
Brasília, federal capital of Brazil
Brazil, rep., S. America; cap. Brasília
Brazzaville, town, cap. of People's Rep. of the Congo, Central Africa
Bremen, town, W. Germany
Bridgetown, cap. of Barbados
Bridgeport, city, Long Island Sd., Conn.
Brighton, seaside tn., E. Sussex, England
Brisbane, port and cap. of Queensland
Bristol, city and port, Glos. and Som., Eng.
British Columbia, prov., W. Canada

British Solomon Is., group, Pacific Oc.
Brunei, state, N.W. Borneo
Brussels (Bruxelles), cap. of Belgium
Bucuresti (Bucharest), city, cap. of Romania
Budapest, city and cap. of Hungary
Buenos Aires, fed. cap. of Argentina
Buffalo, city, New York, on Lake Erie
Bujumbura, town, cap. of Burundi
Bulawayo, town, S. Rhodesia
Bulgaria, rep., Balkan Pen.; cap. Sofia
Burma, rep., E. of India; cap. Rangoon
Burundi, rep., central Africa
Byelorussia, rep., U.S.S.R., cap. Minsk.
Caicos Islands, W. Indies, N. of Hispaniola
Cairo, cap. of A.R.E., on the Nile
Calcutta, city, port and cap. of W. Bengal
Calgary, city, Alberta, S. of Edmonton
California, state, W. U.S.A.; cap. Sacramento
Cambodia, Khmer Republic
Cambridge, co. town, Cambs., England
Cambridge, city, Mass., suburb of Boston
Camden, city, New Jersey, on Delaware River
Cameroun, republic, Central Africa, cap. Yaoundé
Canada, state, N. America, cap. Ottawa
Canary Islands, Span. group, off N.W. Africa
Canberra, fed. cap. of Australia
Canton, town, Ohio
Cape of Good Hope (Cape Province), prov. of Republic of South Africa
Cape Town, port and cap. of Cape Prov.
Cape Verde Islands, group, Atlantic Oc., off N.W. Africa
Caracas, cap. of Venezuela
Cardiff, city and cap. of Wales

Casablanca, port and naval base, Morocco
Cayenne, port and cap. of French Guiana
Cayman Islands, group, W. Indies
Ceará, state, N.E. Brazil
Central African Rep., cap. Bangui
Ceuta, port and naval base, Morocco
Ceylon, I. off S. India
Chad, rep., Africa; cap. Fort Lamy
Chad, Lake, Africa
Channel Islands, off N.W. coast of France
Charles Louis, Mt., New Guinea
Charlotte, city, N. Carolina, S.W. of Raleigh
Chattanooga, tn., Tennessee, on Tennessee R.
Chekiang, prov., China
Chelyabinsk, prov. and town, U.S.S.R.
Chengtu, city, Szechwan, China
Chicago, city, Illinois, on L. Michigan
Chile, rep., S. America; cap. Santiago
Chimborazo, peak in the Andes, Ecuador
China, rep., cap. Peking
Chinghai, prov., China
Christchurch, city, S. Island, New Zealand
Christmas Island, Polynesia, Pacific Ocean
Chumalhari, mt., Bhutan; 23,996 ft.
Chungking, port, Szechwan, China, on Yangtse Kiang
Cincinnati, city, Ohio, on Ohio River
Citlaltepetl, mt., Mexico, 17,879 ft.
Cleveland, city, Ohio, on L. Erie
Cocos Is., group, Pacific Ocean
Cologne (Köln), city, W. Germany, on Rhine
Colombia, rep., S. America; cap. Bogotá
Colombo, port and cap. of Sri Lanka
Colorado, state, W.-cent. U.S.A.; cap. Denver

Columbus, cap. of Ohio, U.S.A.
Columbus, town, Georgia
Comoro Islands, Mozambique Channel
Conakry, port and cap. of Guinea, W. Africa
Congo, Dem. Rep. of, Africa; cap. Kinshasa
Congo, People's Rep. of, W. Africa; cap. Brazzaville.
Connecticut, state, N.E. U.S.A.; cap. Hartford
Cook Islands, Polynesia, Pacific Ocean
Cook, Mt., N.Z.
Copenhagen (København), cap. of Denmark
Cork, city and co., Rep. of Ireland
Corpus Christi, town, Texas
Costa Rica, republic, Central America, cap. San José
Cotapaxi, mt., Ecuador; 19,344 ft.
Coventry, city, Warwicks, England
Cuba, island and rep., West Indies, cap. Havana
Cyprus, island and rep., E. Mediterranean, cap. Nicosia
Czechoslovakia, rep., central Europe, cap. Prague
Dacca, city, E. Bengal, cap. of Bangladesh
Dahomey, rep., W. Africa; cap. Porto Novo
Dakar, port and cap., Senegal, West Africa
Dallas, city, Texas, E. of Forth Worth
Damascus, city and cap. of Syria
Damavand, mt., Iran, 18,934 ft.
Danube, river of Cent. Europe, length 1740 m.
Dar es Salaam, port, and cap., Tanzania
Dayton, city, Ohio, W.S.W. of Columbus
Dearborn, town, Michigan
Delaware, river, rises in New York and flows to Delaware B.
Delaware, Atlantic state, U.S.A.; cap. Dover
Delhi, city and cap. of India

Denmark, kingdom, Europe; cap. Copenhagen
Denver, cap. of Colorado, U.S.A.
Derby, co. town, Derbyshire, England
Descabezado, mt., Chile
Des Moines, city and cap. of Iowa
Detroit, city and port, Michigan
Dikh-tau, mt., U.S.S.R.
Djakarta, tn. and port, Java; cap. of Indonesia
Dnepropetrovsk, town, Ukraine, S.W. of Kharkov
Dominica, island, Leeward Is., W. Indies
Dominican Rep. (Santo Domingo), Hispaniola West Indies, cap. Santo Domingo
Donetsk, town, Ukraine, S.E. of Kharkov
Dortmund, town, W. Germany, N.E. of Cologne
Dresden, tn., E. Germany, E.S.E. of Leipzig
Dublin, city, port, county and cap. of Rep. of Ireland
Dudley, town, Worcester, England
Duluth, city and lake port, Minnesota
Dundee, cy. & pt., Angus, Scot., on R. Tay
Dunedin, town, South I., New Zealand
Durban, port, Natal, on Indian Ocean
Düsseldorf, tn., W. Germany, on the Rhine
East London, port, Cape Province
Ecuador, rep., S. America
Edinburgh, cap. of Scotland, on Firth of Forth
Edmonton, cap. of Alberta, Canada
Elbrus, highest peak, Caucasus, U.S.S.R.
Elizabeth, city, New Jersey, W. of Brooklyn
Ellice Islands, British group in the Pacific, N. of Fiji
El Paso, town, Texas, on Rio Grande
El Salvador, rep., Cent. Amer., cap. San Salvador
England, kingdom, with Wales forms the S. portion of Great Britain

Equatorial Guinea, state, W. Africa
Erie, Lake, between Ontario and U.S.A.
Erie, town, Pennsylvania
Espírito Santo, state, Brazil
Essen, town, W. Germany
Estonia, rep., U.S.S.R.; cap. Tallinn
Ethiopia (Abyssinia), kingdom, E. Africa, cap. Addis Ababa
Etna, Mount, volcano, Sicily, 10,741 feet
Euphrates, river, W. Asia, flows 1700 m. to The Gulf
Evansville, town, Indiana, on Ohio river
Everest, mt. peak, Himalayas, highest in the world, 29,028 ft.
F.T.A.I.=French Territory of the Afars and the Issas
Faerøerne, Dan. islands in N. Atlantic Oc.
Falkland Islands Dependency, Brit. col., S. Atlantic
Fernando de Noronha, state, Brazil
Fernando Póo, isl., Equat. Guinea, W. Africa
Fès, town, Morocco, E. of Rabat
Fiji Islands, state, in Pacific Ocean
Finland, republic, Europe; cap. Helsinki
Finsteraarhorn, Switzerland, Bernese Alps
Flint, town, Michigan
Florida, a S. Atlantic state, U.S.A.; cap. Tallahassee
Fort Lamy, tn. and cap. of Chad, Africa
Fort Wayne, city, Indiana, S.E. of Chicago
Fort Worth, city, Texas, W. of Dallas
France, republic, W. Europe; cap. Paris
Frankfurt-am-Main, city, W. Germany
Freetown, cap. of Sierra Leone, Africa
French Guiana, prov., S. America
French Terr. of the Afars and the Issas (F.T.A.I.); cap. Djibouti

Fresno, town, California
Fuji-san, mt., Japan, S.W. of Tokio, 12,388 ft.
Fukien, province, China
Gaborone, cap. of Botswana
Gabon, rep., Cent. Africa ; cap. Libreville
Gambia, The, river and rep., W. Africa; cap. Banjul
Ganga, river, India, flows 1,500 miles into B. of Bengal
Ganges=Ganga
Gangtok, town and cap. of Sikkim
Gary, town, Indiana
Gateshead, town, Durham, opp. Newcastle upon Tyne
Geelong, city, Victoria, S. of Bendigo
Genova, city and port, N.W. Italy, on G. of Genoa
Georgetown, cap. of Guyana
Georgia, S. Atlantic state, U.S.A. ; cap. Atlanta
Georgia, republic, U.S.S.R. ; cap. Tbilisi
Germany, E., rep., Europe
Germany, W., rep., Europe
Germiston, town, S. Africa
Ghana, rep., W. Africa ; cap. Accra
Gibraltar, Br. fortress and town, S. Spain
Gilbert Islands, British group, Pacific Ocean
Glasgow, city and port, Scotland, on the Clyde
Glendale, town, California
Goiás, state, Brazil
Gorkiy (Nizhni Novgorod), city, U.S.S.R., E. of Moscow
Göteborg, port, Sweden, on Gota river
Grand Rapids, city, Michigan, N.W. of Detroit
Grays Thurrock, town, Essex, England
Great Salt Lake, Utah, U.S.A.
Greece, kingdom, S.E. Europe ; cap. Athens
Greenland, Danish island, N. America
Greensboro, town, N. Carolina

Grenada, island, W. Indies, Windward Is.
Guadalajara, city, Mexico
Guadeloupe, island, Leeward Is., W. Indies
Guam, island, Marianas Is., Pacific Ocean
Guanabara, state, Brazil
Guatemala, rep., central America
Guatemala City, cap. of Guatemala
Guinea, rep., W. Africa; cap. Conakry
Gujarat, state, W. India; cap. Ahmedabad
Guyana, rep., S. America; cap. Georgetown
Hague, The ('s-Gravenhage), cy., seat of govt., Netherlands
Haiti, rep., Hispaniola, W. Indies; cap. Port-au-Prince
Halifax, port and cap. of Nova Scotia
Hamburg, city and port, W. Germany, on Elbe
Hamilton, city, Ontario, S.W. of Toronto
Hammond, town, Indiana
Hanoi, cy. and cap. of N. Vietnam
Hannover, town, W. Germany
Harbin, town, N.E. China, on Sungari river
Hartford, town, Connecticut
Haryana, state, N. India
Havana, port and cap. of Cuba, W. Indies
Hawaii, largest of the Hawaiian Islands and state, U.S.A.; cap. Honolulu
Heilungkiang, prov., China
Helsinki, port and cap. of Finland
Himachal Pradesh, state, N. India
Hobart, city and cap. of Tasmania
Honan, prov., Central China
Hong Kong, British Island and col., S. China
Honolulu, cap. of Hawaii, on Oahu Is.

Hopei, prov., China
Houston, town and port, Texas, U.S.A.
Huddersfield, town, Yorks., England
Hull, port, Yorks., England, on the Humber
Hunan, prov., China
Hungary, rep., Cent. Europe; cap. Budapest
Hupeh, prov., China
Huron, Lake, bet. Canada and United States
Hwang Ho, river, China, enters G. of Pohai
Hyderabad, town, Andhra Pradesh, India
Iceland, rep., N.W. Europe; cap. Reykjavik
Idaho, W. state of U.S.A.; cap. Boise
Illampu, mt., Bolivia; 21,490 ft.
Illimani, mt., Bolivia; 22,579 ft.
Illinois, N. cent. state, U.S.A.; cap. Springfield
India, rep., S. Asia; cap. Delhi
Indiana, N. central state of U.S.A.
Indianapolis, city and cap. of Indiana
Indonesia, rep., E. Indies; cap. Djakarta
Indus, river, Pakistan, flows to Arabian Sea
Inner Mongolia, aut. reg., China
Iowa, N. cent. state, U.S.A.; cap. Des Moines
Ipswich, co. town of Suffolk, England
Iran (Persia), kingdom, W. Asia; cap. Tehran
Iraq, rep., Asia; cap. Baghdad
Ireland, island, W. of Great Britain, comprising Rep. of Ireland and N. Ireland
Islamabad, fed. cap. of Pakistan, N. of Rawalpindi
Israel, rep., S.W. Asia
Istanbul (Constantinople), town, Turkey
Italy, rep., S. Europe; cap. Rome
Ivory Coast, republic, W. Africa; cap. Abidjan
Jackson, town and cap. of Mississippi

Jacksonville, city, Florida, N.E. of Tampa
Jamaica, island, West Indies; cap. Kingston
Jammu & Kashmir, state, India
Jan Mayen, island, Arctic Ocean
Jersey City, town, New Jersey, on Hudson R.
Jerusalem (El Quds esh Sherif), city, Israel-Jordan
Johannesburg, largest city of Transvaal, S. Africa
Jordan, kingdom and river, W. Asia; cap. Amman
Juncal, mt., S. America; 20,367 ft.
Jungfrau, mt., Bernese Alps, Switzerland
K2, mt., Kashmir, W. Himalayas; 28,250 ft.
Kabul, cap. of Afghanistan on Kabul river
Kamet, mt., Uttar Pradesh; 25,447 ft.
Kampala, town and cap. of Uganda, N.E. of Entebbe
Kangchenjunga, mt., Himalayas; 28,146 ft.
Kanpur, city, Uttar Pradesh, India
Kansas, S. central state of U.S.A.; cap. Topeka
Kansas City, town, Missouri, on Missouri river
Kansas City, town, Kansas, E.N.E. of Topeka
Kansu, prov., China
Karachi, town and port, West Pakistan
Karnataka, state, S. India; cap. Bangalore
Kathmandu, cap. of Nepal, E.N.E. of Lucknow
Kazakhstan, republic, central U.S.S.R.
Kazan, town, U.S.S.R., N.E. of Volgograd
Kazbek, mt., U.S.S.R.
Kentucky, an E central state, U.S.A.; cap. Frankfort
Kenya, rep., E. Africa; cap. Nairobi
Kenya, Mt., Africa
Kerala, state, S. India; cap. Trivandrum
Khan Tengri, mt., China; 23,620 ft.
Kharkov, city, Ukraine, S. of Moscow
Khartoum, cap. of Sudan

Khmer Republic, state, S.E. Asia, cap. Phnom-Penh
Kiangsi, prov., China
Kiangsu, prov., China
Kiev (Kiyev), city, cap. of Ukraine
Kigali, town and cap. of Rwanda
Kilimanjaro, mt., Tanzania; 19,340 ft.
Kingston, port, naval base and cap. of Jamaica, W. Indies
Kinshasa, cap. of Dem. Rep. of Congo
Kirgizia, rep., U.S.S.R.; cap. Frunze
Kirin, prov., China
Kitakyushu, city, Kyushu, Japan
Kitchener, town, Ontario, W. of Toronto
Knoxville, city and river port, Tennessee
Kobe, town, Honshu I., Japan
Korea, N. and S., reps., E. Asia
Kota Kinabalu, town and cap. of Sabah, E. Malaysia
Kraków (Cracow), city, Poland, on R. Vistula
Krasnoyarsk, town, U.S.S.R., E. of Tomsk
Krivoi Rog, town, Ukraine, N.E. of Odessa
Kuala Lumpur, tn., Selangor, cap. of W. Malaysia
Kuching, town and cap. of Sarawak, E. Malaysia
Kuwait, state on The Gulf
Kuwait City, cap. of Kuwait
Kuybyshev (Samara), tn., on Volga, U.S.S.R.
Kwangchow (Canton), city and port, S.E. China
Kwangsi-Chuang, aut. reg., China
Kwangtung, prov., China
Kweichow, prov., China
Kyoto, city, Honshu I., Japan, N.E. of Osaka
Ladoga, Lake, U.S.S.R., on border of Finland
Lagos, port, cap. of Nigeria, S. of Ibadan
Lahore, cap. of W. Pakistan, on Ravi River
Lansing, cap. of Michigan, U.S.A.

Laos, kingdom, S.E. Asia; cap. Vientiane
La Paz, city and dep., Bolivia, S. America
La Plata, river, Argentina
Latvia, rep., U.S.S.R.; cap. Riga
Lebanon, state, W. Asia; cap. Beirut
Leeds, city, Yorks, England
Leeward Islands, Lesser Antilles, W. Indies
Leicester, co. town of Leicestershire, England
Leipzig, city, E. Germany, S.S.W. of Berlin
Lena, river, U.S.S.R., flows to Arctic Ocean; 2,850 m. long
Leningrad, city, U.S.S.R., near Lake Ladoga
Lesotho (Basutoland), state, S. Africa
Liaoning, prov., China
Liberia, rep., West Africa; cap. Monrovia
Libreville, tn. and cap. of Gabon, Cent. Africa
Libya, rep., N. Africa; caps. Tripoli and Benghazi
Liechtenstein, princ., E. Switz.; cap. Vaduz
Lille, town, France, S.E. of Calais
Lima, city and cap. of Peru
Lincoln, town, cap. of Nebraska
Lisbon (Lisboa), city, naval base and cap. of Portugal, on River Tagus
Lithuania, rep., U.S.S.R.; chief town Vilnius
Little Rock, cap. of Arkansas, U.S.A.
Liverpool, city and port, Lancs, England
Llullaillaco, mt., Chile; 22,057 ft.
Lódz, town, Poland, S.W. of Warsaw
Logan, Mount, Yukon, N.W. Canada; 19,850 ft.
Lomé, cap. of Togo, W. Africa
London, cap. of England and U.K., on the Thames
London, port of entry, Ontario, S.W. of Toronto
Londonderry, co. and town, N. Ireland

Long Beach, town, California, U.S.A.
Los Angeles, city, California, S.E. of San Francisco
Louisiana, state, U.S.A.; cap. Baton Rouge
Louisville, city, Kentucky, on the Ohio River
Lourenço Marques, town and cap. of Moçambique
Lower Hutt, town, N. Island, N.Z.
Luanda, port and cap. of Angola, W. Africa
Lubbock, town, Texas
Lusaka, cap. of Zambia, central Africa
Lü-ta, port, Kwangtung, China
Luton, town, Beds., England
Luxembourg, grand Duchy and town, W. Europe
L'vov, town, Ukraine
Lyons, city, France, S.E. of Paris
Macao, island (Portuguese), S. China
Mackenzie, river, N.W. Terr., Canada
McKinley, Mount, Alaska; 20,320 ft.
Madeira, river, Brazil; flows into Amazon
Madhya Pradesh, state, India; cap. Bhopal
Madinat ash Sha'b, town and cap. of People's Dem. Rep. of Yemen
Madison, cap. of Wisconsin, W. of Milwaukee
Madras, city, port and cap. of Tamil Nadu state, India
Madrid, cap. of Spain, on Manzanares River
Maharashtra, state, India; cap. Bombay
Maine, N.E. state of U.S.A.; cap. Augusta
Maipo, mt., Argentina
Makalu, Mt., Tibet/Nepal; 27,790 ft.
Malagasy Rep., state, Indian Ocean
Malawi, rep., central Africa
Malaya, states, W. Malaysia; southern part of Malay Pen.; cap. Kuala Lumpur

Malaysia, federation, S.E. Asia
Maldive Islands, Indian Ocean, S.W. of Sri Lanka
Mali, rep., cent. Africa; cap. Bamako
Malta, island and state, in cent. Mediterranean; cap. Valletta
Man, Isle of, Irish Sea; cap. Douglas
Managua, town and cap. of Nicaragua
Manchester, city, Lancashire, England
Manila, port, Luzon I., Philippines
Manitoba, prov., Canada; cap. Winnipeg
Maranhão, state, Brazil
Marseilles, port, France, S. coast
Martinique, French island, W. Indies
Maryland, Atlantic state of U.S.A.; cap. Annapolis
Maseru City, cap. of Lesotho
Massachusetts, state, U.S.A.; cap. Boston
Mato Grosso, state, Brazil
Matterhorn, alpine peak, Switzerland; 14,705 ft.
Mauritius, state and I., Indian Ocean
Mauritania, rep., W. Africa; cap. Nouakchott
Meghalaya, state, N.E. India
Mekong, river, S.E. Asia; length 2,750 miles
Melbourne, cap. of Victoria, Australia
Melilla, port and settlement, N. coast of Morocco
Memphis, town, Tennessee, on Mississippi
Mexico, state, N. America
Mexico City, cap. of the rep. of Mexico, N. America
Miami, city and winter resort, Florida
Michigan, state of U.S.A.; capital Lansing
Michigan, Lake, N. America
Milan, city, Lombardy, N. Italy
Milwaukee, city and port, Wisconsin
Minas Gerais, state, Brazil

Minneapolis, city, Minnesota, on Mississippi
Minnesota, north-central state, U.S.A.; cap. St Paul
Minsk, cap. of Byelorussia, U.S.S.R.
Miquelon, island, off S.W. Newfoundland
Mississippi, great river of U.S.A., flows to G. of Mexico; length 3160 miles
Mississippi, state of U.S.A.; cap. Jackson
Missouri, state, U.S.A.; cap. Jefferson City
Missouri, river, 3000 m. long; joins Mississippi
Mobile, port city, Alabama
Moçambique , Portuguese province, E. Africa; cap. Lourenço Marques
Mogadishu (Mogadiscio), town and cap. of Somali Rep.
Moldavia, rep., U.S.S.R. in S.W.
Monaco, small principality and town, on Mediterranean Riviera
Mongolia, rep., central Asia; cap. Ulaanbaatar
Monmouth, co., Wales
Monrovia, cap. of Liberia, W. Africa
Montana, N.W. state of U.S.A.; cap. Helena
Mont Blanc, France-Italy, highest peak of Alps; 15,772 ft.
Montevideo, cap. and chief port, Uruguay
Montgomery, cap. of Alabama, U.S.A.
Montreal, city, Quebec, E.N.E. of Ottawa
Montserrat, island, Leeward Is., W. Indies
Morocco, kingdom, N.W. Africa; caps. Rabat and Tangier
Moscow (Moskva), prov. and cap. of the R.S.F.S.R.
Mulhacen, mt., Spain
Munich (München), cy., W. Germany, on R. Isar
Muscat, cap. of Oman, Arabia, on G. of Oman

Nagaland, state of N.E. India
Nagoya, town, Honshu I., Japan
Naha, town and cap. of Ryukyu Is.
Nairobi, cap. of Kenya, East Africa
Namibia=South West Africa
Nanda Devi, mt., Himalayas, Uttar Pradesh
Nanga Parbat, mt., Kashmir; 26,620 ft.
Nanking, city, China, on the Yangtze Kiang
Naples, city and naval base, Italy, S.E. of Rome
Nashville, cap. of Tennessee, on Cumberland R.
Nassau, cap. of Bahamas, New Providence I.
Natal, prov., S. Africa; cap. Pietermaritzburg
Nauru Island, Pacific, N.E. of Solomon Islands
Nebraska, state, U.S.A.; cap. Lincoln
Nepal, independent state, in the Himalayas
Netherlands, kingdom, W. Europe; caps. Amsterdam and The Hague
Nevada, west. state, U.S.A.: cap. Carson City
Nevis, I., Leeward Is., W. Indies
Newark, city, New Jersey, N.W. of Staten I.
New Bedford, town, Massachusetts
New Brunswick, E. maritime prov. of Canada
New Caledonia, French island, in S. Pacific
Newcastle, port, New South Wales, N. of Sydney
Newcastle upon Tyne, city and port, Northumberland, England
Newfoundland, island and prov. of E. Canada; cap. St John's
New Guinea, island in W. Pacific
New Hampshire, New England state, U.S.A.; cap. Concord
New Haven, port, Connecticut, N.E. of N.Y.
New Hebrides, island group, W. Pacific

New Jersey, a New England state of U.S.A.; cap. Trenton
New Mexico, state, U.S.A.; cap. Santa Fé
New Orleans, port and cap. of Louisiana
Newport, tn. and port, Monmouthshire, Wales
Newport News, port, Virginia, N.W. of Norfolk
New South Wales, state, Aust.; cap. Sydney
New York, state, U.S.A.; cap. Albany
New York, city and port, U.S.A.
New Zealand, state, S. Pacific; cap. Wellington
Niagara Falls, city, New York, at falls of Niagara river
Niamey, town and cap. of Niger, West Africa
Nicaragua, rep., Cent. America; cap. Managua
Nicaragua, Lake, S. America
Nicosia, cap. of Cyprus, Mediterranean
Niger, river, W. Africa, flows 2600 m. to G. of Guinea
Niger, republic, W. Africa; cap. Niamey
Nigeria, rep., West Africa; cap. Lagos
Nile, river, N.E. Africa, flows 3600 miles to Mediterranean
Ningsia-Hui, aut. reg., China
Niue, island, one of Cook Is.
Norfolk, city, port and naval base, Virginia
Norfolk Island, Pacific Oc., N.N.W. of N.Z.
Northampton, co. town, Northants, England
North Carolina, state, U.S.A.; cap. Raleigh
North Dakota, a N. central state, U.S.A.; cap. Bismarck
Northern Ireland, prov., U.K.
Northern Territory, territory, Australia; cap. Darwin
Northwest Territories, prov., Canada
Norway, kingdom, Scandinavia, W. Europe; cap. Oslo
Norwich, town, Norfolk, England
Nottingham, co. town of Notts, England

Nouakchott, cap. of Mauritania, W. Africa
Nova Scotia, E. maritime prov., Canada; cap. Halifax
Novosibirsk, town, on Ob river, U.S.S.R., E. of Omsk
Nyasa, Lake, S.E. Africa
Oakland, city, California, on San Francisco B.
Ob, river, U.S.S.R., flows 2420 m. to Arctic Oc.
Odessa, city and port, Ukraine, on Black Sea
Ohio, state, U.S.A.; cap. Columbus
Oklahoma, state, U.S.A. cap. Oklahoma City
Oklahoma City, cap. of Oklahoma state, U.S.A.
Oldham, town, Lancashire, England
Omaha, city & riv. port, Nebraska, on Missouri
Omsk, town, U.S.S.R., S.E. of Sverdlovsk
Onega, Lake, U.S.S.R., E. of Lake Ladoga
Ontario, E., province, Canada; cap. Toronto
Ontario, Lake, between Canada and U.S.A.
Oporto, city, Portugal, on the Douro
Orange Free State, prov., S. Africa; cap. Bloemfontein
Oregon, N.W. state of U.S.A.; cap. Salem
Orissa, state, India; cap. Bhubaneswar
Osaka, city and port, Honshu, Japan
Oslo, city and cap. of Norway, on Oslo Fjord
Ottawa, cap. of Canada, on Ottawa riv., Ontario
Ouagadougou, town and cap. of Upper Volta
Oxford, univ. and co. town of Oxfordshire, England
Pakistan, state, S. Asia; cap. Islamabad
Palermo, port and cap. of Sicily
Panama City, port & cap. of the rep. of Panama
Panama, republic, cent. America
Papua, S.E. part of the island of New Guinea; cap. Port Moresby
Para, state, Brazil
Paraguay, republic, S. America; cap. Asuncion

Paraíba, state, Brazil
Paramaribo, cap. of Surinam, S. America
Paraná, state, Brazil
Paraná, river, Brazil
Paris, cap. of France, on the River Seine
Pasadena, town, California
Paterson, city, New Jersey, N.W. of New York
Peking, city, Hopeh prov., cap. of China
Pennsylvania, state, U.S.A., cap. Harrisburg
Peoria, city, Illinois, S.W. of Chicago
Perm, town, U.S.S.R., on river Kama
Pernambuco, state, Brazil
Perth, cap. of W. Australia, S.W. coast
Peru, rep., S. America
Philadelphia, city, Pennsyl., S.W. of New York
Philippines, ils., rep. E. Indies, cap. Manilla
Phnom Penh, cap. of Cambodia, Indo-China
Phœnix, cap. of Arizona, N.E. of Tucson
Phœnix Islands, group, N.E. of Fiji, Pacific Oc.
Piaul, state, Brazil
Pietermaritzburg, cap. of Natal, S. Africa
Pitcairn Island, E. Pacific, S.E. of Tuamotu Archipelago
Pittsburgh, city, Pennsylvania
Plymouth, port, Devon, England
Poland, rep., central Europe; cap. Warsaw
Popocatepetl ("smoking mountain"), Mexico, S.E. of Mexico, height 17,887 ft.
Port-au-Prince, cap. and chief port, Haiti
Port Elizabeth, port, on Algoa B., Cape Prov.
Portland, city, Oregon, on Williamette river
Port Louis, town and cap. of Mauritius
Port of Spain, cap. of Trinidad, W. Indies
Porto Novo, cap. of Dahomey, W. Africa

Portsmouth, city, port and naval base, Hants, England
Portsmouth, town, Virginia
Portugal, republic, S.W. Europe, cap. Lisbon
Portuguese Guinea, colony, W. Africa; cap. Bissau
Prague (Praha), city, Bohemia, cap. of Czechoslovakia
Preston, town, Lancs, England, N.E. of Liverpool
Pretoria, town and cap. of S. Africa
Prince Edward Island, prov., Canada; cap. Charlottetown
Principe, Portuguese island, in G. of Guinea, W. Africa
Providence, city & cap. of Rhode Is., U.S.A.
Puerto Rico, Is., Greater Antilles, W. Indies
Punjab, state, N.W. India
Pusan, port, S. Korea
Pyongyang, city and cap. of N. Korea
Qatar, sheikdom, Arabia, in The Gulf
Quebec, tn. and cap. of Quebec prov., Canada
Quebec, prov., Canada
Queensland, state, Australia; cap. Brisbane
Quezon City, cap. of the Philippines
Quito, city, cap. of Ecuador, S. America
R.S.F.S.R.= Russian Soviet Federated Socialist Republic
Rabat, tn. & cap. of Morocco, S.W. of Tangier
Rajasthan, state, N.W. India; cap. Jaipur
Rangoon, city and port; cap. of Burma
Rawalpindi, dist. and town, Pakistan
Reading, town, Berkshire, England
Recife, city, Brazil, N.E. Brazil
Regina, cap. of Saskatchewan, W. of Winnipeg
Réunion, I., Indian Ocean
Reykjavik, cap. of Iceland, on S.W. coast
Rhode Island, New England state, U.S.A.; cap. Providence

Rhodesia, state, central Africa, cap. Salisbury
Richmond, cap. of Virginia, U.S.A.
Riga, port and cap. of Latvia, on G. of Riga
Rio de Janeiro, city, Brazil
Rio de Janeiro, state; Brazil
Rio del Norte, river, Brazil
Rio Grande do Norte, state, Brazil
Rio Grande do Sul, state, Brazil
Riyadh, Najd, cap. of Saudi Arabia
Robson, Mt., Brit. Columbia
Rochester, city, New York, near L. Ontario
Rockford, town, Illinois
Rome (Roma), city, cap. of Italy, on River Tiber
Romania, rep., S.E. Europe, cap. Bucharest
Rondônia, state, Brazil
Roraima, state, Brazil
Rosa, Monte, Pennine Alps, Switzerland and Italy, height 15,216 ft.
Rostov, town, U.S.S.R., at mouth of the Don
Rotterdam, cy. & pt., Netherlands, on R. Maas
Russia=R.S.F.S.R.
Ruwenzori, Mt., Zaire/Uganda; 16,794 ft.
Rwanda, republic, central Africa, cap. Kigali
Ryukyu Archipelago, chain of Is., from Japan to Formosa
Sabah (North Borneo), state, E. Malaysia, cap. Kota Kinabalu
Sacramento, city and cap. of California
Saigon, port and cap. of S. Vietnam
St Christopher=St Kitts
St Helena, island, S. Atlantic Ocean
St Helens, town, Lancs, Eng., near Liverpool
St John, town and port, New Brunswick
St John's, town & port, cap. of Newfoundland

St Kitts, island, Leeward Is., W. Indies
St Lawrence, great riv. of N. America; 2340 m.
St Louis, city, Missouri, on the Mississippi
St Lucia, island, Windward group, W. Indies
St Paul, city, Minnesota, on Mississippi
St Petersburg, town, Florida
St Pierre, island, Atlantic, S. of Newfoundland
St Vincent, island, Windward Is., W. Indies
Salford, town, Lancs., England
Salisbury, cap. of Rhodesia, central Africa
Salt Lake City, cap. of Utah, on River Jordan
Salvador, El, rep., Cent. Amer.; cap. San Salvador
San'a, cap. of Yemen, Arabia
San Antonio, city, Texas, W. of Houston
San Diego, city and naval base, California
San Francisco, city and port, California
San José, city and cap. of Costa Rica
San Jose, town, California
San Juan, cap. of Puerto Rico, W. Indies
San Marino, rep., N.E. Italy
San Salvador, cap. of El Salvador, Cent. America
Santa Ana, town, California
Santa Caterina, state, Brazil
Santiago, city, cap. of Chile, S. America
Santo Domingo, town and cap. of Dominican Rep., West Indies
São Francisco, river, Brazil
São Paulo, city, Brazil, N.W. of Santos
São Paulo, state, Brazil
São Tomé, island in G. of Guinea, W. Africa
Saratov, town, U.S.S.R., S.E. of Moscow
Sarawak, state, E. Malaysia
Saskatchewan, W. prov. of Canada; cap. Regina

Saskatoon, town, Saskatchewan, N.W. of Regina
Saudi Arabia, kingdom, S.W. Asia; cap. Riyadh
Savannah, port, Georgia, U.S.A.
Scotland, northern part of Great Britain; kingdom, cap. Edinburgh
Scranton, city, Pennsyl., N.W. of Philadelphia
Seattle, port, Washington, on Puget Sound
Senegal, republic and river, N.W. Africa; cap. Dakar
Seoul (Kyongsong), city and cap. of S. Korea
Sergipe, state, Brazil
Seychelles, Is., Indian Ocean
Shanghai, port, Kiangsu prov., China
Shansi, prov., China
Shantung, prov., China
Sheffield, city, Yorks, England
Shensi, prov., China
Shenyang (Moukden), city, N.E. China
Shreveport, town, Louisiana, U.S.A.
Sian (Changan), cap. of Shensi prov., China
Sierra Leone, rep., W. Africa; cap. Freetown
Sikkim, state, N.E. India; cap. Gangtok
Singapore, island, rep., port and naval base, S. of Malaya
Sinkiang-Uighur, aut. reg., W. China; cap. Urumchi
Slave Lake, Great, N.W. Territories, Canada
Sofia, city, cap. of Bulgaria
Solihull, town, Warks., England
Solomon Islands, Melanesia, Pacific Ocean
Somali Republic, state, E. Africa; cap. Mogadishu
Southampton, port, Hampshire, England
South Africa, rep., cap. Pretoria
South Australia, state, Aust.; cap. Adelaide
South Bend, town, Indiana, E. of Chicago
South Carolina, state, U.S.A.; cap. Columbia

South Dakota, state, U.S.A.; cap. Pierre
Southend-on-Sea, seaside resort, Essex, England
South Shields, port, Durham, England
South West Africa (Namibia), state, S. Africa
Spain, state, S.W. Europe; cap. Madrid
Spanish Sahara, prov., W. Africa
Spitsbergen, islands, Arctic Oc., N. of Norway
Spokane, town, Washington, N.E. of Portland
Springfield, town, Massachusetts, S.W. of Boston
Sri Lanka (Ceylon), rep., I. off S. India; cap. Colombo
Stanley, port and cap. of Falkland Is.
Stewart Island, to south of South I., N.Z.
Stockholm, port, and cap. of Sweden
Stockport, town, Cheshire, England
Stoke-on-Trent, city, Staffs, England
Stuttgart, city, W. Germany
Sucre, town and cap. of Bolivia
Sudan, rep., N.E. Africa; cap. Khartoum
Sudbury, town, Ontario, N.W. of Montreal
Sunderland, port, Durham, England
Superior, L., Canada and U.S.A.; length 360 m.
Surabaja, port, Java, Indonesia
Surinam, prov. of Netherlands, S. America
Svalbard, arch., Arctic Ocean
Sverdlovsk, town, in Ural Mts., U.S.S.R.
Swansea, port, Glamorganshire, Wales
Swaziland, kingdom, S. Africa
Sweden, kingdom, Scandinavia, W. Europe; cap. Stockholm
Switzerland, rep., central Europe, cap. Berne
Sydney, city, cap. of New South Wales
Syracuse, town, New York, E. of Rochester
Syria, rep., W. Asia; cap. Damascus

Szechwan, prov., China
Tacoma, town, Washington, N.E. of Olympia
Tadzhikistan, rep., U.S.S.R.; cap. Dushanbe
Taipei, town and cap. of Taiwan
Taiwan (Formosa), island and rep., to E. of China
Taiyuan (Yangku), city, Shansi prov., China
Ta'izz, town, Yemen
Tamil Nadu, state, S.E. India, cap. Madras
Tampa, town, Florida, on Tampa Bay
Tananarive, cap. of Malagasy Rep.
Tanganyika, Lake, E. Africa
Tanzania, rep., E. Africa, cap. Dar es Salaam
Tashkent, city, cap. of Uzbekistan, N.E. of Samarkand
Tasman, Mt., N.Z.
Tasmania, island state, Commonwealth of Aust.
Tbilisi, cap. of Georgian rep., U.S.S.R.
Teesside, town, England, S. of Newcastle
Tegucigalpa, cap. of Honduras, Cent. America
Tehran, cap. of Iran, S. of Caspian Sea
Tennessee, state, U.S.A.; cap. Nashville
Texas, a southern state of U.S.A.; cap. Austin
Thailand, kingdom, S.E. Asia; cap. Bangkok (Krung Thep)
Thimphu, town and cap. of Bhutan
Tibet, aut. reg., W. China; cap. Lhasa
Tientsin, port, Hopeh, China, S.E. of Peking
Timor, prov., Indonesia, S.E. of Celébes
Tinguiririca, Mt., Chile
Tiranë, cap. of Albania, Europe
Titicaca, Lake, Peru and Bolivia, in the Andes
Tobago, island, Trinidad and Tobago
Togo, rep., W. Africa, cap. Lomé
Tokelau Is., group, Pacific Ocean

Tokyo, city and cap. of Japan, Honshu I.
Toledo, town, Ohio, W. of Cleveland
Tolima, mt., Colombia
Tonga Islands, Polynesia, Pacific Ocean
Topeka, city, cap. of Kansas, U.S.A.
Torbay, town, Devon, England
Toronto, city, cap. of Ontario, Canada
Torrance, town, California
Transvaal, prov., S. Africa; cap. Pretoria
Trenton, city and cap. of New Jersey
Trinidad, island, W. Indies, part of rep. of Trinidad and Tobago; cap. Port of Spain
Tripoli, port and naval base, Libya
Tristan da Cunha, volcanic island, S. Atlantic Oc.
Tsingtao, port, Shantung, on Kiaochow Bay
Tucson, town, Arizona, S.E. of Phoenix
Tulsa, town, Oklahoma
Tunis, town and cap. of Tunisia
Tunisia, rep., North Africa; cap. Tunis
Tupungato, mt., S. America
Turin, town, Piedmont, N. Italy
Turkey, rep., Europe and Asia; cap. Ankara
Turkmenistan, rep., U.S.S.R.; cap. Ashkhabad
Turks Islands, group of islands, S. of the Bahamas
U.A.R.=United Arab Rep. now Arab Republic of Egypt
U.K.=United Kingdom of Great Britain and Northern Ireland
U.S.A.=United States of America
U.S.S.R.=Union of Soviet Socialist Republics
Ufa, town, U.S.S.R., S.W. of Sverdlovsk
Uganda, state, Africa; cap. Entebbe
Ukraine, rep., U.S.S.R.; cap. Kiev (Kiyev)
Ulaanbaatar, town and cap. of Mongolia

Union of Soviet Socialist Republics, state, Europe and Asia; cap. Moscow
U.A.R. (Egypt) now A.R.E. Africa; cap. Cairo
United Kingdom of Great Britain and Northern Ireland, state, W. Europe; cap. London
United States of America, state, N. America; cap. Washington
Upper Volta, rep., W. Africa; cap. Ouagadougou
Uruguay, rep. and river, S. America; length 950 m. cap. Montevideo
Utah, inland state, U.S.A.; cap. Salt Lake City
Uttar Pradesh, state, India; chief tn. Lucknow
Utica, town, New York, N.W. of Albany
Uzbekistan, rep., U.S.S.R.; cap. Tashkent
Vaduz, cap. of the principality of Liechtenstein
Valencia, port, Spain, on east coast
Valletta, port and cap. of Malta
Vancouver, city, Brit. Columbia, N. of Victoria
Vänern, lake, SW Sweden; length 95 m.
Venezuela, rep., S. America; cap. Caracas
Vermont, a New England state, U.S.A.; cap. Montpelier
Vesuvius, Mount, vol., Italy, on B. of Naples
Victoria, state, S.E. Aust.; cap. Melbourne
Victoria, cap. of Br. Columbia, on Vancouver I.
Victoria, cap. and chief port, Hong Kong
Victoria, Lake, Africa, between Uganda, Tanzania and Kenya
Vienna (Wien), city, cap. of Austria, on Danube
Vientiane, town and cap. of Laos, on Mekong R.
Vietnam, N. and S., reps., S.E. Asia
Virgin Islands, group in West Indies
Virginia, a S. Atlantic state, U.S.A.; cap. Richmond

Volga, river, U.S.S.R., falls into Caspian Sea; length 2320 m.
Volgograd, town, U.S.S.R., N.W. of Astrakhan
Voronezh, town, U.S.S.R., S.S.E. of Moscow
Wales, principality, W. of England
Walsall, town, Staffs., England
Wallasey, town, Ches., England
Warley, town, Worcs, England
Warsaw (Warszawa), cap. of Poland, on the River Vistula
Washington, city, Dist. of Columbia; cap. of United States
Washington, Pacific state, U.S.A.; cap. Olympia
Waterbury, town, Connecticut
Wellington, city and cap. of New Zealand, on North Island
Western Australia, state, Aust.; cap. Perth
West Bengal, state, India
West Bromwich, town, Staffs., England
Western Samoa, state, Pacific Ocean; cap. Apia
West Virginia, state, U.S.A.; cap. Charleston
Whitney, Mt., California
Wichita, town, Kansas, on Arkansas River
Wichita Falls, town, Texas
Windsor, port, Ontario, Canada
Windward Islands, part of the Lesser Antilles
Winnipeg, city, cap. of Manitoba, Canada
Winnipeg, Lake, Canada
Winston Salem, town, N. Carolina
Wisconsin, state, U.S.A.; cap. Madison
Wollongong, port, New South Wales, S. of Sydney
Wolverhampton, town, Staffordshire, England
Worcester, town, Mass., W.S.W. of Boston

Wuhan (Hankow), river port, China, on Yangtze Kiang, in Hupeh prov.

Wyoming, N.W. state, U.S.A.; cap. Cheyenne

Yangtze Kiang, river, China, rises in Tibet; length 3000 m.

Yaoundé, cap. of Cameroun, Africa

Yemen, rep., S.W. Arabia; cap. San'a

Yemen, People's Dem. Rep. of, S. Arabia; cap. ash Sha'b

Yenisey, river, U.S.S.R., flows to Arctic Sea

Yerevan, town and cap. of Armenia

Yokohama, port, Japan, Honshu Island

Yonkers, town, New York

York, city and co. town of Yorkshire, England

Youngstown, town, Ohio

Yugoslavia, republic, S.E. Europe, in Balkans; cap. Belgrade

Yukon, river, Yukon and Alaska, flows S.W. to the Bering Sea

Yukon, territory, N.W. Canada; cap. Dawson

Yunnan, prov., China

Zagreb, town, Croatia, Yugoslavia, on R. Sava

Zaire, river, Central Africa, flows 3000m to Atlantic Oc.

Zambezi, river, S. Africa, flows 1600 m. into the Indian Ocean

Zambia, republic, central Africa; cap. Lusaka

Zanzibar, island & town, Tanzania

Zaporozh'ye, town, Ukraine, W.S.W. of Donetsk

Zomba, town and cap. of Malawi